Shameful Flight

SHAMEFUL FLIGHT
The Last Years of the
British Empire in India

STANLEY WOLPERT

OXFORD
UNIVERSITY PRESS

2006

OXFORD
UNIVERSITY PRESS

Oxford University Press, Inc., publishes works that further
Oxford University's objective of excellence
in research, scholarship, and education.

Oxford   New York
Auckland   Cape Town   Dar es Salaam   Hong Kong   Karachi
Kuala Lumpur   Madrid   Melbourne   Mexico City   Nairobi
New Delhi   Shanghai   Taipei   Toronto

With offices in
Argentina   Austria   Brazil   Chile   Czech Republic   France   Greece
Guatemala   Hungary   Italy   Japan   Poland   Portugal   Singapore

Copyright © 2006 by Stanley Wolpert

Published by Oxford University Press, Inc.
198 Madison Avenue, New York, NY 10016
www.oup.com

Oxford is a registered trademark of Oxford University Press

Library of Congress Cataloging-in-Publication Data
Wolpert, Stanley A., 1927–
Shameful flight : the last years of the British Empire in India / Stanley Wolpert.
p. cm.
Includes bibliographical references and index.
ISBN-13: 978-0-19-515198-5
ISBN-10: 0-19-515198-4
1. British—India—History—20th century.
2. India—History—Partition, 1947.
3. India—History—Quit India movement, 1942.
4. India—History—20th century. I. Title.
DS480.45.W55 2006
954.03'59—dc22
2006040121

1 3 5 7 9 8 6 4 2
Printed in the United States of America
on acid-free paper

To the memory of the million defenseless
Hindu, Muslim, and Sikh victims of British India's Partition

CONTENTS

Acknowledgments   ix

Participants   xi

Introduction   1

1   From the Fall of Singapore to the Failure of Cripps's Mission, February–April 1942   13

2   From Cripps's Failure to the Failure of the Congress Party's "Quit India" Movement, April–October 1942   35

3   From Gandhi's Fast through the First Year of Wavell's Viceroyalty, January 1943–July 1944   53

4   Summit Failures and Cabinet Obstacles, August 1944–July 1945   67

5   From the End of World War II through the Cabinet Mission, August 1945–June 1946   89

6   The Interim Government, June–December 1946   109

7   Lord Mountbatten's Last Chukka, December 1946–June 1947   129

8   Partitioned Transfer of Power, June–August 1947   153

9   Freedom's Wooden Loaf, September–October 1947   173

10   Indo-Pak War over Kashmir, October 1947–July 1948   183

Notes   195

Bibliography   223

Index   233

Illustrations follow page 114.

ACKNOWLEDGMENTS

Khushwant Singh's searing novel *Mano Majra* (*Train to Pakistan*, New York, 1956), first made me aware of the human impact of Partition's tragedy on Punjab. I became more acutely conscious of the historic dimensions of Britain's irresponsibly hasty withdrawal from India and the economic and political consequences of Partition when I worked on my *Jinnah of Pakistan* twenty years later. Interviewing Lord Mountbatten in London, I sensed hidden sources of that multifaceted debacle but failed fully to grasp its poison roots until I focused on Mountbatten's role in Britain's "Shameful Flight" six years ago. I am indebted once again to my oldest and wisest friend, John Kenneth Galbraith, for urging me to write "a new history" of Partition's genesis and its disastrous consequences.

Many other wise gurus, first among whom was W. Norman Brown who taught me Sanskrit in his Department of South Asian Studies at the University of Pennsylvania, helped me to fathom India and the depths of this complex and tragic story. My dear departed friends Raja Dinesh Singh and Justice Nagendra Singh taught me the power of modern India's courtly patience and ancient political roots. Former Prime Minister Inder Gujral taught me to understand the beauty and pain of Punjab's poetry and history. I thank my most hospitable friend, Dr. A. S. Marwah, for introducing me to so many luminaries of India's Punjab over the last half century. Three of Pakistan's greatest diplomats, Sahibzada Yaqub Khan, Jamsheed Marker, and Akbar Ahmed, have helped me appreciate the best of Islamic culture, as did my dear departed friend Gustave von Grunebaum. There are too many other kind friends to list in this brief acknowledgment of lifelong debts to those who have helped me understand the history of India and Pakistan. I must, however, also thank two of my finest students, both now Professors of Indian History, Sita Anantha Raman, and Ravi Kalia.

I am indebted to Oxford University Press for its faith in my work for more than thirty years. I thank my editor, Susan Ferber, for her painstaking critique of my manuscript, and senior production editor Joellyn Ausanka for so efficiently expediting its reincarnation as a book. To my son Adam and his bride, Katy, thanks for restoring my faith in the limitless powers of love, as to Dan and Debra, and grandfatherly thanks to Sam and Max. Finally, to my better self, Dearest Dorothy, goes all my love.

S.W.
March 2006

PARTICIPANTS

Ambedkar, Dr. B. R. (1891–1956), "untouchable" leader, barrister; Nehru's minister of law; chaired the government of India's constitution-drafting committee.

Amery, Leopold Charles (1873–1955), secretary of state for India, 1940–45.

Attlee, Clement Richard (1883–1965), earl; deputy prime minister, war cabinet, 1942–45; prime minister of Britain's Labor government, July 1945–50.

Auchinleck, Field Marshal Sir Claude (1884–1981), commander-in-chief, India, June 1943–47.

Azad, Maulana Abul Kalam (1888–1958), president of Indian National Congress, 1939–46; minister of education, government of India, 1947–58.

Churchill, Sir Winston Leonard Spencer (1874–1965), prime minister, 1940–July 45; leader of the opposition from August 1945.

Cripps, Sir Richard Stafford (1889–1952), Labor member of Parliament; leader of the House of Commons and lord privy seal; war cabinet, 1942–45; sole mission for cabinet to India, 1942; member of cabinet mission in 1946; president of board of trade, 1947–48.

Gandhi, Mohandas Karamchand (1869–1948), *Mahatma* ("Great Soul"); spiritual leader of India and of the Indian National Congress.

Ismay, Hastings Lionel, Baron Ismay of Wormington (1887–1965), chief of Mountbatten's staff.

Jenkins, Sir Evan Meredith (1896–1985), P.S.V., 1943–45; governor of Punjab, 1946–47.

Jinnah, Muhammad Ali (1876–1948), *Quaid-i-Azam* ("Great Leader") and president of the Muslim League; also serving until his death as first governor-general of Pakistan.

Khan, Liaquat Ali (1895–1951), Jinnah's deputy leader of the Muslim League; finance member of the interim government, 1946–47; first prime minister of Pakistan, 1947–51.

Participants

Linlithgow, Lord Victor Alexander John (1887–1952), viceroy of India, 1936–October 1943.

Mountbatten, Rear-Admiral Viscount Lord Louis Francis Albert Victor (1900–1979), viceroy of India, March–August 1947; first governor-general of dominion of India, 1947–48.

Nehru, Jawaharlal (1889–1964), president of Indian National Congress, 1929–30, 1946; first prime minister of India, 1947–64.

Pant, G. B. (1887–1961), Congress political leader; chief minister of Uttar Pradesh; home minister of India.

Patel, Sardar Vallabhbhai (1875–1950), Gandhi's disciple; Nehru's home member of the interim government; first deputy prime minister of India, 1947–50.

Pethick-Lawrence, Lord (1871–1961), secretary of state for India, 1945–April 1947; chair of 1946 cabinet mission, 1945–April 1947.

Radcliffe, Sir Cyril (1899–1977), chairman, Punjab and Bengal boundary commissions, 1947.

Rajagopalachari, C. (1878–1972), south Indian leader of Congress; chief minister of Madras; governor of Bengal (1947); governor-general of India (1948–50).

Roosevelt, Franklin Delano (1882–1945), president of the United States, 1933–1945.

Singh, Master Tara (1885–1967), Sikh political leader of the Akali Dal; first to demand a separate Sikh nation-state of "Sikhistan" in 1946–47.

Suhrawardy, H. S. (1893–1963), Muslim League chief minister of Bengal, 1946; founding leader of the Awami League; prime minister of Pakistan (1956–57).

Wavell, Field Marshal Sir Archibald Percival (1883–1950), commander-in-chief, India, 1941; supreme commander South-West Pacific, December 1941–June 1943; viceroy of India, October 1943–47.

Shameful Flight

Introduction

I N MID-AUGUST OF 1947 the world's mightiest modern empire, on which "the sun never set," abandoned its vow to protect one-fifth of humankind. Britain's shameful flight from its Indian Empire came only ten weeks after its last viceroy, Lord Louis ("Dickie") Mountbatten, took it upon himself to cut ten months from the brief time allotted by the Labor government's cabinet to withdraw its air and fleet cover, as well as the shield of British troops and arms, from South Asia's 400 million Hindus, Muslims, and Sikhs.

Prime Minister Clement Attlee and his cabinet gave Mountbatten until June of 1948 to try to facilitate agreement between the major competing political party leaders of India to work together within a single federation. But adrenaline-charged Mountbatten scuttled that last best hope of the British Imperial *Raj* (Sanskrit for "King" or "Ruler" and by extension "Rule" or "Government") to leave India to a single independent government, deciding instead to divide British India into fragmented dominions of India and Pakistan. The hastily and ineptly drawn lines of partition of North India's two greatest provinces, Punjab and Bengal, slashed through their multicultural heartlands. They were drawn by an English jurist who had never set foot on the soil of either province. Following Britain's flight, a tsunami of more than ten million desperate refugees swept over North India: Hindus and Sikhs rushed to leave ancestral homes in newly created Pakistan, Muslims fled in panic out of India. Each sought shelter in next-door's dominion. Estimates vary as to the number who expired or were murdered before ever reaching their promised land. A conservative statistic is 200,000; a more realistic total, at least one million.[1]

Many books have been written about British India's Partition, even more about the genesis and birth of Pakistan. Why then have I chosen to add another volume? Because I believe that the tragedy of Partition and its more than half century legacy of hatred, fear, and continued conflict—capped by the potential of nuclear war over South Asia—might well have been avoided, or at least mitigated, but for the arrogance and ignorance of a handful of British and Indian leaders. Those ten additional months of postwar talks, aborted by an impatient Mountbatten, might have helped all parties to agree that cooperation was much wiser than conflict, dialogue more sensible than division, words easier to cope with and pay for than perpetual warfare. When asked how he felt about his Indian viceroyalty eighteen years after Partition, Mountbatten himself admitted to BBC's John Osman, when they sat next to one another at dinner shortly after the 1965 Indo-Pakistani War, that he had "got things wrong." Osman felt "sympathy" for the remorseful sixty-five-year-old ex-viceroy and tried to cheer him, but to no avail. Thirty-nine years after that meeting he recalled: "Mountbatten was not to be consoled. To this day his own judgment on how he had performed in India rings in my ears and in my memory. As one who dislikes the tasteless use in writing of . . . 'vulgar slang' . . . I shall permit myself an exception this time because it is the only honest way of reporting accurately what the last viceroy of India thought about the way he had done his job: 'I fucked it up.'"[2]

Although I could more politely and at much greater length summarize the central thesis of my book, and what I have now long believed to be the primary cause of the tragedy of Partition and its aftermath of slaughter and ceaseless pain, I could not more pithily, nor aptly, state my own view of Mountbatten's work in India. If for no other reason than to counter the many laudatory, fawning accounts of Lord Mountbatten's "splendid," "historically unique," "brilliant and wonderful" viceroyalty that have for more than half a century filled shelves of Partition literature and Mountbatten hagiography,[3] I feel justified in adding my *Shameful Flight* to history's list of the British Raj's last years. World War II, British politics, personal ambitions, and simple ignorance each added complexity to the picture, and I shall also have much to say about the roles of Muhammad Ali Jinnah, Mohandas Karamchand Gandhi, Jawaharlal Nehru, Vallabhbhai Patel, and viceroys Lord Linlithgow and Lord Wavell, as well as prime ministers Winston Churchill and Clement Attlee, and president Franklin D. Roosevelt, though none of them played as tragic or central a role as did Mountbatten.

Ironically, it was the impact of World War I that brought the two major political parties of British India—the Indian National Congress and the Muslim League—together, though only briefly, on a single platform in 1916. Both parties supported the Allied War effort and jointly called for "dominion status" as their national goal after the war ended. It was a golden opportunity for India as a whole. The architect of that 1916 Lucknow Pact

was barrister M. A. Jinnah, the most brilliant Anglophile Muslim nationalist leader, who had first joined the National Congress Party in 1906, and
seven years later the Muslim League. The League was inspired by conservative British officials, who feared the Congress Party's growing popular opposition to their Raj and encouraged a number of Muslim feudal princes,
led by the Aga Khan, to launch their own separate "Muslim Party" in 1906,
competing for Muslim membership and support with India's older National
Congress Party, which accepted as members Indians of every faith. Jinnah
was uniquely admired, respected, and courted by the leadership of both
major political parties as a potential president of each, and hailed by his
liberal Congress Party mentor, Gopal Krishna Gokhale, as "the Best Ambassador of Hindu-Muslim Unity."[4] Gokhale's more famous disciple was
Mahatma ("Great Soul") M. K. Gandhi, who had returned to India during
World War I after twenty years in South Africa, where he led the Indian
community's struggle for equality.[5] Regrettably, Jinnah and Gandhi, who
both became barristers at London's Inns of Court and were inspired by the
same "political guru" to advocate Indian freedom from British Imperial
rule, could never agree on the best tactics to win India's liberation. Nor did
they really like or completely trust one other.

Mahatma Gandhi had transformed himself in South Africa, abandoning his barrister dress and Western sophistication for the naked simplicity
and poverty of rural India. He embraced this image with a passion that
made him the revolutionary hero of India's Hindu masses, depending as he
did on ancient Hindu symbols and ideas to launch his *satyagraha* ("Hold
fast to the truth") campaigns of noncooperation against the British Raj.
Jinnah cautioned Gandhi against the dangers of his revolutionary tactics,
warning him of the potential for violence that could erupt from exciting too
many illiterate, impoverished people to take to the streets or to lie down on
railroad tracks as a way to oppose British rule and Western civilization.
Though Jinnah came from a traditional Muslim family he developed a mind
that was modern and secular, and was as brilliant and sharp as any of his
adversaries or colleagues, whether Indian or British. Like the best pre-
Gandhian leaders of India's National Congress Party, such as Gokhale, Jinnah
continued to work toward and hoped to win India's freedom by his brilliant
mastery of secular Western law and parliamentary rules of governance. He
eloquently appealed to both the British viceroy in India and the British cabinet in London for expanding opportunities for more qualified Indians to
take over jobs that Englishmen held at much higher costs, socially as well as
financially, for India. Gandhi considered Jinnah's old-fashioned liberal appeals to Britain's Parliament, or to viceregal sympathy, a waste of energy
and time. Jinnah thought the Mahatma's revolutionary calls to action irresponsibly provocative madness. Had either of British India's two greatest

modern leaders been willing to subordinate his own ambitions to the leadership of the other, India might well have won its freedom much earlier and without Partition.

After World War I ended in Allied victory, the British no longer needed the million valiant Indian soldiers who had been shipped to the Western and Near Eastern fronts. Great Britain's generals and India's civil servants were more terrified by than grateful to demobilized "native" Indian troops. So instead of granting India the virtual sovereign independence of "dominion status" (within the British Commonwealth) that India's National Congress Party and the Muslim League both demanded and expected as their reward for loyal service, Viceroy Lord Chelmsford extended India's invidious wartime "martial law" ordinances. Those "Black Acts," as Gandhi labeled them, removed the shield of British civil liberties and legal rights of due process from India, allowing any Indian subject to be arrested by a British officer of the Raj and held indefinitely under "preventive detention," without being charged with any violation of law. Gandhi called upon Indians to "refuse civilly" to obey such "Satanic laws" as "unjust." Jinnah, who had recently been elected to Bombay's seat on the viceroy's legislative council, resigned, because, as he informed the viceroy: "The fundamental principles of justice have been uprooted and the constitutional rights of the people have been violated . . . by an over-fretful and incompetent bureaucracy which is neither responsible to the people nor in touch with real public opinion."[6] Gandhi then launched his first nationwide *satyagraha* campaign. The British cracked down hard on the Mahatma's nonviolent followers, arresting many in Delhi and Bombay. Then in April 1919, Brigadier R. E. Dyer ordered his troops to open fire on thousands of unarmed Indians penned inside a walled "garden" (Jallianwala *Bagh*) in Punjab's Amritsar, unleashing a massacre that left 400 innocents dead and over 1,200 wounded.[7]

Indian nationalist dreams of imminent dominion status evaporated as "martial law" closed down the Punjab, its tough Lieutenant Governor Michael O'Dwyer issuing "crawling orders" to all Indian residents who lived in the quarter of Amritsar, where several English missionary women had been attacked. Indians who failed to crawl within those specified streets were harshly lashed by British officers for daring to walk upright to or from their own houses. Jinnah's hope of becoming the first Indian viceroy dissolved in the deadly fire that turned Amritsar's garden into a national morgue and monument. Millions of moderate Indians, including Jinnah's wealthy lawyer friend Motilal Nehru, abandoned their faith in British justice. The National Congress Party abandoned its faith in Jinnah's Lucknow Pact and constitutional tactics of cooperation and instead embraced Mahatma Gandhi's revolutionary noncooperation, boycotting British goods and institutions, setting fire to pyres of British cotton cloth and silk imports, and demanding *Swaraj* ("freedom"). But in 1919 no British minister in London, nor English official in the Raj's two capitals of Calcutta or Simla, had any intention of leaving India to its own political leaders.

The decades between 1919 and 1939, when World War II started, witnessed increasingly bloody Hindu-Muslim conflicts in many parts of India. Antipathy grew between India's National Congress Party—under the leadership of Gandhi and his most brilliant young disciple, Jawaharlal Nehru, Motilal's only son—and conservative Muslim League feudal princes and landlords, whose only leader of true national stature was Jinnah. Britain's Tory Party leaders, Lord Birkenhead and Sir John Simon, and prime ministers Stanley Baldwin and Winston Churchill, encouraged and supported India's Muslim League. Like princely India's rulers, they considered them useful imperial counters to the claims of "half-naked fakir" Mahatma Gandhi and his cohort of radical Hindu and Socialist Muslim followers in the Congress Party, who insisted that *they* alone represented India's "nation."

In March of 1930, Gandhi launched the Congress Party's second nationwide satyagraha campaign, leading almost a hundred male disciples from his ashram ("rural community") in Gujarat on a "salt march" of more than a hundred miles to Dandi at the seashore, where they broke the onerous British monopoly on salt, which was heavily taxed by the Raj and could be purchased by Indians only at government salt outlets. When Mahatma Gandhi stooped to "steal" a lump of natural salt drying on the beach he was "hailed" by Congress poetess Sarojini Naidu as India's "deliverer"[8] from the tyranny of British oppression. Soon 60,000 Congress Party members, women as well as men, were arrested by British India's police for following their Mahatma's example, breaking what Gandhi called Britain's "cruelest and meanest law." Millions of India's poorest peasants, who perspired so profusely as they worked in blazing sunlight, required salt to survive India's intense heat. After filling every prison cell in India, the British government decided it might be a good idea to try to reach agreement with Gandhi and his Congress Party. At Jinnah's suggestion, and with the agreement of Viceroy Lord Irwin (later Lord Halifax), Labor Prime Minister Ramsay MacDonald launched his first Round Table Conference in London in December 1930. India's National Congress Party leaders, as well as Jinnah and other Muslim League leaders and Indian princes, were invited to sit around a large table with leaders from Whitehall and New Delhi to discuss how best to bring popularly elected representative Indian leaders into the central and provincial council chambers of the Raj. Gandhi refused to leave the "temple" of his prison cell, however, unless all other political prisoners were released. No other leader of the Congress Party would go to London without him, so the first conference proved a futile exercise. A year later Viceroy Irwin invited Gandhi to his New Delhi mansion for a series of talks, leading to their truce-"pact," which included amnesty for most prisoners and a reduction of the salt tax.

Gandhi reached London in September 1931 to attend the second Round Table Conference as the sole representative of the Congress Party, imposing an impossible burden on himself, since that meant he alone would have to attend every meeting and read every proposal or salient paper circulated at the conference. He would also be expected to argue against every criticism of the Congress Party raised by British officials, or by the leaders of the Muslim League. For two months of the talks, the Mahatma lived in London's East End, winning admiration and cheering support from radical British friends, who rallied around him wherever he spoke. Most of the other hundred-odd delegates to London's Constitutional Conference, all of whom came from India or were members of the British government of India, found it impossible to understand much of what Gandhi whispered in a hoarse voice or to agree with anything he demanded. When he addressed the Federal Structure Committee, he angered many by saying, "I would rather be called a rebel than a subject."⁹ And to the Minorities Committee he brought smiles to British lips when he confessed his "utter failure" to reach agreement with any of the Muslim or Sikh delegates on how to resolve India's "communal question" that kept exploding in violent Hindu-Muslim or Muslim-Sikh conflicts in Punjab and elsewhere. By mid-October, Gandhi expected "nothing" good to come of the conference and wired Jawaharlal Nehru to prepare the Congress Party to take whatever "steps"¹⁰ were deemed necessary to counter growing British repression and stop the ejection of Indian peasants unable to pay land taxes. He knew, of course, that the British response would be harsh, but he could not indefinitely restrain younger Congress radicals like Nehru. By the time Gandhi returned to India at year's end, Lord Irwin had gone home and been replaced by a much tougher Tory viceroy, Lord Willingdon, who ordered Gandhi's arrest shortly after he disembarked in Bombay.

Conservative Lord ("Hopie") Linlithgow chaired the Joint Committee on Constitutional Reform, which turned resolutions adopted during the three round table conferences (the third was held without Gandhi in 1932) into a new Government of India Act of 1935. That act was to remain the constitution of British India until the end of the Raj. Its central new principle was to have been to create a "Federation of India," meant to include all eleven provinces of British India and some 560 princely states, but those rulers could never agree to cooperate, either with one another or with the British governors or Congress ministers of the provinces. So it was only the new act's democratic "provincial autonomy" principle that was to be introduced, its central federal ideal to unite British India and the princely states left to die untested. Linlithgow's patient work in bringing the new Government of India Act to partial fruition, however, sufficed to assure his appointment as viceroy in 1936. His first major task was to prepare for India's first provincial elections, held in all eleven of British India's provinces early in 1937.

Introduction

More than half of some thirty-five million Indians enfranchised under the new act trekked to polling stations established throughout British India. Gandhi, who had been released from prison, devoted his time primarily to cotton spinning and rural uplift work in his central Indian ashram. The reclusive Mahatma was, however, lured back by his old disciples on Congress's working committee to help them convince Congress Party president Jawaharlal Nehru to remain at the helm of his party to lead his colleagues in contesting elections, rather than resigning to launch a "real revolution" of workers and peasants. Nehru was depressed and frustrated by his older conservative colleagues and by the stately pace of constitutional change so grudgingly doled out to India by its imperial rulers. But thanks to Gandhi's goading, Nehru campaigned so vigorously, barnstorming the country for the Congress Party, that its candidates won clear majorities in six of the eleven provinces. Though many provincial parties ran candidates, who contested elections, the only two national parties were the Indian Congress Party and the Muslim League.

Jinnah's Muslim League, however, failed to win a single province, despite "separate Muslim electorate" seats reserved under the Raj's religious minority formula, which the Congress Party always viewed as a blatant example of British "divide and rule." Jinnah appealed to Nehru to agree to coalition Congress-League ministries in India's most populous multicultural provinces, primarily the United Provinces (UP). But Nehru refused. The elections had proved, Nehru insisted, that there were only "two parties" left, "the British and the Congress."[11] Outraged, Jinnah replied: "There is a third Party—the Muslims." He devoted the next ten years of his life to proving just that, siring South Asia's first Muslim nation, Pakistan.

On September 3, 1939, when Viceroy Lord Linlithgow broadcast to inform all the people of British India that they were "at war with Germany," it seemed never to have occurred to him that Congress Party leaders, especially Nehru and Gandhi, might feel offended not to be informed first, privately, about that most momentous decision. Or perhaps it did occur to him, and he deliberately chose to ignore them as a sign of how irrelevant he considered their views, and those of all revolutionary Hindu Congress Party leaders. A month later, the Congress's high command reacted by ordering all seven of its provincial cabinets to resign their posts, resolving no longer to cooperate with a viceroy and British officials so disinterested in the views of National Congress leaders. Imperialist Tory contempt for all Congress leaders was too well known by now to Gandhi as well as to Nehru. "The dogs bark, the caravan moves on," Secretary of State Sir Samuel Hoare remarked when Gandhi had informed him he would have to "fast unto death" if Hoare insisted in 1932 on establishing "separate electorates" for Hindu untouchables.[12] Now Linlithgow's autocratic hauteur in announcing that India was at war dealt so harsh a blow to the Congress Party's sensitivities as to provoke its leaders to weaken their own party by abandoning its hard-won posts of responsible provincial power.

By mid-November 1939, all provincial Congress Party cabinet ministers had resigned, returning India to its preelection autocratic British governor's rule, in response to which Jinnah said "Thank God!" He proclaimed December 22, 1939, Muslim India's "Day of Deliverance" from the "Hindu" Congress Raj's "tyranny, oppression and injustice."[13] After two years of responsible provincial rule, mostly under Congress Party ministries, British India's government thus reestablished its autocratic Raj, each province ruled by a British governor or lieutenant-governor and his official appointees, and the central government in New Delhi ruled by its viceroy, who also held the title of governor-general and chose his own council. British India was governed far less responsibly during World War II than it had been before the war started, and most of its former Congress ministers would soon be locked behind prison bars.

Congress opposition to the British Raj from the start of World War II was thus the polar opposite of the Muslim League's strongly supportive approach, naturally inducing British officials, from the viceroy and commander-in-chief down to the youngest members of the Indian civil service and subalterns in the British Indian Army, to view India's Muslims much more favorably than they did the Hindu leaders of the Congress Party. Muslim soldiers and officers continued, moreover, to play a vital role in British India's Army, unlike India's Hindu majority, most of whom were neither recruited, nor permitted to volunteer to serve, since India's 1857 "Sepoy Mutiny."[14] Jinnah was wise enough to take full advantage of official British favoritism directed toward its friendly Muslim quarter of India's population. Five months after the war started, Jinnah addressed his Muslim League's largest and most important meeting in Lahore, announcing the new goal of his premier Muslim Party to be an independent nation-state of Pakistan. Congress Party leaders were outraged by that League demand, Gandhi denouncing it as nothing less than a call for the "vivisection of India." The first years of World War II, however, were fought in Europe and North Africa, so remote from India, it seemed, that few British officials worried about the anger or rising levels of alienation toward the Raj felt by most Hindus, especially politically active ones. It was only after the war reached Singapore in 1942, with Japan's invasion of that premier base of British Pacific air and sea power, that Great Britain's war cabinet and Whitehall's India office focused attention on the possible imminent threat posed by the newest Axis power to their finest imperial "jewel," India. This book focuses on the following half decade of diplomatic missions and intense political negotiations launched by the British Raj to try to keep India secure, while devising constitutional plans to permit its people to enjoy all the benefits of responsible democratic government after the war ended.

My title is borrowed from Opposition Leader Winston Churchill's prophetic warning to Prime Minister Clement Attlee's government in the British House of Commons during the first debate over Labor's Indian Independence Bill. Though I have long disagreed with Churchill's harsh and outmoded imperialist views of India and its nationalist leaders, in this particular instance he was quite right. Mountbatten's hyperactive frenzy in accelerating the initially tight withdrawal schedule, mandated by Britain's cabinet to extend to June 1948, triggered Britain's "shameful flight, by a premature hurried scuttle" that left South Asia vulnerable to hatred and terror, compounded by ignorant fears and ugly rumors, multiplied by hundreds of millions.

How was it possible for the leaders of Great Britain, barely two years after defeating, with U.S. support, the armies of Hitler and Mussolini, to withdraw its 14,000 British officers in such unseemly haste from India? A combination of historic causes contributed to that tragic error of judgment, only the most immediate of which was Mountbatten's incompetence. Mounting British frustrations with Indian political leaders, their endless squabbling, escalating demands, and lack of gratitude or reliability, made even their closest British wartime friends in the Labor Party lose faith in them, especially after the collapse of Sir Stafford Cripps's mission, launched immediately following Singapore's surrender. The failure of Congress leaders to appreciate what Cripps tried to do damaged India much more than Britain. Churchill treacherously assisted Cripps's collapse, even while using his mission as "proof positive" to Roosevelt of Britain's "best intentions" toward India. In August 1942, Congress Party leaders launched their brutally smothered "Quit India" campaign, giving Viceroy Linlithgow the opportunity he keenly coveted to lock all of them up, including Gandhi and Nehru, leaving them to rust behind British bars for the remaining years of the war. *Quaid-i-Azam* ("Great Leader") Jinnah, the League's permanent president, took advantage of his wartime freedom to enhance the prestige of his Muslim constituency. Jinnah kept demanding nothing less than a sovereign Muslim nation of *Pakistan* ("Land of the Pure"), as Muslim India's postwar reward for the service of its loyal Muslim troops on all fronts and for the support Muslim leaders like himself gave the viceroy and his governors.

Britain's dependence on Indian supplies of food grains and iron and steel manufactured goods throughout the war reversed the previous century's balance of payments position, turning England into India's major debtor-state. By war's end, the Bank of England owed hundreds of millions of pounds sterling to the Reserve Bank of India. Trouble-strewn India was no longer a rich source of career opportunities for English graduates of Oxford and Cambridge, who for decades had taken Indian civil service exams, headed east on Peninsula & Orient steamers to make their fortunes in Bengal, and won fame fighting along India's northwest frontier.

Britain's first postwar elections, held in 1945, brought Clement Attlee's Labor Party a thumping majority and stripped Winston Churchill and his Tory Party of control of the House of Commons. Prime Minister Attlee tried again to bring the Congress Party and the Muslim League together within a single federal union of India, sending Stafford Cripps back to India with two other cabinet colleagues. That 1946 cabinet mission inched closer to success than Cripps alone had done four years earlier, but it ultimately failed to break India's political deadlock. Preoccupied as they were with Britain's own growing postwar domestic problems and diminishing resources, Labor's cabinet all but lost interest in India's problems.

Then Attlee appointed Admiral "Dickie" Mountbatten, the favorite cousin of King George, to serve as Britain's last viceroy. The prime minister hoped that with his famous "irresistible charm," Mountbatten might within fourteen months bring Gandhi, Nehru, and Jinnah round his viceregal table, teasing agreement from them to resolve their own problems. Britain could then withdraw its troops with dignity and take credit for leaving independent India unified. But Mountbatten was neither wise enough nor patient enough to accomplish what many older and more experienced British predecessors had failed to do. Nor did he have the humility or good sense to listen to India's two wisest political leaders, Mahatma Gandhi and Quaid-i-Azam Jinnah, both of whom tried their frail best to warn him to stop the runaway juggernaut to Partition before it was too late.

I met Lord Mountbatten only once, when I interviewed him while working on *Jinnah of Pakistan* in 1979, in what was to be the last year of his life. I hoped he would offer some fresh insights into the personality of the dominion of Pakistan's first governor-general. But Mountbatten brushed aside all my questions about Jinnah, hardly giving any a moment's consideration, advising me to "Ask Alan" [Campbell-Johnson] about him, at one point "wondering" aloud "why" I would bother to write about so "humorless" a man? He suggested I should, instead, write about "What [General] Slim and I did for Southeast Asia and the Commonwealth." I explained that I found Jinnah fascinating and was committed to writing his biography before I tackled anything else. From the sourness of his face at every mention of Jinnah's name, I could see how negatively Mountbatten felt about the Muslim leader. A few days earlier, moreover, I had read one of Mountbatten's "Top Secret and Personal" reports to King George, in London's India Office Library, in which he referred to Jinnah as "psychopathic." What I hadn't realized then, however, and have only recently appreciated since restudying the *Transfer of Power*[15] documents and many more recent memoirs of the period and of Partition's impact, was the monumental importance of Mountbatten's negativity toward Jinnah and its tragic significance for all of South Asia in the aftermath of Partition.

Partition maps revealing the butchered boundary lines drawn by Sir Cyril Radcliffe through the Sikh heartland of Punjab and east of Calcutta in Bengal were kept under lock and key on Mountbatten's orders, hidden from any other eyes for precious days within New Delhi's viceregal palace. If only the governors of Punjab and Bengal had known what to anticipate, they could with that early knowledge have saved countless refugee lives by dispatching troops and trains to what soon became lines of fire and blood. But Mountbatten had resolved to wait until India's "Independence Day" festivities were all over, the flashbulb photos all shot and transmitted worldwide, Dickie's medal-strewn white uniform viewed with admiration by millions, from Buckingham and Windsor Palaces to the White House. What a glorious charade of British Imperial largesse and power "peacefully" transferred.

Only in the desperate days and weeks after those celebrations of mid-August did the horrors of Partition's impact begin to emerge. No viceregal time had been wasted in planning for the feeding and housing and medical needs of ten million refugees. No British officers or troops remained to keep the peace in shattered Punjab, or in Bengal, nor in the state of Jammu and Kashmir, left in deadly limbo to become the source of increasingly violent conflicts between India and Pakistan, the cause of three wars to be waged between them over the next fifty-five years.

1

From the Fall of Singapore to the Failure of Cripps's Mission, February–April 1942

THE FALL OF SINGAPORE to a Japanese force one-third the size of the British-Indian garrison, in mid-February of 1942, sent shock waves of fear for India's security from what had been Britain's insular bastion of Southeast Asian naval and air power, directly to 10 Downing Street. So integral was that city to imperial defense that when Prime Minister Winston Churchill learned of the Japanese invasion on February 10, he telegraphed General Sir Archibald Wavell, British Supreme Commander of Allied Forces in Southeast Asia: "There must . . . be no thought of saving the troops or sparing the population. The battle must be fought to the bitter end at all costs. . . . The honour of the British Empire and of the British Army is at stake."[1]

The morale of the some 60,000 British Indian troops on Singapore was so low, however, that their commanding officer, General Percival, desperately requested permission of Wavell to surrender his men only six days after General Yamashita's force of 20,000 had crossed the Malay Peninsula's gorge and invaded Singapore's unprotected north shore. Permission was granted and the troops all became Japanese prisoners of war. That night Churchill reported to his closest ally, President Franklin D. Roosevelt (FDR), that Britain had "suffered the greatest disaster in our history."[2] For British India's imperial rulers, the fall of Singapore proved the first knell to toll the death, half a decade later, of its Raj. Churchill knew that without Singapore's fleet to defend the Indian Ocean from Japanese ships and planes, the Bay of Bengal and India's Eastern littoral, from Calcutta to Madras, were "now in danger of attack."[3]

Two months earlier, Japan had followed up its bombing of Pearl Harbor by sinking Britain's finest battleship, *Prince of Wales,* and its escort cruiser *Repulse,* the pride of Singapore's fleet, off Malaya's coast. The success of a swarm of Japanese suicide and torpedo bombers had come as the most "horrible shock" to Churchill prior to Singapore's loss. Britain's fleet was stretched so thin in defense of Anglo-American Atlantic convoys and the British Isles that there were neither battleships nor aircraft carriers left for Southeast Asia. Churchill understood too well that Japan, with two new 45,000-ton battleships, could dominate both the Pacific and Indian Oceans. Even though the Japanese flew few sorties over India, there was cause for concern. British Indian military intelligence reported that many "left wing speakers" in Bengal appeared ready to support the Japanese, if they should attempt to invade India. Antiwar and "defeatist rumors" were also now often heard in Calcutta's bazaars. Yet Prime Minister Churchill focused primarily on the defense of England and its Anglo-American Atlantic lifeline, secondarily on recapturing Egypt and North Africa, and on plans for an Allied invasion of Western Europe. India remained his lowest strategic priority until Singapore's fall. He had once hoped to convince Roosevelt to transfer the U.S. battle fleet from Hawaii to Singapore, but after the *Prince of Wales* was sunk he knew how little chance he had of doing so. Instead he stressed the theme of "Anglo-American unity" during his first wartime visit to Washington, condemning Japan for its "sneak attack" on Pearl Harbor in a speech that brought a joint session of the U.S. Congress to enthusiastic ovations. Britain had been obliged to spend over $4.5 billion "in cash" for American planes, tanks, ships, and machines since the war started. Roosevelt resolved to help save America's most-valued partner from bankruptcy by announcing his Lend-Lease plan in mid-December 1940. Isolationist Republicans denounced Roosevelt as a "dictator," trying to "drag" America into a "foreign War," when he proclaimed his plan to send Britain whatever food or equipment it needed to survive, without requiring any cash payments. A reluctant U.S. Congress withheld its passage of the Lend-Lease Act until March 11, 1941.[4]

Roosevelt and Churchill had established strong, cordial bonds of personal friendship even before the United States entered the war in the wake of Pearl Harbor's disaster. They met for nine summits during the war, conversing many hours alone. "Former Naval Person" Churchill sent 1,161 wartime messages and telegrams to "Former Naval Secretary" Roosevelt, the president personally responding 788 times.[5] Their friendship and mutual respect remained the single most important human anchor of the Anglo-American Alliance. The only diplomatic area over which they were deeply divided was India. Roosevelt never agreed with Churchill's inflexible position on keeping India in the British Empire, nor with his malignant mistrust of Mahatma Gandhi. FDR was too much the pragmatist to risk rupturing his relationship with Churchill, however, over a point so peripheral to their wartime Grand Alliance of twenty-six nations against the Axis powers.

Roosevelt understood, moreover, that Churchill's political popularity and personal charisma in wartime England was unique. Britain's Tory Party reflected outmoded values of Britain's conservative aristocracy in the pre-war years of Neville Chamberlain's pathetic appeasement of Nazi Germany, but after Winston Churchill became prime minister in May 1940 he inspired all of England to take heart. To broaden the spectrum of his political support, he invited the opposition Labor Party's leader, Clement Attlee, to join his wartime coalition cabinet as deputy prime minister. Attlee, who chaired the cabinet's India-Burma Committee, had visited India in 1927 when he served on Ramsay MacDonald's Indian Statutory Commission. What Attlee learned then of the complexity of India's multicultural Hindu-Muslim society strongly influenced his lifelong thinking about India. He was less disposed than his more radical Labor colleagues to accept oft-repeated claims of India's National Congress leaders to speak for India's *entire* "Nation."

In the aftermath of Singapore's fall, however, Attlee understood, and Churchill agreed, that it was vital for Britain's cabinet to launch a diplomatic initiative to try at least to win the support of India's National Congress Party for the Allied war effort. Without the backing of Mahatma Gandhi and Jawaharlal Nehru, the British government of India had no chance of mobilizing the vast majority of India's 400 million people effectively to resist attack by Japanese armed forces. Four days after the loss of Singapore, therefore, Churchill invited Sir Stafford Cripps into his war cabinet as lord privy seal and leader of the House of Commons.

Cripps was at once admired and reviled by colleagues for his radical brilliance and austere lifestyle. He was dubbed "Red Squire" by Churchill, who well knew how brilliant he was yet considered him "a lunatic."[6] Cripps had recently returned from Moscow, where he served as British ambassador, and had earlier visited India, where he met with Nehru and also traveled to Gandhi's remote central Indian village ashram to meet with the mahatma alone. Like Nehru, he was an ardent Socialist; and, like Gandhi, he was a strict vegetarian. Cripps seemed, therefore, the ideal cabinet minister to dispatch to India at this time of extreme danger and mounting anxiety over the possibility of a Japanese invasion. Nor did Attlee have to convince his radical Labor comrade to take on the job. Cripps was so eager that he volunteered to go alone on his official "mission" to India on behalf of the war cabinet less than a month after Singapore had been lost.

Viceroy Linlithgow, graduate of Eton and an avid fox hunter, was as conservative an imperialist as Cripps was a radical Socialist. When he learned of Cripps's mission from secretary of state for India Leopold Amery, Linlithgow's first question was "Why?" He felt nothing but disdain for Cripps before his mission started and, by its bitter end, considered his judgment justified. Leo Amery was the only secretary of state for India to have been born there, his father stationed on the northwest frontier. Like Churchill and Nehru, Amery had gone to Harrow, then trained as a classical scholar at Oxford, and went on to become a barrister. He taught himself India's ancient classical language, Sanskrit, one of half a dozen languages in which he was fluent.[7] Amery reassured Linlithgow he had no need to fear that Cripps was being sent to India by the cabinet to usurp or undermine his viceregal powers, but merely to "help" him rule India more effectively by winning the support of noncooperating National Congress Party leaders.

Churchill and Attlee agreed, insisting, however, that the offer Cripps carried to India in his attache case include one option that would almost certainly preclude the possibility of winning the Indian Congress Party's support. The offer promised what Indians had long demanded and what most still eagerly awaited: "dominion status"—complete independence within the British Commonwealth, much the same as Canada, Australia, and New Zealand had long enjoyed—only India's would not come until after the war ended. Any province of British India whose elected representatives voted against joining the new dominion, however, could "retain its existing constitutional position." That "opt-out" clause was read by Gandhi and Nehru as the war cabinet's invitation to Jinnah's Muslim League to carve its own separate Muslim dominion of Pakistan out of North India.

Some two years earlier the Muslim League had, on March 23, 1940, adopted its "Pakistan" resolution in Lahore, where Jinnah presided over its largest annual meeting ever held. That resolution asserted that "no constitutional plan" put forward by the British for India would be "acceptable" unless those areas in which Muslims were a majority, "as in the north-western and north-eastern zones of British India, should be grouped to constitute independent States in which the constituent units shall be autonomous and sovereign."[8] The resolution was ambiguous, probably initially meaning two Muslim states: Pakistan and Bangladesh, though when Jinnah was questioned on this point by journalists the next morning he insisted it meant *one Pakistan*. That remained his League's single most important demand, further bolstered by Cripps's "opt-out" clause in 1942.

In early March of 1942, the war cabinet unanimously agreed to back the offer to be made by Cripps, which Churchill himself offered to broadcast to the Indian people, in his own inspiring voice. But when Linlithgow learned of this he threatened to resign.[9] So Churchill withdrew his offer, knowing that Linlithgow's negative views of India's National Congress Party and Mahatma Gandhi faithfully reflected his own and anxious to keep his like-minded viceroy in place.[10] Both men preferred to leave the government of India unchanged, its autocratic powers undisturbed by Cripps or any one else, at least until the war ended. But with the United States helping Britain to survive Axis assaults on every front, Churchill dared not ignore Roosevelt's concerns about India. Cripps also had substantial British popular backing, having returned from Moscow to a diplomatic hero's welcome, for his strong support of Russia's valiant resistance against the Nazi army's invasion. Some of his supporters viewed Cripps as Britain's most effective wartime prime minister-in-waiting. Sending him off to India could, therefore, be the easiest way for Churchill to solve two of his most thorny problems with a single deft stroke, both appeasing Roosevelt and undermining Cripps's popularity by letting him prove how inept he would be at global diplomacy.

Roosevelt's close friend and personal envoy to Churchill, Averell Harriman, wrote FDR that he was "worried about the Prime Minister," whose "confidence" had been badly shaken by Singapore "to such an extent that he has not been able to stand up to this adversity with his old vigor."[11] He added, however, that "Cripps wears the hair shirt and wants everyone else to do the same." Harriman reported to Roosevelt's other personal envoy in London, Harry Hopkins, that "Cripps' star has risen high on the backs of the fighting Russian armies . . . but he lacks, I believe, an understanding of the British people. . . . His intimate friends tell me he thinks he is the Messiah."[12] Roosevelt closely monitored what Churchill was doing to generate more "public enthusiasm" in India for the war effort. "The Prime Minister will not take any political steps which would alienate the Moslem population of over 100 million," Harriman replied.[13] Churchill himself told the president: "We are considering whether any declaration can be made which will strengthen defence of India against approaching invasion. Danger is of offending Moslems who, besides being a hundred million strong, constitute the main fighting part of the Army. . . . They will not allow themselves to be governed by majority produced by the Congress Caucus and the Hindu priesthood."[14]

Given military exigencies, Roosevelt could hardly insist to his partner that he must now "risk" losing India by undermining the loyalty of the British Indian Army's major religious bloc. Nor did FDR understand enough about India's multicultural society to be able to argue against Churchill's personal favoring of India's Muslim minority against the majority "Congress-Hindu priesthood." Roosevelt hoped, nonetheless, to use personal envoys to India to keep him accurately informed of what was happening there, just as Harriman and Hopkins informed him on Churchill's moods. The first Roosevelt envoy to India was Colonel Louis Johnson, who had been assistant secretary of war, and arrived in India as head of America's technical mission in April of 1942.

Sir Stafford's plane landed in Karachi, Sind's provincial capital, on March 22, 1942. He and his entourage were quarantined overnight, as all wartime flights arriving in India from Africa were subject to that medical delay as a public health precaution. Angry at the waste of his time, Cripps tried to get on the night flight from Karachi to Jodhpur, but was dissuaded by British officials, who warned that they had no proper mosquito netting there and a number of recent visitors had caught malaria. Resigned to that symbolic "Welcome to India," Cripps met with Sind's governor and found him "optimistic" about his chances of success. In their discussion of Cripps's mission to win the support of India's political leaders for postwar reforms, Muslim Chief Minister of Sind Allah Bakhsh was also "very pleased"[15] that Sir Stafford had taken on this task.

The next day, when he reached Delhi, Cripps was surprised to see thousands of Muslims marching with green flags, shouting *"Pakistan Zindabad!"* ("Victory to Pakistan!") to celebrate the second anniversary of the League's adoption of its Lahore Resolution. Jinnah's followers saluted as they marched past the platform on which he stood, thus giving Cripps a dramatic demonstration of how united Muslims were in their Pakistan demand. Neither Churchill nor Linlithgow could have picked a better date for Cripps's arrival in terms of strengthening Jinnah's hand while weakening the position of Gandhi, Nehru, and the Congress Party in their talks over the next few weeks.

"I have come to India to discuss with the leaders of Indian opinion conclusions which the War Cabinet have unitedly reached in regard to India," Cripps told the press on his first evening in Delhi.[16] The proposals he brought were "practical steps" to fulfill past British "promises of self-government to the Indian peoples." As soon as India's political leaders understood his proposals, Cripps felt "confident" that they would all put forth their "maximum effort" to defend India during the remainder of the war. Sir Stafford added that he personally had always been "a great friend and admirer of India." He planned to gain swift support, announcing his intention to stay in Delhi for only two weeks, before returning to many "urgent and important matters" in London.

During his first two days in Delhi, Cripps met with the viceroy and his executive council. He initially found Linlithgow "very helpful," and the viceroy promised to give Cripps "every possible assistance" to "make a success of his mission."[17] But "whether the scheme succeeds or fails," Linlithgow added, agreeing with Amery's earlier assessment, the "propaganda value involved in [the] face of American opinion" would leave "a balance of credit to our side." Even before Cripps left England, Amery had recognized the public relations value of "sending out someone who has always been an extreme Left Winger and in close touch with Nehru."[18] He told Linlithgow that the "alarming" immediate effect on "your Muslims, as with my Tory friends here" would "in the end . . . mitigate any blame thrown upon the Government as a whole for failure."

Most of Raj's senior British civil servants agreed with Amery and Linlithgow, though some, like Central Provinces Governor Sir Henry Twynam felt cautiously hopeful about Cripps's mission and its prospects for success. Twynam favored "the fullest measure of Self-Government for India after the war."[19] He feared, however, that Congress would "pitch its demands" too high, as Nehru was apt to be "stiff and uncompromising," foolishly "convinced" that the British government was about to collapse. The "morale" in his own Central Provinces was steadily "declining," Twynam reported, yet he felt "confident" law and order could be maintained. He had no illusions though about "arousing a national spirit in India" to help win the war. "I have little doubt that the vast majority would acquiesce in Japanese rule without hesitation sooner than risk their lives or property."

Linlithgow invited Cripps to meet with his executive council, and Cripps read out his proposed declaration, giving council members time to question him as soon as he finished. The nonaccession clause immediately elicited discussion; it would have permitted any province with a Muslim majority to refuse to join a postwar dominion of India, leaving each of them free to unite if they wished to create a dominion of Pakistan. The Muslim League's supporter, Sir Firoze Khan Noon, wanted to know if "non-acceding provinces . . . would have their own constitution . . . not inferior *vis-à-vis* the British Government? (At this Mr. Aney looked glum.)"[20] Dr. Madhao Shrihari Aney was a devout Hindu who clearly understood, even before Sir Firoze asked his next question as to "whether non-acceding provinces could amalgamate," that Noon envisaged "Pakistan" emerging from Cripps's "opt-out" clause. Dr. Raghavendra Rao, civil defense member of council, inquired as to what arrangements would be made for "joint services" like the railways and currency, to which Cripps replied that would be "done by agreement." Law Member of Council Sir Sultan Ahmed asked if there would still be "any Centre," meaning India's central government under the viceroy and his council, but Cripps did not reply. When the commander-in-chief next asked about "the future of the army," Sir Stafford shocked him and other British members of the council by answering that it would "cease to exist as a British Army."[21]

General Sir Archibald Wavell attended that council meeting as commander-in-chief of the British Indian Army, the position he had held in 1941 before he was promoted to supreme commander of Britain's South-West Pacific forces. He returned to India and his former job soon after the fall of Singapore. Now, after listening to Cripps, Wavell told Linlithgow he believed the "effect" of those proposals on India's "fighting services" would be "disastrous." The trouble, Wavell feared, was that given the multi-communal character of Muslim-Sikh-Hindu Punjab, which alone supplied some 50 percent of the army's total number of recruits, any future constitutional announcement "will take soldier's mind . . . off fighting our enemies and start him looking over his shoulder."[22] In his first long talk with Cripps, Wavell reiterated his anxieties about Punjab. "He seemed to think that it was the Pakistan idea which would cause them most concern," Cripps noted.[23] The governor of Punjab, Sir Bertram Glancy, was "anxious" about Muslim-Sikh relations in his province. "The Sikhs were troublesome anyway," he explained, "and if there were a hint of [Punjab's] secession they would concentrate on getting ready to fight the Moslems."[24] Glancy agreed with Cripps that "something should be done" to encourage greater Sikh security as well as more overall Hindu and Muslim support for the war, suggesting that a postwar body be established, consisting of representatives of the United States as well as the commonwealth dominions and Great Britain, to "work out a constitution for India." Sir Stafford was certain no "section of Indian opinion" would agree to that.

On March 25 Cripps began to meet with Indian leaders, beginning with Congress Party president Maulana Abul Kalam Azad. Nehru had stepped aside to allow Muslim Azad to preside over the Congress Party throughout the war, as proof of Congress's multicommunal secular nature. (Fully understanding his symbolic role, Azad stepped down as soon as Nehru was ready to take back his presidential powers after the war ended.) Jinnah bitterly resented Azad, so outraged by his "sham" elevation to the Congress presidency that he refused ever to shake hands with him and publicly condemned him as a "showcase Muslim." Azad brought his secretary, Asaf Ali, whose command of English was better than his own, that afternoon. "I read the document slowly [aloud]," Cripps noted after they left, "asking for any interruptions upon points that did not seem too clear or satisfactory."[25] The only points they [Azad and Ali] questioned were those dealing with "Defence," insisting that to "mobilise effectively" all of India's people, the Congress Party felt it must be given control over the ministry of defense. Cripps argued that "strategically" India was part of a much larger "theatre of war," and decisions as to the disposition of troops, ships, and planes on that stage could only be made by London's war cabinet. Azad reiterated his point, however, insisting some "great gesture" would be required to mobilize Indians, and appointing an Indian minister of defense would possibly serve that purpose. The Congress Party was prepared to leave the current commander-in-chief in charge of "matters of strategy." Azad made no other suggestions, and Cripps reportedly found him "extremely friendly."[26]

As president of the Muslim League, Jinnah came next. Cripps thought him "rather surprised," after he read the document, "in the distance it went to meet the Pakistan case."[27] Though Jinnah was not immediately prepared to give his own "views" of the proposal, he did ask whether Bengal and Punjab, both of which had narrow Muslim majorities, would have "the effective right to opt out of the constitution." Cripps replied that "in the case of such narrowly divided provinces, the minority should have the right to" demand a plebiscite, an impartially monitored vote, of the total adult population of the province. Jinnah agreed that a "plebiscite was the only absolutely fair idea." Cripps found him "extremely cordial. . . . I was hopefully impressed by his general attitude." Jinnah's only suggestion for alteration of the document was to clarify its phraseology "as regards the possibility of a second Dominion being set up."[28] Jinnah's "clarification" language [adding the "possibility of a second Dominion being created"] was approved by Attlee's India Committee in London the very next day.[29]

On that same afternoon in New Delhi, March 27, Cripps showed Mahatma Gandhi his altered document. "In the first instance he expressed the very definite view that Congress would not accept the document [which he called] . . . an invitation to the Moslems to create a Pakistan."[30] Though Gandhi had resigned from the Congress Party several years earlier and reminded Cripps that "officially" he had no position in the party, Sir Stafford should have known how powerful and supremely important this "Great Soul's" influence remained on the Congress leaders as well as rank-and-file membership throughout most of India. But Cripps had already invested a week of his life in this mission and wanted to believe it was going "well," as he had been told optimistically by everyone he had until now met with. Both presidents of the major parties, Azad and Jinnah, had been very "friendly" and "amiable," after all, as was the viceroy and his council and governors, not to mention Attlee, Amery, and Churchill. They all encouraged him and were rooting for him to succeed, confirming how important his mission was. Why should this one half-naked old man's harshly negative assessment make him lose faith in its outcome? "I expressed a doubt as to whether, when it came to the question of practical application, there would be much support for the Pakistan idea as there was at the present time," Cripps told him. A great barrister, he thought he could convince Gandhi that there was no sound reason to be negative about his proposal. "I went through the document with him, pointing out that it was primarily based upon the conception of a united India."[31]

Cripps tried his best to convince Gandhi that it would really be up to the Congress Party to reach "agreement" with the Muslims, after the British were "out of the way," and a constitution-making body had been elected. Then they could all sit together—Gandhi, Nehru, Azad, and Jinnah—and work out their differences and find a way to live peacefully, productively, in a happy, united, independent India. "After very lengthy discussion," Cripps optimistically noted, "he seemed to be rather less certain of the antagonism of Congress on this point."

"I then asked him frankly as a friend,"—for that was why Cripps had come all this way, because he was, he thought, a true friend of Gandhi and

Nehru and of their Congress Party, and of India—"to tell me what he thought was the best method of proceeding." His relationships with Congress leaders were the reason Churchill and Attlee had sent him out to serve Britain's war cabinet on this vital mission. "He (Gandhi) said he thought it would have been better if I had not come to India with a cut and dried scheme to impose upon the Indians."[32] Somewhat surprised by that sharp criticism, Cripps "reminded him that the first time I had met him he had told me that once it was made absolutely clear that India would achieve self-government on some ascertained date, what happened in the intervening period was of comparatively small importance." Cripps thought "he seemed inclined to accept the view that this document was merely a finalising of the date and the method which might be adopted pending the agreement of the parties upon any other or better one." He believed he had changed Gandhi's mind on this crucial matter. Cripps noted to himself, after the Mahatma had left the room, "He accepted, I think, this approach to the document and then said he thought it was extremely inadvisable to have the document published in any way whatsoever unless first agreement had been obtained from both the major communities."

On that Friday, Cripps told Gandhi he intended to publish it on Monday. It was first to be made public in India and shortly afterward by the BBC in London. Still Gandhi "asked me many times to see that it was not so published."[33] But it was too late. Sir Stafford had already cleared the precise hour of his announcement to the press and subsequent broadcast of his document in Delhi, in London, and to the United States. The Mahatma pleaded, convinced that his Congress colleagues would reject the proposal as an invitation to the birth of "Pakistan," but Cripps moved on. So deluded was he that he recorded of the incident, "He expressed, I think quite sincerely, his hopes that I should succeed in spite of what he had said." Sir Stafford had failed to understand that even though he would still have two more exhausting, sweltering weeks of arduous talks and heated discussion in Delhi, his mission had failed.

Cripps met with a deputation of four Sikh leaders the same day he saw Gandhi. They were interested "naturally" in questions concerning the "protection of the Sikh minority" and of possible redistribution of several portions of Punjab "in order to carve out a province in which the Sikhs would have the decisive voice."[34] Master Tara Singh, the most extreme of his bearded-and-turbaned visitors, called for the creation of a separate "Sikhistan," a Sikh nation-state within Punjab, where the majority of Sikhs lived and where their founder, Guru Nanak, was born. "I pointed out to them the successive stages at which they might hope to exert pressure that would enable them either to remain part of the single Indian Union or to get some provincial autonomy within the second Union if such was formed," Cripps noted. He hadn't given serious thought to the Sikhs wanting their own dominion. They were, after all, only six million strong. Like Punjabi Muslims, Sikhs had long been pandered to by British recruiting officers as a "martial race" of fearless soldiers, their regiments sustaining the highest number of casualties in the British army. Hindu Brahmans considered Sikhism no more than an "offshoot" of Hinduism, but Sikhs worshiped their own scripture of the sacred "True Words" of their gurus, which was daily read aloud in the Golden Temple in Punjab's Amritsar, Mecca of Sikhism.

"If, when the constitution was finally settled, the Moslems decided that they had not got sufficient concessions to enable them to remain within the Indian Union," Cripps tried to explain to his quartet of skeptical Sikh visitors, "then it would be necessary for them to obtain a vote of non-accession . . . in the Punjab (and) they would no doubt be anxious to . . . try to get the Sikh vote to support their action . . . possibly . . . agreeing to . . . a semi-autonomous district."[35] None of the Sikhs seemed satisfied with that quarter loaf of what they expected for their valiant community. Without Sikh soldiers, after all, British officers a century earlier might never have recaptured Delhi after the 1857 "Sepoy Mutiny," led by Bengali Hindus and Muslims of Oudh. They raised the point made by Azad, insisting how "essential" it was to have an "Indian Minister" associated with "Defence." Summing up the meeting, Cripps optimistically noted, "Although they were obviously anxious, I think they appreciated that we had done our utmost in the circumstances to provide protection."

The next day nine princes, a delegation from the chamber of princes, arrived. The chamber consisted of 562 feudals, who enjoyed virtual autonomy over their own princely states as long as they accepted British paramountcy and did nothing "subversive" or "treacherous" to alienate the viceroy or his agents. The major concern of the princes was to retain the martial and diplomatic support of Britain's paramount power, to whose king-emperor each of them swore allegiance. "So far as the undertaking of our obligations of defence of the States was concerned," Cripps told them, that would depend on "the number and position of States that were left out of the Union." There was, however, "no insuperable difficulty from the naval point of view so long as we held Ceylon (Sri Lanka), or from the Air point of view. . . . We should stand by our treaties with the States, unless they asked us to revoke them, so far as all matters of paramountcy were concerned."[36] That solemn promise would expire half a decade later, when British paramountcy was to die with the Raj. The Muslim nizam of Hyderabad, the most populous princely state, was deeply worried about his future, hoping either for complete independence from India, or for continued British protection. Hyderabad's diwan (prime minister) anxiously questioned Cripps again that afternoon, after all the other princes had left, but "This was merely a repetition . . . of the interview which had been held . . . in the morning . . . and therefore requires no further record," weary Cripps noted.[37]

Hindu-first extremists, led by Hindu Mahasabha Party's president, Vinayak Damodar Savarkar, came after the Hyderabad delegation departed. Savarkar had been charged with treason and transported for "life" to Britain's Andaman Island prison before World War I. Recently released, he was hailed as a national hero by Hindu extremists, including the man who was to assassinate Mahatma Gandhi. "Savarkar . . . spent most of his time lecturing me upon the principles of majority determination and of the fallacies within the document," Cripps noted. "I am afraid I made little or no impression on him and his colleagues who . . . were in favour of an immediate declaration in the terms of the first paragraph but were opposed to the right of non-accession."[38] Cripps insisted that his proposal must either be accepted or rejected "as a whole." Savarkar and his party rejected it as another example of British duplicity.

Congress President Azad returned next, "depressed at the apparent cheerfulness of the Muslim League and at first raised again the question of the right of non-accession but very quickly gave up," focusing instead on the importance of appointing an Indian minister of defense.[39] For over an hour and a half they argued, Cripps trying to convince the depressed Azad that unless Congress accepted his scheme they would get nothing until the end of the war, and "possibly a good deal longer." Cripps also warned him that if the Congress Party rejected his offer they would lose their "best friends" in "British political circles." But Cripps sensed that what Gandhi had earlier warned him appeared to reflect the sensitivities of other Congress leaders as well.

Jawaharlal Nehru came to breakfast alone on Sunday, March 29, 1942. Nehru said he had not as yet spoken with his Congress colleagues about Cripps's proposals, which he claimed to have "only just seen," having been in "strict isolation in bed for two days to try to get over his fever."[40] Cripps stressed to his old "friend" the "need" to reach agreement, but they had little time alone, since "a great gathering of Congress people" awaited them at Birla House, where Mahatma Gandhi stayed in Delhi. Azad led Cripps into Birla's rear bedroom, where Gandhi sat on the floor spinning cotton. He "had nothing more to add" to what he had told Cripps two days earlier, urging him to speak to other members of the Congress Party Working Committee, who were waiting to see him in another room.

Pandit Pant, who had served as Congress Premier of the United Provinces (UP) from 1937 to 1939, argued vigorously against Cripps's nonaccession clause for over an hour. Cripps explained that his "task was to create a solution between the Muslim League and Congress," which could not be done without trying to meet the Muslim League demand. [41] He came no closer to convincing Pant on that point than he had Gandhi. Pant also argued that Britain's "paramountcy" over all Indian states should be transferred to the Indian Union. Cripps insisted that could not be done, "except by the consent of the States." Then he met for two more hours with Nehru and Azad, who both disliked the term "dominion," and wanted Congress's radical States's Peoples parties, which Nehru himself had been active in organizing , rather than the state princes, to lead "democratic" states into the Indian union. They also opposed a nonaccession clause. "I pointed out that Nehru and other Congress leaders had said they were prepared to envisage the possibility of Pakistan and that was all the scheme was doing." [42] Finally, they insisted that an Indian minister of defense was a prerequisite for arousing Indian support for the war.

Undeterred by the uneven support he had received, Cripps held his press conference, as planned, that Sunday afternoon. When asked how soon the new Indian Union might be achieved, he said that provincial elections would be held "immediately" after the termination of hostilities, and as a result of those elections "the constitution-making body will be set up." [43] Asked to explain the name "Indian Union" he said it was the name they gave to "the new India which will have a constitution made by Indians." One reporter bitterly remarked that the "history of Britain" in India was of "broken pledges," and went on to request that President Roosevelt be asked to "guarantee" these proposals. Cripps said that would not be possible. Asked if a "non-acceding Province" in the north might form "a separate union" with another such province in the south, Cripps replied, "That would be impracticable. Two contiguous provinces may form a separate union." [44] That, of course, was what the Congress Party feared most.

As to the possibility of holding a plebiscite, Cripps said, " I proposed it. Democratically, the plebiscite is to ascertain the will of the population in a given area, if is doubt." [45] Would it be "obligatory" for a province to decide either to accede or not before it was permitted to send representatives to the constituent assembly? "The process is completely different," Cripps explained, laying out his plan.

> All provinces have got to send representatives to the constituent assembly. There will be discussions . . . with everybody present and at the end of a period (say, during the course of a year) a constitution will be framed. When it is finally, definitely framed all provinces will be able to say 'in spite of all our efforts to get what we wanted, fair treatment, in the constituent assembly we have failed. We do not, therefore, wish to accede.' The legislature will then vote upon it. If there is a majority of less than 60 per cent the minority will demand that a plebiscite should decide. If for a year in the constitution-making body the Indian communities meet together in order to forge a united constitution for India they will probably

succeed. If they do not, we can do nothing more to help them to succeed. If after having done that, some of them want to separate, nobody in the world can stop them.[46]

Asked about what would happen to the Indian states and who would decide, their "people" or their princes, Cripps said: "We have got to deal with facts as they are. We cannot create Governments that are not there. The Indian States are governed by treaties. The treaties . . . will continue to exist unless somebody wants to alter them . . . . States, if they do not join in this Union, will remain in exactly the same situation as they are today."[47] Asked "at what stage" the British government "propose to leave this country," Cripps replied, "At the stage when the constitution-making body have decided upon the constitution." After that press conference, Cripps more realistically recognized how many Indians questioned his good faith in proposing what he did, for he was sensitive enough to see how the reporters often shook their heads or shrugged off his answers as too vague and unclear.

Nehru came to dine alone with Cripps the next day. He was very "worried about the Indian situation," primarily expressing how much Indian "opinion" against the British had recently grown because of the harsh treatment of Indian refugees from the eastern seaboard, fleeing for fear of an imminent Japanese invasion, compared to the treatment of European refugees from the same region, who were all housed at British clubs. Increased unemployment, especially among the weavers of Benares, also worried him, as did shortages of food grains. Nehru frankly expressed a "growing disbelief in the capacity of Great Britain to make any defence effective" since the fall of Singapore.[48] There was much greater "sympathy for Japan," as during the Russo-Japanese War in 1905, when Indians took great pride in their tiny fellow Asian power's defeat of the huge Russian fleet. Nehru then gave Cripps the impression that Congress's working committee would "not accept the proposals, largely, I think . . . due to the influence of Gandhi." Linlithgow's private secretary, Leonard Pinnell, had just been told by an informant on the Congress working committee that Gandhi was "dead against" Cripps's proposal, calling it a "blank cheque on a crashing bank."[49]

That evening, Cripps attempted to sell his plan directly to the Indian people, broadcasting to India as well as to England and America. "I want tonight to give you a short explanation of the document which was published in the Press this morning," Cripps began.

The British Government and the British people desire the Indian peoples to have full self-government, with a constitution as free in every respect as our own in Great Britain or as of any of the great Dominion members of the British Commonwealth of Nations . . . so we propose that immediately [after] hostilities are ended a Constitution-making body will be set up

[26]

consisting of elected representatives from British India, and if the Indian States wish . . . they too will be invited to send their representatives to this Constitution-making body.[50]

He went on to note that "there is more than one people, there are many peoples and races" in India, and that in addition to those "who claim that India should form a single united country, there are others who say it should be divided up into two, three or more . . . countries."[51] But he repeated the hope that elected representatives of all those Indian "religions and races" would come together, as soon as the war ended, to frame their own constitution. "We hope and expect to see an Indian Union strong and united because it is founded upon the free consent of all its peoples; but it is not for us Britishers to dictate to you, the Indian peoples, you will work out and decide that problem for yourselves."[52] For the "immediate future," he hoped the viceroy would do everything in his power to bring leaders of Indian opinion onto his executive council, and thus most effectively organize India's resources for India's defense as part of the world war effort.

> There will still be difficulties . . . the result of the distrust which has grown up between us in past years, but I ask you to turn your back upon that past, to accept my hand, the hand of friendship and trust to allow us to join with you . . . in working to establish and complete your freedom and your self-government. . . . Let us enter upon this primary task of the Defence of India in the now sure knowledge that when we emerge from the fire and travail of war it will be to build a free India . . . and to forge a long-lasting and free friendship between our two peoples. . . . Let the dead past bury its dead! And let us march together side by side through the night of high endeavour and courage to the already waking dawn of a new world of liberty for all the peoples.[53]

These were brave and noble words, but the next morning, when Cripps went to see Linlithgow, he confessed that he knew "he was finished."[54] Mahatma Gandhi's words echoed in his mind, as India's heat and dust took its toll on his tired body, and Cripps wondered, indeed, why he had "come so far." He made plans now to fly home on April 5, wiring Churchill on April 1 to say that it seemed "certain that Congress will turn down the proposals."[55] In a last effort to satisfy the Congress Party's demands for an Indian minister of defence, however, he asked if the viceroy would be willing to meet Congress leaders with the commander-in-chief to discuss a possible role for an Indian in "some office connected with the Government of India's defence responsibilities without . . . impinging upon the functions and duties of the Commander-in-Chief."[56] So he concluded his telegram to Churchill by asking: "If some adjustment can be so arrived at will you give me full authority subject to agreement of Commander-in-Chief and Viceroy." But Churchill would not make that decision alone and would have to submit the question to his cabinet. To bolster Cripps's flagging spirits, Churchill wrote, "Everyone admires the manner in which you have discharged your difficult mission and the effect . . . has been most beneficial in the United States."[57]

As Cripps had anticipated, Azad and Nehru brought the Congress Party's negative response to him on April 2. They found his proposals "vague and altogether incomplete and it would appear that no vital changes in the present structure are contemplated."[58] Cripps then invited them to speak with the commander-in-chief as soon as he could meet with them. They agreed, so Cripps delayed his departure until April 12.

Churchill brought Cripps's request before the war cabinet on April 2, and though they approved the idea of inviting Azad and Nehru to meet with Wavell, they were "disinclined to depart from the published text of the Declaration or to go beyond it in any way."[59] Churchill then wired Linlithgow and Wavell, asking each of them "to send their own views . . . on the proposals under consideration."[60] He used their negative replies to reenforce his own negative feelings about Cripps's attempts to expand his proposals far beyond the limits initially set by the cabinet, repeating them to FDR and others. Sir G. S. Bajpai, "Agent" of the viceroy in Washington, was called in to see President Roosevelt that same afternoon. Bajpai reported to Linlithgow: "Mr. Roosevelt seems to think (Cripps's) plan regarding immediate federation does not go far enough. His idea . . . seems to be that complete autonomy, including power to raise armies, should be given to provinces. I tried to explain dangers in time of war of such change . . . but the President is not a good listener."[61]

Meanwhile, the Japanese fleet advanced forcefully into the Indian Ocean, having taken the Andaman Islands, and was heading west toward Ceylon (Sri Lanka) on April 4. With five aircraft carriers, the Japanese delivered "severe air attacks" on Sri Lanka's capital of Colombo and the great naval base at Trincomalee, destroying nineteen British planes and four heavily armed British warships, while losing twenty-one of their own planes.[62] Some 500 British sailors were drowned that day, and 300 more a day later, when the second Japanese air attack on Trincomalee harbor sank the aircraft carrier *Hermes* and the British destroyer *Vampire*. Luckily, Colombo was not invaded by a Japanese army. A relieved Churchill wired Cripps in Delhi, "it is lucky we did not withdraw fighter forces," as the viceroy had earlier requested. Pressure on Ceylon diminished as swiftly as it began. The Japanese returned their fleet to the Pacific and landed troops on the Solomon Islands on April 6.

Cripps took Nehru and Azad to meet with Wavell on the evening of April 4. The commander-in-chief listened silently to both Congress Party leaders, neither of whom really trusted him. The feeling was mutual. Wavell had lost one eye in combat, and his glass eye made his impassive square-jawed face appear even more "wooden." Wavell reassured Cripps, as well as Churchill, that "I am doing my utmost . . . to go to furthest limit possible on question of defence in order to secure acceptance of scheme put forward by H. M. G.[His Majesty's Government]."[63] He knew that Churchill blamed him for the loss of Singapore and was, therefore, doubly determined not to risk losing India. Cripps was equally determined to do everything in his power to ensure the safety and protection of India, but he would approach the problem from a different direction. "The time has now arrived when a final decision must be arrived at as to how far we are prepared to go on the chance of getting a settlement," Cripps wired Churchill on April 4 as the bombs fell on Ceylon. The Congress Party was divided, he explained, into a Gandhi-wing of "non-violence who are against the scheme altogether . . . and regard Great Britain as defeated and unimportant so far as the future of India is concerned."[64] Cripps believed that wing was "definitely a minority." The rest favored "fighting the Japanese," though some felt the non-accession clause in his proposal was a fatal flaw, while others would "swallow" that and the rest of his scheme so long as they could be reassured on the matter of Indian partnership with the commander-in-chief, or at least "participation" in running the ministry of defense. If Congress rejected the proposal, Cripps informed Churchill that even the Muslim League would turn it down, though he had just learned it received "unanimous" approval of Jinnah's working committee. The League could not, however, risk public ridicule as a "lackey" of the British by openly accepting an offer that the much larger Indian National Congress rejected.

Cripps hoped that if Nehru and Azad could convince a majority of the Congress working committee to support his scheme, then Gandhi and his followers would "retire" from the party for the rest of the war. He was "satisfied" that once they came in, Nehru, Azad, and C. Rajagopalachari, South India's foremost member of the Congress Party, "will go all out to maximise Indian resistance to Japan and will fight with courage and determination to galvanise the Indian people to action."[65] If Congress rejected the proposals, however, a "hostile atmosphere" would grow throughout British India, Cripps feared, and a "great deal of suppression will be necessary" to maintain order, intensifying nationalist antipathy to the Raj for the rest of the war. Cripps preferred, therefore, to "take the risks entailed" in handing over the ministry of defense to an Indian, subject to "a convention in writing that the Defence Minister will not in any matter affecting the prosecution of the war act contrary to the policy laid down by His Majesty's Government and communicated through the Commander-in-Chief."[66] He was willing, if Churchill "approved" of that in principle, to stay on in India to help the viceroy and commander-in-chief "work out details" of the new system.

The Congress Party's resolution in response to the war cabinet's proposals was so negative and hostile in reiterating the "perfidy" and "divide and rule" policies of the British, that as soon as Amery read it, he wrote to Linlithgow:

> It is certainly difficult to imagine a more purely negative document . . . looks as if Gandhi had once again persuaded them that wrecking is the best policy. I am not sure that these people really want responsibility. . . . They must know . . . that they are quite incapable . . . of 'galvanizing the people of India to rise to the height of the occasion'. All this is bunk for external consumption, material for proving us in the wrong if we refuse to hand the whole show over to them. . . . I must say that the more I look at the Resolution the more doubtful I am whether people of that type would ever run straight, even if they could be brought for the moment to agree. [67]

Linlithgow noted in the margin next to that line: "*They could never run straight. One will have to plough through the old gang down to better and younger stuff.* "[68]

Wavell and Linlithgow did, nonetheless, agree that there were "no serious risks" involved in appointing an Indian member to the viceroy's council to handle a newly created department they might call "Defence Co-ordination,"[69] under which such things as public relations, demobilization, amenities for troops and their dependents, and all canteen organizations could be handled. Everything having to do with the troops and the equipment needed to fight the war would remain under direct control of the commander-in-chief. In a MOST SECRET, personal telegram to Cripps on April 6, Amery cautioned: "It is unnecessary to remind you of the danger of antagonising other elements [Muslim League] in your efforts to secure adhesion of Congress in respect of the immediate position."[70]

Roosevelt's personal envoy, Colonel Louis Johnson, reached India at this time. Nehru was eager to meet with Johnson, to inform him that the Congress Party was ready to hitch "India's wagon to America's Star and not Britain's."[71] Johnson told Nehru of Roosevelt's "determination" to support Great Britain "to the end of the war, to the utmost and to preserve the integrity of the British Empire." As long as America believed that the Congress Party was "solidly supporting the war effort," American sympathy for Congress would continue, and Johnson would do all he could to see that India attained "her ambitions" after the war. But if Americans ever felt that their soldiers' "blood" was "spilt unnecessarily" because Indian "shilly-shallying" prolonged the war, then American feelings about India would be "far otherwise." Johnson thought he had "created some impression" on Nehru, who would "assist the war effort."

Cripps wrote to Azad on April 7 to propose that an Indian member be added to the viceroy's council to take charge of defense coordination, listing all the subjects that new department could oversee. Yet even as Cripps tried his best to win Congress support for the war effort and his plan, Linlithgow sent Amery a report of Nehru's speech that day to the Congress, charging that the "Government of India were incapable of defending the country and were not allowing Indians to defend it." Britain, he said, claimed it "wanted freedom for the world, but that would be meaningless unless it meant freedom for India also."[72] Nehru added that Congress had never hidden its sympathy with the "democracies" or its antipathy to Hitler's Germany, but they were opposed to a "system that enslaved India." British imperialism "could never survive the war," in his opinion, and declarations regarding future changes of India's constitutional status were, therefore, of "very little value." Nonetheless, Nehru added that if India were invaded by Japan, India would "go down fighting" hoping to rise "again," and meanwhile laying the "foundation of India's freedom."

Feeling more optimistic, Cripps wired Churchill after midnight on April 9, 1942, telling him: "Owing to very efficient and wholehearted help of Col. Johnson, I have hopes scheme may now succeed."[73] Johnson just finished meeting with Nehru and Cripps again, devising a formula that all three felt certain would bring the Congress Party to accept the offer. Instead of putting an Indian member in charge of an insignificant, newly created department, they would give him the old "Defence Department" itself to run. At the same time they would create a new "War Department," which the commander-in-chief could control, thus allowing him to enjoy all his former powers under a different department's name. Indians would then think that their representative minister was, indeed, in charge of "Defence," never knowing that the old shell game had been played on them. Johnson's other brainstorm was to have Nehru write the formula in his own hand and present it to the Congress working committee as his own idea. As soon as the working committee agreed, Nehru would bring the written plan back to Cripps, who could then show it to the viceroy and commander-in-chief. A jubilant Cripps ended his telegram to Churchill with "I should like you to thank the President for Col. Johnson's help on behalf of H. M. G., and also personally on my own behalf."

Cripps and Johnson had informed the viceroy of what they had devised and assured him of Nehru's enthusiasm about the prospect of the Congress working committee agreeing. The viceroy, feeling both outraged and impotent, "asked how Congress had come to know about this formula. Cripps replied that Johnson had shown it to them. . . . I at once protested against Congress having been shown the draft, and said that . . . if I were now to differ from the draft, my position might well be rendered intolerable, as I ran the risk of being held up to the U.S.A. as the obstacle to a settlement."[74] After Cripps left, Linlithgow telegraphed Amery, "You can imagine my own feelings, but they are neither here nor there, and if Wavell is able to accept this . . . and the Cabinet approve . . . I will do my utmost, and fully recognise the paramount importance of the war situation and our relations with United States."[75]

Meanwhile, Churchill urged Cripps to slow down, explaining that the entire cabinet still had to "study your latest formula," and warning "You must not commit us in any way." Churchill then called in Harry Hopkins, FDR's personal envoy to him, to ask whether Roosevelt gave Johnson authority to "be drawn into the Indian constitutional issue." Hopkins thought not. A few hours later, the war cabinet sent a MOST SECRET, personal message to Cripps, "greatly concerned to find that latest formula was propounded to Nehru and to Working Committee without previous knowledge and approval of Viceroy and Wavell . . . . It is essential to bring the whole matter back to Cabinet's plan which you went out to urge."[76] Cripps had gone too far out on a limb, and Churchill was not offering him unconditional support. Still Cripps refused to give up. That evening he went back to show Linlithgow the formula he had redrafted, incorporating changes Wavell had insisted upon. He assured Congress they were not substantive changes, "purely legal points of drafting."[77] Linlithgow asked if the Congress Party had accepted the entire original proposal, and Cripps said "No," but they were now willing to "come in on the basis that they refused to agree to the long-range scheme," only to the immediate change in the viceroy's executive council. That was "good enough," Cripps informed Linlithgow. The viceroy was unhappy, but he did not want to be "held up as the bad boy responsible for wrecking . . . the wonderful settlement arrived at by Sir Stafford Cripps."

Congress promised to give Cripps their answer by April 11, the day before he was scheduled to fly home. Cripps knew by now, from the questions raised by the war cabinet in its most recent telegram to him, that Linlithgow and Wavell were undercutting him. Both were privately sending negative messages to Churchill about his actions, bringing his negotiations under more criticism from the war cabinet. "I am sorry that my colleagues appear to distrust me over this matter," he wrote to the cabinet. "Unless I am trusted I cannot carry on with the task."[78] There was "no question of want of confidence" Churchill assured him, "but we have our responsibilities as well as you. We feel that in your natural desire to reach a settlement with Congress you may be drawn into positions far different from any the Cabinet . . . approved before you set forth."[79]

None of the tricky changes proposed by Johnson and agreed to by Nehru and Cripps sufficed, however, to win over the Congress working committee. "The future, important as it is, will depend on what happens in the next few months and years," Azad wrote to Cripps on April 10. "We concentrated therefore on the present. . . . Defence at any time, and more particularly in war time, is of essential importance; and without it, a National

Government functions in a very limited field . . . the whole purpose of your proposals and our talks centered round the urgency of the problems created by the threat of the invasion of India. . . . Popular resistance must have a national background and both the soldier and the civilian must feel that they are fighting for their country's freedom under National leadership."[80] The working committee did not understand why constitutional changes could not be made during the war, since "everything that helps in the war . . . must be done with speed . . . . A recognition of India's freedom and right to self-determination could easily be made if it was so wished. . . . War accelerates change." The new formula for the defense department, with its list of responsibilities, was considered trivial and unacceptable by Congress. India's "National Government" should be one in which a "Cabinet" of ministers shared power with the viceroy, acting as its " constitutional head," not leaving every decision to his "sole discretion." They also called for an end to the secretary of state's India Office in London, "which has been a symbol of evil to us."

"There is clearly no hope of agreement," a defeated Cripps admitted to Churchill; " I shall start home on Sunday."[81] "You have done everything in human power and your tenacity, perseverance and resourcefulness have proved how great was the British desire to reach a settlement," Churchill responded. "You must not feel unduly discouraged or disappointed by the result. The effect throughout Britain and in the United States has been wholly beneficial. . . . Even though your hopes have not been fulfilled, you have rendered a very important service to the common cause and the foundations have been laid for the future progress of the peoples of India."[82]

2

From Cripps's Failure to the Failure of the Congress Party's "Quit India" Movement, April–October 1942

CRIPPS MISTAKENLY BELIEVED that his mission, "despite failure," had definitely improved the attitude of India toward the war and made the National Congress Party more sympathetic toward the Raj's struggles against the Japanese.[1] On the eve of his departure, he wrote Churchill that he believed there was "a chance" the Congress Party might soon see the wisdom of their cabinet's offer just as Jinnah's Muslim League and most of the Sikhs did. Cripps felt "sad," though "not depressed," ending his message on a note that sounded more like one Churchill might have sent to him: "Now we must get on with the job of defending India."

As Cripps prepared to leave, Azad expressed how "surprised and pained" he was over the "progressive deterioration" in their negotiations. "What we were told in our very first talk with you is now denied," Azad noted. "You told me then that there would be a National Government which would function as a Cabinet and that the position of the Viceroy would be analogous to that of The King in England."[2] He insisted that the Congress Party was not interested in gaining power for itself, wanting only for the Indian people as a whole to achieve freedom.

In a farewell broadcast, Cripps spoke directly to the Indian people, telling them how "sad" he felt that "this great opportunity of rallying India for her defence and her freedom has been missed." British governments in the past had "been accused of using vague terms to cloak a lack of purpose," Cripps told them, yet when the war cabinet drafted a unanimous and straightforward declaration, sincerely hoping to convince the Indian peoples of their desire to offer freedom to India at the earliest practicable moment, India's political leaders failed to accept it. Every leader wanted, it seemed, to draft his own declaration and express his own point of view. "Criticism has been showered on the scheme from all sides," Cripps concluded. "But . . . those vital parts of the document with which all agree have never been mentioned. Full and free self-government for India—that is its central feature." Some day, he insisted, "the great communities and parties in India will have to agree upon a method of framing their new constitution."[3] Failure brought out the best in Cripps, but the price he had to pay was high. His dreams of British premier glory, or at least of helping India win its freedom, died that night.

"What a relief now that it is over!" Amery wrote Linlithgow that same evening. "It does seem to me that the longer he [Cripps] stayed out there, the more his keenness on a settlement drew him away from the original plan on which we had all agreed. . . . Cripps was getting very near giving the whole case away . . . prepared to go that far with Congress without realising that this was the very thing against which Jinnah said the Muslims would rise in revolt."[4] Among Linlithgow's notes to himself in the margins of Amery's letter is one that reads: "Cripps told me that Cabinet had given him permission to go the length of 100 per cent Indianization, if necessary."[5] Either Linlithgow misunderstood Cripps or he had an exaggerated view of his own mandate. The impact of Cripps's mission outside India, however, seemed "all to the good," Amery felt. "For the first time America will have learnt something about the complexities of Indian affairs and of the intransigence of Congress politicians." Linlithgow and Amery both wondered now if the Congress Party leaders would drift into a position of "definite antagonism" against the Raj, in which case, as Amery put it, "we shall have to be absolutely firm in locking them all up," or " will they be at heart a little ashamed of themselves and give a certain measure of co-operation?"[6]

Roosevelt immediately sent his reaction to Churchill, worried about the consequences of the mission's failure on the war and urging Churchill to give it one more try, ominously reporting on American opinion.

> I regret to say that . . . in the United States . . . the feeling is held almost universally that the deadlock has been due to the British Government's unwillingness to concede the right of self-government to the Indians notwithstanding the willingness of the Indians to entrust to the competent British authorities technical military and naval defence control. It is impossible for American public opinion to understand why, if there is willingness on the part of the British Government to permit the component parts of India to secede after the war from the British Empire, it is unwilling to permit them to enjoy during the war what is tantamount to self-government.[7]

If India were to be invaded by the Japanese, with attendant serious defeats, FDR solemnly added, it would be "hard to over-estimate" the "prejudicial reaction on American public opinion." He urged Churchill, therefore, to ask Cripps to postpone his departure and to make one final effort to find "a common ground of understanding" with India's leaders.

Churchill responded that it was not his decision alone.

> I could not decide such a matter without convening the Cabinet. . . . I did not feel I could take responsibility for the defence of India if everything has again to be thrown into the melting-pot at this critical juncture. That I am sure would be the view of Cabinet. . . . As your telegram was addressed to Former Naval Person I am treating it as purely private, and I do not propose to bring it before the Cabinet officially unless you tell me you wish this done. Anything like a serious difference between you and me would break my heart and would surely deeply injure both our countries.[8]

Churchill knew how strongly Roosevelt felt about granting India more freedom and cleverly used this specious argument about the "private" nature of FDR's message to absolve himself of the necessity of having to tackle its content head-on. Roosevelt understood, of course, what Churchill was doing, but in the interests of preserving Allied wartime unity, he kept silent.

During his flight home, Cripps drafted the speech he would make in the House of Commons, blaming himself and India's National Congress Party for his mission's failure. When he delivered it a week later few of his colleagues bothered to listen. Amery made his own speech about the mission, again summarizing the cabinet's proposal, and warmly congratulating Cripps for his hard work.[9] Cripps made no formal "report" directly to the cabinet, nor was he even summoned to appear before its India Committee, which preferred to let his mission quietly fade away, though as Amery later told Linlithgow, Cripps may have discussed the subject with the prime minister on a weekend visit with him just after his return.[10]

The launching of Britain's diplomatic mission to seek Indian support for the war had not deterred the Japanese from steaming their fleet toward south India. Governor Sir Arthur Hope of Madras sent an anxious "SECRET" report on April 18 to Linlithgow of word he had just received from the Southern Command of a large Japanese force heading toward his province. Two Japanese air raids on the south Indian ports of Vizagapatam and Cocanada on April 7 had resulted in many casualties and completely emptied both towns. Several cargo ships sunk off the coast of Madras also gave rise to much alarm, as their survivors landed to tell their terrified tales.[11] Governor Hope evacuated Madras's offices and courts, moving his provincial government's civil servants and their documents as far inland as possible. "I am sorry to say that some of the Europeans [British residents] . . . gave way to sheer terror," Governor Hope reported. As for south India's Congress Party leaders, including Rajagopalachari, "they all are very upset, and say that Congress have made a fatal mistake."[12] Rajagopalachari understood Cripps's self-righteous liberal mind better than Gandhi or Nehru did, knowing now that there would be no further British offers until after the war ended.

Gandhi still tried, however, to justify his own rejection of Cripps's offer, sensing perhaps that Rajagopalachari was right in his criticism. "It is thousand pities that the British Govt. should have sent proposal for dissolving the political deadlock which on the face of it was too ridiculous to find acceptance," Gandhi wrote in his *Harijan* weekly journal on April 19. "And it was a misfortune that the bearer should have been Cripps, acclaimed as the radical . . . friend of India. I have no doubt about his goodwill . . . [but] Cripps having become part of the imperial machinery unconsciously partook of its quality . . . [and] loyalty to the Moloch of imperialism. Had Sir Stafford remained detached he would have conferred with his radical friends in India and secured their approbation before undertaking the mission."[13] Gandhi reiterated what he had often said before, that India could attain its independence only by solving its communal tangle, Hindus and Muslims working together to arrive at amicable agreement. If most Muslims really wanted a "separate nation no power on earth can compel them to think otherwise." If Hindus wanted to "fight" against such a division, "That way lies suicide. . . . In that case goodbye to independence."[14]

Rajagopalachari now called a meeting of Madras's Legislative Congress Party, over which he presided, carrying a resolution that "regretted" the failure of Cripps's mission. He insisted it was "impossible for the people to think in terms of neutrality or passivity" during any invasion by an "enemy power."[15] Thirty-seven Madras Congress members of the assembly voted to do all that Congress could to remove every obstacle to the creation of a national administration that would work with the British government and the Muslim League. In another resolution, the Madras Congress Party recognized the League's "right of separation" and the creation of Pakistan, if that proved to be the preference of its majority, when a constitution for India was framed. Two days later, on the eve of the All-India Congress Committee's national meeting, Nehru called a press conference in Calcutta and announced: "We prefer to perish rather than submit to arrogant imperialism or [a] new invader. [The] Gulf is greater today than before Cripps' visit. We will have nothing to do with co-operating with the British efforts in India."[16] Nehru "entirely disagreed" with the Madras Congress Party's resolutions, as did Azad, who was "astonished and pained" by Rajagopalachari's position, reprimanding him for going beyond the powers of any provincial congress committee. A few days later Rajagopalachari resigned from the working committee of the Congress Party and later lost the support of most of his former provincial backers. Congress frustrations at Cripps's unexpectedly swift departure left them to fight among themselves, each faction trying to justify its own rigid position, both sensing that their once strongly supportive Labor Party friends no longer really cared about what they said.

When the All-India Congress Committee convened in Allahabad on April 29, 1942, only about 100 of its 370 members attended that first session, reflecting the apathy of most members and the alienation of many from their leadership. Azad repeated what he had earlier said about Cripps having retreated from his initial offer to Congress of a national government within which the viceroy would function much the way Britain's king did, in relation to his all-Indian cabinet.[17] He also insisted that Cripps "made it plain" that the India Office as such would not continue, saying it should be absorbed within London's Dominion Office. Whitehall's old India Office had become not just the busy work center of the secretary of state for India's power, but the very symbol of British imperial dominance over everything Indian, including New Delhi's central government, whose pro-India fiscal and other financial policies were usually rejected by more conservative India Office imperialists. Adding insult to such inequitable fiscal injury, the inordinately high costs of running London's India Office were all charged to New Delhi's budget. If the Japanese invaded, the Congress Party agreed not to support them by "active welcome" or "silent welcome," but to greet them with the "weapon of non-violence." Asaf Ali added that Cripps's proposals were not sincere, merely a facade to satisfy world opinion. The working committee's resolutions passed unanimously, since Rajagopalachari had resigned.

The government of India prohibited India's press from reporting any of those Congress resolutions, the first of which noted the shameful behavior of the British government in Burma, even though the Japanese army was still some distance away from Rangoon. "The whole civil administration suddenly collapsed and those in charge sought their own safety. . . . Private motor cars were commandeered for the evacuation of . . . Europeans, leaving their owners stranded. . . . The police force was discharged or withdrawn . . . criminals were released from prisons, and lunatics allowed to go out of their asylum." The city of Rangoon was thus left at the mercy of "lunatics, hardened criminals, and other anti-social elements," its terrified citizens living without protection in "utmost misery and desolation." Rangoon and Lower Burma were thus held up to Congress Party members as examples of what Indians could expect to see in Calcutta and Bengal, "for the same type of official wields authority here, as [the] recent astonishing exhibition of panic and incompetence in Madras demonstrates."[18] British officials of Madras had all been swiftly evacuated to safety, but no thought was given to evacuating civilians, or arranging for their transport, housing, and food supplies. "It is [the] misfortune of India at this crisis in her history not only to have a foreign Government, but a Government which is incompetent and incapable of organising her defence properly or of providing for safety and essential needs of her people."

The Congress Party urged all its members to work on developing programs of "self-sufficiency and self-protection," preparing food and medical supplies in cities threatened by potential invasion. The final All-India Congress Committee resolution stated: "In view of the imminent peril of invasion that confronts India, and the attitude of the British Government . . . the A.-I.C.C. is convinced that India will attain her freedom through her own strength and will retain it likewise. . . . Britain must abandon her hold on India. It is on the basis of independence alone that India can deal with Britain or other nations."[19]

Small wonder that so honestly critical a Congress Party resolution as this would be deemed "too dangerous" by Linlithgow and his Home member, Sir Reginald Maxwell, to be published in India's newspapers. Delhi's Home Department justified its ban on the reporting of the Congress proceedings in the press on the grounds "that deliberate object of resolutions was to bring Government into hatred and contempt, to undermine public confidence in Government's ability to defend India, to excite hostility against forces British . . . and to encourage establishment of [a] parallel administration."[20] Amery now told Linlithgow that he hoped that such extreme Congress Party resolutions, "telling us to clear out bag and baggage, will have opened the eyes of most people here and in America."[21]

In light of these resolutions, the governor of United Provinces, Sir Maurice Hallett, reported to Linlithgow that it appeared inevitable to him that "we must have another fight with Congress and take drastic action against their fifth-column activities."[22] Hallett's intelligence reports indicated growing "alarm, despondency and defeatism over the war situation," despite the arrival of American troops in India and news of American bombing of Japan. Linlithgow sent a copy of Gandhi's latest *Harijan* article to Amery.

> To deprive people in East Bengal of boats is like cutting off vital limbs. As out and out war resister, it is my duty to ask affected people to resist, nonviolently of course. . . . I feel convinced that British presence is incentive for Japanese attack. If British wisely decided to withdraw and leave India to manage her own affairs, Japanese would be bound to reconsider their plans. The very novelty of [such a] British stroke will confound Japanese, dissolve subdued hatred against British, and set up atmosphere for ending unnatural state of things that have . . . choked Indian life.[23]

Denys Pilditch, Indian police director of intelligence, informed Governor Hallett, after the Congress Party session ended in Allahabad, that "75 per cent of Congress workers were pro-Japanese and 100 per cent anti-British." Rajendra Prasad, Bihar's Congress leader, expressed the view that it would be easier to oust the Japanese from India after ridding themselves of the British."[24] Prasad wrote in a letter "intercepted" by Pilditch from Mahatma Gandhi's ashram in central India, to report that though Gandhi did "not like" the final Congress Party resolution, *"He thinks there can be no other way than to go*; that the British should leave India alone."[25]

Gandhi thus finally agreed with Congress's most radical members that the time had come

for British and Indians to be reconciled to complete separation from each other. . . . I feel British cannot suddenly change their traditional nature; racial superiority is treated not as vice but as virtue not only in India but in Africa, Burma and Ceylon. This drastic disease requires drastic remedy—complete and immediate orderly withdrawal from India. . . . I must devote whole of my energy to realisation of this supreme act. Presence of British in India is invitation to Japan to invade India. Their withdrawal removes the bait.[26]

The Mahatma was ready to launch the last of his great satyagraha movements, demanding that the British "quit India." He spent a week in Bombay, conferring with his leading Gujarati lieutenant, the Congress Party's strong man, Sardar Vallabhbhai Patel, who had helped him launch earlier such movements. Bombay's governor, Sir Roger Lumley, aware that "he [Gandhi] is more bitter against Great Britain than ever," gave Linlithgow his prediction that Congress was planning "some openly hostile move."[27]

On May 17 Gandhi's lead article in his *Harijan* journal was addressed "To every Briton," asking for their support "in my appeal to British at this very hour to retire . . . from India."[28] He noted that India was never consulted about the declaration of war, nor about the war taxes they must pay. "Britain may be said to be at perpetual war with India, which she holds . . . through army of occupation." British troops took any dwellings they liked, ejecting the Indian owners summarily, usually without compensation. "Indian life is suffocating; almost every Indian is discontented, but will not own it publicly. Government employees high and low are no exception. . . . I am asking for . . . a bloodless end of an unnatural domination and a new era."[29] Gandhi also endorsed a new suggestion by Azad that representatives of the Congress working committee and the Muslim League meet as soon as possible to resolve their deadlock without further British involvement. A week later, *Harijan*'s lead offered Gandhi's response to "British friends" who asked how they could "retire" from India without knowing to whom they should leave their Raj. "Leave India to God," he told them. "If that is too much, then leave her to anarchy."[30]

He maintained, as he would until the end of his life, that the reason Hindus and Muslims could not reach agreement was the "artificial division" resulting from the intrusive presence of Britain's "third party." In late May, Director of Intelligence Pilditch concluded that Gandhi's new movement would demand "immediate and complete separation of Britain from

India not after but during the war."[31] He expected it to start in one or two months, an estimate that proved only a month premature.

"If Nehru and Co. are really prepared, Gandhi consentient with them, to embark on a policy of real mischief," Amery said, in urging Linlithgow, "then I hope you will not hesitate or lose a moment in acting firmly and swiftly. Don't refer to me if you want to arrest Gandhi or any of them, but do it and I shall back you up."[32] Leo Amery feared now that there was real danger of "old" Gandhi's "wounded vanity" and young Nehru's "unreasoning bitterness" drawing them together into "open revolution." News reports that Nehru might be going to America, at Roosevelt's "invitation," led Linlithgow to urge Amery to alert Halifax in Washington to check the accuracy of those reports, which proved false. Agent-General Bajpai met with Roosevelt on May 26 and reported that the "President did not seem to realise that Indian iron ore and manganese may tempt the Japanese to attempt an invasion. . . . He is alive to strategic importance of India but will limit aid only to what His Majesty's Government . . . will ask for."[33] Gandhi's recently revealed [increasingly anti-British] "attitude" displeased FDR, who thought of Nehru as Gandhi's "victim rather than a political Hamlet."

Linlithgow and Amery both believed that Gandhi's recent articles in *Harijan* did more harm to himself and the Congress Party than to the Raj, but they did not wish to prematurely arrest him for fear of losing the propaganda struggle in Washington. Governor Twynam congratulated Linlithgow for being careful not to help Gandhi "to consolidate his position by premature action."[34] Recent U.S. air and naval victories against the Japanese in the Coral Sea and at Midway relieved fears of possible imminent invasion of India, and many of those who had fled to hill stations or remote villages now began returning to Bombay, Madras, and Calcutta. By mid-June the war cabinet decided that "quick and decisive action" would be best once it became clear that Gandhi's activities must be "repressed." Amery's personal preference was "to put him in an aeroplane [*sic*] for Uganda."[35]

Rajagopalachari kept trying to bring leaders of the National Congress Party and the Muslim League together to "save the nation, " as he said in mid-June.[36] Britain was "guilty of many crimes" against India, but at least she now realized her past errors and would not add to them the "crowning offence of leaving [the] country in chaos to become certain prey to foreign ambition." He argued forcefully against the "snare and temptation" of "escape" to British prison, which would be the only "achievement" of Gandhi's new campaign. If Great Britain left immediately, Rajagopalachari predicted that Japan would rush into the "power vacuum" and turn India into a "slave factory." He no longer had faith in Gandhi's extreme non-violent "position," calling upon Nehru and Jinnah to "come together" to break the deadlock, to bring a united India into the war effort in order to save the country. If Nehru or Jinnah was listening, however, neither chose to act on this advice. Nehru went to Bombay a few days later, and from what Governor Lumley heard of Nehru's "private talks," he reported to Linlithgow that "Nehru has convinced himself that the present situation is intolerable and that action is necessary . . . that Hindus must face up to the fact that they must fight the Muslims, or any other minority which 'revolts' against a Congress attempt at domination."[37]

Jinnah's statements at this time only underscored how little chance there was now of achieving unity between the Congress Party and the League in the aftermath of Cripps's failure. In a statement issued to the press in Bombay on June 22, Jinnah said

> Gandhi has at last openly declared that unity and Hindu-Muslim settlement can only come after achievement of India's independence. . . . Gandhi never wanted to settle Hindu-Muslim question except on his own terms of Hindu domination. . . . [H]e wants British Government to accept that Congress means India and Gandhi means Congress, and to come to terms with him as spokesman of all-India with regard [to] transfer of power of government to self-styled Indian National Congress, and to keep in power by means of British bayonets, so that Hindu Congress raj can dominate Muslims and other minorities.[38]

Jinnah called it libel to say that his League favored continuation of the British Raj, insisting that the Muslim League would welcome an immediate British withdrawal. Gandhi's threat of a "big move," Jinnah argued, was intended to distress and coerce the British to agree with Congress Party demands, but Britain would be making its "greatest blunder if she surrenders to Congress in any manner detrimental to . . . Muslim India."[39] He reiterated that nothing would move his League from its purpose of achieving Pakistan.

The Congress working committee met at Gandhi's ashram on July 14, resolving that

> British rule in India must end immediately . . . because India in bondage can play no effective part in defending herself. . . . The abortive Cripps' proposals showed . . . there was no change in the British Government's attitude towards India and that the British hold on India was in no way to be relaxed. . . . Congress is anxious to avoid the experience of Malaya, Singapore, and Burma and desires to build up resistance to any aggression on or invasion of India. . . . On the withdrawal of British rule in India, responsible men and women of the country will come together to form a provisional government . . . which will later evolve a scheme by which a constituent Assembly can be convened in order to prepare a constitution for . . . India acceptable to all sections of the people.[40]

If the British refused to withdraw, then Congress would have to resort to full use of its "non-violent strength," under the leadership of Mahatma

Gandhi, to compel that withdrawal. Gandhi, seventy-two years old and suffering from high blood pressure, was now ready to launch the most difficult struggle of his life.

British India's Home Department worked hard over the next few weeks to lessen the impact of the Congress Party's resolution, encouraging and then planting as many anti-Congress statements as they could in daily papers throughout India, reporting and broadcasting criticisms of Gandhi and the Congress Party by such prominent Muslims as Jinnah and Firoz Khan Noon and by Hindu Untouchable leader Dr. B. R. Ambedkar. Phase two of the home department's strategic plan was to abort implementation of the resolution as soon as it was passed in Bombay by the All-India Congress Committee. Immediately after ratification, they plotted, "Gandhi and all members of Working Committee should be simultaneously arrested in Bombay."[41]

To launch his satyagraha campaign, Gandhi traveled from his central Indian ashram to Bombay on August 3, carrying his confidential draft of "instructions" for civil resisters. "Every satyagrahi should understand . . . that he is to ceaselessly carry on the struggle till independence is achieved."[42] The Mahatma's mantra, coined for this "Quit India" satyagraha, was "We will do or die!" (*"Karega ya marega!"*).

On the evening of August 8, the All-India Congress Committee of the Congress Party unanimously adopted its most famous resolution, urging "the immediate ending of British rule in India" as a "necessity." Rather than issuing yet another appeal to Britain, the Congress Party decided "to sanction . . . the starting of a mass struggle on non-violent lines on the widest possible scale . . . under the leadership of Gandhiji."[43] The committee "appeals to the people of India to face the dangers and hardships that will fall to their lot with courage and endurance, and to hold together under the leadership of Gandhiji and carry out his instructions as disciplined soldiers of Indian freedom." Gandhi still hoped to meet with the viceroy in the days ahead, to "plead with him for the acceptance of the Congress demand." He planned before that to meet with Congress's working committee to discuss points to be raised in his negotiations with Linlithgow. But the viceroy had no interest in meeting with Gandhi.

"Zero hour" was just before dawn on Sunday, August 9. Mahatma Gandhi and his entourage of intimates were arrested, as was the entire working committee of the Congress Party. With this action, Linlithgow thus ended the Raj's political negotiations with India's National Congress Party for the remainder of the war years.

Gandhi and his frail wife, Kasturba, his secretary, Mahadev Desai, and adoring disciples Mira Behn, British Admiral Slade's daughter Madeleine, and Congress "Song-bird" poetess Sarojini Naidu were picked up by the police and driven to Bombay's central Victoria Station, where they and the working committee were put on trains bound for prisons in Pune and Ahmednagar. For the next two years Gandhi was forced to live in the Aga Khan's mosquito-infested palace-prison. Less than a week after his nonviolent coterie of innocents was locked up in Pune, Mahadev Desai, Gandhi's brilliant, gentle secretary, died of heart failure at age fifty-five. A year and a half later, on February 22, 1944, his devoted wife of sixty-three years, Kasturba, also died a prisoner of the British Raj. Nehru, Patel, Azad, and the other members of Congress's working committee were incarcerated in the old Mughal Fort of Ahmednagar, which since World War I had been converted to a British prison. The Raj kept their places of detention secret and tried to defuse U.S. and other Allied criticism by insisting, "Our action was taken in the interest of the United Nations—not merely for the protection of British interests in India."[44]

Despite the top secret arrests of those Congress Party leaders, news spread swiftly throughout the city and angry protests erupted within hours on the streets and roads of Bombay, with crowds throwing "stones and soda water bottles at trains, buses and cars."[45] Several buses were burned, and a few post offices attacked and looted. Police opened fire, killing twenty-four people and injuring a hundred in the first two days of street fights. The fighting would soon escalate into civil war across British India and never totally die down until the end of World War II. Strikes shut down cotton mills and factories in Ahmedabad and Pune, as well as Bombay. Some eight thousand mill workers in Ahmedabad alone left their jobs. Students stopped attending schools and joined with workers in marching down roads of major cities and small towns, shouting Gandhi's mantra "Quit India" at every English person they passed. Before the end of 1942, 250 railway stations had been attacked, telegraph wires cut, tracks uprooted, and more than a hundred police stations burned to the ground, some with police still trapped inside. Some 60,000 Indians were jailed, 600 of them flogged, and 900 officially reported killed, though Congress's unofficial estimate was several times higher. British Air Force planes were used to machine-gun unarmed protesters in Bihar. Never before had those deadly airborne weapons been used against civilians in British India, except along the north-west frontier, where planes had strafed armed tribals.

By mid-August of 1942, "saboteurs" completely cut off railway traffic to and from Patna, the crowded capital of Bihar in eastern India. From the air, the British attacked Indian satyagrahis lying down on the tracks. Some protesters threw spears in futile rage at the British planes that strafed them. In the neighboring United Provinces cities of Banares and Allahabad, mass meetings were organized by local Congress Party members. Energetic students became leaders of the movement overnight, shouting "Do or Die!" while attacking government buildings and railway stations. Linlithgow informed Amery that he had "authorised machine-gunning" around Patna from the air but had carefully "given instructions that any reference to this . . . must be kept out of statements to Press."

The viceroy hoped by mid-September to have the situation under control. But on the last day of August, he was less sanguine, admitting to Churchill:

> I am engaged here in meeting by far the most serious rebellion since that of 1857, the gravity and extent of which we have so far concealed from the world for reasons of military security. Mob violence remains rampant over large tracts of the countryside and I am by no means confident that we may not see in September a formidable attempt to renew this widespread sabotage of our war effort. The lives of Europeans in outlying places are today in jeopardy. If we bungle this business we shall damage India irretrievably as a base for future allied operations and as a thoroughfare for U.S. help to China.[46]

Republican presidential candidate Wendell Willkie and the YMCA's missionary secretary for Asia, Dr. Sherwood Eddy, had expressed interest in visiting India, possibly to see Gandhi, which Linlithgow viewed as zealous, sentimentalist American interference in "our own business," appealing to Churchill to do what he could to dissuade them.

Gandhi contemplated a fast, possibly "unto death," from his prisoner's palace in Pune, but first wrote to Linlithgow to protest that "the Government of India should have waited" before launching its attacks on the Congress Party.

> I had publicly stated . . . an appeal to you for an impartial examination of the Congress case. . . . The precipitate action of the Government leads one to think that they were afraid . . . world opinion [might] veer round to the Congress . . . and expose the hollowness of the grounds for the Government's rejection of the Congress demand. . . . I venture to suggest that it is a long draft upon the credulity of mankind to say that the acceptance of the demand "would plunge India into confusion." Anyway the summary rejection of the demand *has* plunged the nation and the Government into confusion. The Congress was making every effort to identify India with the Allied cause. . . . Violence was never contemplated at any stage. . . . Was it wise . . . to seek to suppress a popular movement avowedly non-violent? . . . But however much I dislike your action I remain the same friend you have known me. I would still plead for reconsideration of the Government of India's whole policy. . . . Heaven guide you![47]

Gandhi always tried, through a sweet reasonableness of expression, to encourage his worst enemies as well as his friends to act compassionately and live in accordance with the "Sermon on the Mount."

But Linlithgow had no intention of reconsidering his harsh actions against the Congress Party, nor of opening any political dialogue with Gandhi.

Nor did Churchill, who insisted at his war cabinet meeting on September 1 that "Congress really represents hardly anybody except lawyers, money-lenders and the 'Hindu priesthood.'" Amery reported: "From this he [Winston] rambled on to the suggestion that it would really pay us to take up the cause of the poor peasant and confiscate the rich Congressman's lands and divide them up. . . . I can well sympathise with your appeal to Winston to try to do something to protect you from peripatetic Americans. I have no doubt he will do what he can . . . [as] with both Roosevelt and Chiang Kai-shek. But it is more difficult to prevent lesser fry from reaching India and . . . writing articles."[48] Discussing those "American invaders" in the cabinet, Foreign Minister Anthony Eden diplomatically suggested that if Linlithgow could find time to talk to the "better type of American" like Willkie, he might help "get our case across." Willkie was specially "amenable to the influence of good champagne." As for Dr. Eddy, he was the "kind of person" who might best be influenced by talking to Dr. Ambedkar about the "position of the Untouchables."

In a press conference on September 13, Jinnah reiterated that the Congress Party's movement was "insensible and a call for civil war."[49] He added that his Muslim League's Pakistan demand was to give the Muslims of India "self-determination." Asked if there was any chance that he might modify his demand, Jinnah replied that he had never been "unreasonable," and that "the Muslim League stands for independence for the Hindus and for the Mussalmans. Hindu India has got three-fourths of India in its pocket and it is Hindu India which is bargaining to see if it can get the remaining one-fourth for itself and diddle us out of it."[50] Jinnah also reminded American reporters at the press conference that almost 65 percent of British India's Army were Muslims, and that every Islamic country from Afghanistan to Turkey and Egypt, the "entire Middle East," were in "full sympathy with the Muslim demand" for Pakistan, and "strenuously supported" it. The next day, Linlithgow wired Amery that "so far as Muslims" were concerned, "Jinnah is the only person [political leader] that matters."[51]

Lord Halifax, who had served as India's viceroy from 1926 to 1931, was alarmed at the growing trend in enlightened American opinion, unofficial as well as official, favoring more positive steps by the Raj to rally the Congress Party and popular support for the war effort. "Harry Hopkins spoke to me last night about this strong pressure being exerted on the President," Halifax reported to Anthony Eden.[52] Much as Eden agreed with his ambassador to Washington, however, neither of them could budge the prime minister. More worrisome to Churchill than the hostile feelings of the Congress Party and the noncooperation of most Indians were the soaring debts Britain's exchequer owed to the government of India for ever increasing wartime demands for Indian goods and services. By mid-September 1942 these had mushroomed to 450 million pounds sterling, reversing the old

Anglo-Indian balance of trade in so alarmingly dramatic a way that many of Whitehall's once ardent empire-builders wanted to rid themselves of the former golden goose colony as swiftly as possible. Each month of war only magnified that debt.[53]

Sir Abraham Jeremy Raisman, finance member of the viceroy's executive council, faced many questions from his Indian colleagues on the council as to why the government of India should be obliged to pay Britain's home government under a war financial settlement agreed to in 1940, when most of the money paid out went to supporting a global war that had nothing to do with India's defense. Linlithgow inquired of Amery as to how Raisman should answer such questions. Churchill himself replied that Japan's entry into the war exposed India to "imminent danger of invasion," demanding more, rather than less, in annual contributions from the government of India to pay for war expenses Britain "incurred in India's defence and in the common task."[54] British industry and British shipping were constantly kept busy "carrying troops and war supplies" to India, Churchill argued. How dare Indians complain about England's paltry contributions to the war effort? A further review, Churchill insisted, would have to be undertaken and "a counter-claim" filed by the war cabinet to reduce the sterling balance debt owed to India by the UK.

Amery as well as Linlithgow feared, however, that Churchill's bellicose reply would lead to the immediate resignation of every Indian member of the viceroy's council and induce such anxiety among India's manufacturers over the possible loss of hundreds of millions in sterling owed to them that all Indian production supporting the war might come to a halt. Two new members of the viceroy's council, untouchable leader Ambedkar and Sikh leader Jogendra Singh, argued, Linlithgow reported, that since Indians were never asked if they wanted "to be at war at all" and since the war was "conducted exclusively by His Majesty's Government," London's government alone should have "to foot any bills that there might be!"[55] Raisman had to meet with most of the other anxious Indian members of the council to mollify and reassure them, while Amery had to work on Churchill and other members of the war cabinet to convince them not to suggest any possible modifications in the current formula to the viceroy's council. "In no event can it help the Exchequer during the war, so why take this fence before we come to it?" Amery cautioned. "What is certain is that put forward now in argumentative and what Indians will undoubtedly regard as dictatorial terms, it is bound to bring about the resignation of the present Government of India. Are we, at this desperately critical moment in India, prepared to face that consequence?"[56] Most of his cabinet colleagues agreed that they were not. Churchill swallowed it, though he never changed his mind about India or the ingratitude of its Hindu leaders. In a letter to Amery he asked:

What have we to be ashamed of in our Government of India? Why should we be apologetic or say that we are prepared to go out at the instance of some jackanapes? Let us tell them what we have done for India. For eighty years we have given it peace and internal security and prosperity such as have never been known in the history of that country for two thousand years. Which country in the world can rival that period of peace and prosperity? The Americans had their civil war, China is torn to pieces, Russia had its revolutions, every European country has been scarred and marred by terrible conflicts, but, thanks to our rule in India, uninterrupted trade and peace and prosperity has prevailed. . . . An Indian maid with bangles on can travel from Travancore to Punjab all alone without fear of molestation. . . . If we have ever to quit India, we shall quit in a blaze of glory, and the chapter that shall be ended then will be the most glorious chapter of that country. . . . No apology, no quitting, no idea of weakening or scuttling.[57]

As American industrial power now played an increasingly important role in bolstering Britain's defenses and the Allied War effort, Linlithgow sent his "personal advice" to Halifax in Washington on how best to respond to "American pressure" calling for a representative government in India.

We must keep the balance even; we must discharge our responsibilities to minorities, to the Princes, and to India as a whole. Subject to that our accepted policy is to see India achieve Dominion Status at the earliest date consistent with agreement between Indians themselves. . . . The Muslims do not, I believe . . . want any change . . . save on terms which no self-respecting Hindu leader can accept, viz., Pakistan, and abandonment of the ideal of Indian unity. . . . Hindus want Hindu domination backed by British bayonets. The Princes want no change. . . . No Indian party had the political courage to accept the Cripps proposals, and none has been able to produce any workable alternative to them. Hindu opinion is substantially behind Congress, and Muslim opinion behind Jinnah.[58]

Halifax used Linlithgow's self-justifying line of imperial argument quite effectively in handling the U.S. state department and press throughout the war, convincing most Americans that India was so hopelessly divided that British force alone kept it from falling apart.

By late September radical Labor members of Parliament, eager for a public discussion of what was happening there, called for a debate on India. Churchill felt this was too risky, however, since "certain big issues" could "hardly be answered without stirring up controversy."[59] Amery agreed, of course, so the parliamentary "discussion" was abandoned. What worried Churchill most about India was not the plight of Congress Party leaders behind bars, nor the desperate state of Bihar, but India's sterling balances. Returning to his earlier demand to drastically change the 1940 formula, he wrote Linlithgow:

I quite see your difficulties and the many arguments in favour of letting sleeping dogs lie. . . . [but] The reason why we are piling up a huge debt to India is because five-sixths of our export trade has been suppressed by us in the interests of war production, and that three-quarters of our shipping is actually engaged on war service and transport of munitions. The British nation is quite unaware of what is taking place and no one dreams . . . that if the war goes on until 1944 or 1945 we may owe India seven or eight hundred million sterling as part of the process of having kept the invader from Indian soil and as the concomitant of our departure.[60]

Amery tried his best to explain to Churchill that a large sterling debt to India might not actually be bad for Britain, but could prove a " valuable stimulus to our heavy industries when they will most need it after the war."[61] India would then need reconstruction and industrial equipment, which, having so much sterling, they would "naturally" buy from Great Britain. But Churchill was not persuaded. "As he [Churchill] talks all the time and does not really read papers, it has been almost impossible to get into his head either the fact that India does pay for British Forces now defending India or likely to go there in future . . . or that most of the debt is incurred in respect of goods supplied for other theatres of war, and . . . that we have no means of altering the situation unless a friendly India were willing after the war to consider some adjustment." When Churchill responded "with a personal indictment against myself," Amery added, "I may say that under considerable provocation to lose my temper I was angelic."[62]

Linlithgow reported that internally all was "going pretty well. . . . A good many minor incidents in Bengal, Bombay and Bihar but nothing of importance. Bihar reports reappearance of gangsters and revival of meetings and processions."[63] The viceroy knew that his optimistic reports were being used by the India Office to mollify anxious members of Parliament, whose Labor Party members continued to ask Amery where Nehru was being held, and if letters could be sent to him. Amery, therefore, wired Linlithgow to ask if Nehru's place of detention had as yet been made public. The viceroy replied in the negative, maintaining that Nehru was permitted to receive letters from "family members" only. Many other questions were asked about Gandhi's health and his whereabouts. The same answer was given to all parliamentary questions as to where each of Linlithgow's most famous prisoners was interned: "in India."

India's Home Department reported on October 2, Mahatma Gandhi's seventy-third birthday, that since August, 312 "rebels" had been shot dead and 151 wounded, while eleven British soldiers were killed and seven wounded. Most provinces had not yet reported numbers of arrests, but 4,800 were incarcerated in the central provinces, 2,600 in Bombay, and 453 in Delhi.[64] Three weeks later, Bombay's Governor Lumley wrote Linlithgow that "I am beginning to entertain the belief that Gandhi is now unlikely to fast . . . for some time to come; . . . [but] I fully agree with the importance of having our plan of action thought out in advance . . . [for] I must make it clear beyond doubt that, if Gandhi dies under arrest, we must be prepared to meet a very serious situation in this Province. . . . I have no doubt at all that the reaction would be so strong that considerable forces would be required to meet it."[65]

Though the "Quit India" movement failed to drive the British out of India, it roused a hornet's nest of opposition to the Raj, opening wider, more violent gulfs of disagreement and fear between British armed masters of India and the vast mass of India's population, whose most beloved leaders were locked behind British bars.

3

From Gandhi's Fast through the First Year of Wavell's Viceroyalty, January 1943–July 1944

G ANDHI HAD RESOLVED to wait half a year, after his arrest in August 1942, before undertaking a fast in protest against his incarceration. On New Year's Eve of 1942 he wrote to Linlithgow: "I have given myself six months. The period is drawing to a close, so is my patience. The law of *Satyagraha* as I know it prescribes a remedy in such moments of trial. . . . [I]t is 'crucify the flesh by fasting'. That same law forbids its use except as a last resort. I do not want to use it if I can avoid it. . . . [C]onvince me of my error or errors and I shall make ample amends."[1] Linlithgow replied early in January that he was most disappointed at Gandhi's failure to condemn "the burning alive of police officials, the wrecking of trains, the destruction of property, the misleading of these young students, which has done so much harm to India's good name, and to the Congress Party. You may take it from me that the newspaper accounts [of those crimes] are well-founded."[2] The viceroy asked if Gandhi had now "changed" his mind and was "ready" to "retrace" his rebellious steps. Gandhi replied negatively to both questions.

"This time, the retracing . . . lies with the Government," Gandhi wrote on January 19. "I am certain that nothing but good would have resulted if you had stayed your hand and granted me the interview."[3] Gandhi had earlier requested a chance to meet with the viceroy before launching his campaign. Linlithgow refused, however, to agree. Then on January 29, Gandhi wrote, "I have pleaded and would continue to plead till the last breath. . . . But you throw in my face the facts of murders by persons reputed to be Congressmen. . . . My answer is that the Government goaded the people to the point of madness. . . . If then I cannot get soothing balm for my pain, I must . . . commence after the early morning breakfast on the 9 February a fast for 21 days."[4]

When Linlithgow informed his council of Gandhi's decision they were very "reluctant" to risk the possibility of his dying in detention, unanimously proposing his immediate release. The viceroy personally "never wavered that Gandhi, if he desired to do so, should be allowed on his own responsibility to starve to death."[5] But he did not feel justified in opposing the unanimous view of his own council, so he agreed that it would be safer to release Gandhi while he fasted than to be held responsible for what might be the fatal outcome. Linlithgow wired that decision to Amery, who then brought it to the war cabinet, chaired by Clement Attlee, while Churchill was en route from the Casablanca summit. The cabinet was "greatly disturbed,"[6] mainly by the potential "public reaction" to Gandhi's release on his mere "threat" of a fast.

When Churchill heard of Linlithgow's decision, he was outraged, calling an "emergency Cabinet" meeting on the Sunday he returned to London, a day before Gandhi's fast was to begin. Amery reported how angry Churchill was from the moment he opened the meeting, and how quickly "he warmed up and worked himself into one of his states of indignation over India . . . and [how] this our hour of triumph everywhere in the world was not the time to cringe before a miserable little old man who had always been our enemy." Attlee alone made a very mild attempt to suggest that imprisoning or releasing Gandhi was not the same thing as "dealing with an ordinary criminal in this country." Amery concluded by alerting Linlithgow to "a telegram to you conveying the War Cabinet's views . . . telling you to suspend action."[7]

Since Gandhi's fast to "capacity" allowed him to drink water and fruit juice, the viceroy estimated he might survive for three weeks. But Lumley had learned that Gandhi would only take enough fruit juice to make the water he drank "palatable," giving him little "nutritive value."[8] Weighing 109 pounds when he began his fast, Gandhi lost eighteen pounds after his twenty-one day ordeal, yet survived, despite Surgeon-General Candy's fear that he could not endure so severe a strain to his system for more than twelve days. Churchill and Linlithgow cynically suspected that Gandhi's Indian doctor added glucose to his water, but no evidence of this was ever discovered.

In a private letter to Linlithgow on the eve of Gandhi's fast, Amery confessed that "nothing has convinced me more than the Cabinet meetings . . . of the fundamental incapacity of a British Cabinet to try and govern India."[9] He was even frank enough to admit that "I am also convinced that it will be right to Indianise the whole Executive by stages sooner or later, and not too much later. I do not believe that you will ever get Indian politicians settling down to a reasonable discussion of their own internal problems so long as they can shirk them by putting the blame on an alien Government. To that extent there really is something in Gandhi's plea that Indians can only agree once we are out of the way." Linlithgow was rather shocked by Amery's daring and, to his mind, impractical suggestion, which sounded more like radical Cripps or meddling Colonel Johnson than his own Tory secretary of state.[10]

Most prominent Indian leaders, except for Jinnah, agreed to attend a nonparty conference in Delhi, called by Rajagopalachari and Sir Tej Bahadur Sapru, to discuss how best to deal with the "situation" arising out of Gandhi's fast. Jinnah, who had never gone to jail, insisted that it was a matter for "Hindu leaders" alone to consider. Bombay's shipping magnate, Sir Cowasjee Jehangir, then a member of the viceroy's national defense council, "severely criticised" Gandhi's action, and his Parsi colleague on the executive council, Sir Homi Mody, told Linlithgow "in confidence" that he thought "the Mahatma's demise would be a real contribution to Indian politics!"[11] Or so the viceroy reported. A few days later, however, Mody joined Dr. M. S. Aney and N. R. Sarkar in tendering his resignation from the viceroy's council when he learned of a serious deterioration in Gandhi's health.[12] Mody was anxious not to be blamed by his colleagues if, indeed, Gandhi did die, and they then learned what he had said.

Fears for Gandhi's health reverberated from Washington. Roosevelt's new personal envoy to India, Ambassador William Phillips, who had initially made a favorable impression on Linlithgow, aroused the viceroy's ire when he conveyed FDR's "deep concern" over the danger of Gandhi's death.[13] In response to Phillips's question about what would happen to India if, indeed, Gandhi died in detention, Linlithgow predicted: "Six months unpleasantness steadily declining in volume. After it was over . . . India would be far more reliable as a base for operations. Moreover the prospect of a settlement would be greatly enhanced by the disappearance of Gandhi."[14] Amery agreed, and hoped, as Linlithgow requested, that Churchill could raise the question of the possibly positive impact of Gandhi's death directly with Roosevelt. But the prime minister, "laid up" with high fever from pneumonia, was unable to do anything, other than to send Anthony Eden to America "to handle the matter firmly as well as tactfully."[15] Amery personally believed, after comparing notes with Halifax, that the inspiration triggering Roosevelt's " intervention" came from the powerful duo "Madame Chiang Kai-shek and Mrs. Roosevelt," who "between them have got at the President."[16] Two days later, Amery learned from Halifax that Roosevelt had told Secretary of State Cordell Hull, "Our biggest desire is not to see the fellow [Gandhi] die in prison."[17] Linlithgow wrote to Churchill of Gandhi as "the world's most successful humbug."[18] Though he found no firm evidence, he still believed, as did Churchill, that the "nervous tension [anxiety] and hysteria engendered by all this Hindu hocus pocus" would have made it quite possible for "Gandhi's own doctors" to "slip glucose" into his water.[19]

"I do not think Gandhi has the slightest intention of dying, and I imagine he has been eating better meals than I have for the last week," Churchill wired Field Marshal Smuts on February 26. "What fools we should have been to flinch before all this bluff and sob-stuff. Opinion here has been very steady, and the Viceroy has been very good."[20] To Linlithgow, Churchill wrote, it seemed "almost certain that the old rascal [Gandhi] will emerge all the better for his so-called fast." He credited the viceroy's strong, cool, sagacious handling of the matter with giving him "the greatest confidence and satisfaction."[21] That so cheered Linlithgow, obviously unconcerned about Gandhi's health, to recover from a brief "attack of influenza" to go "out for a shoot over the weekend," bagging "415 snipe in one day and 246 the next."[22]

Gandhi broke his three-week fast on March 3, 1943, sipping six ounces of orange juice. "It is difficult to say what permanent damage may have been caused by the fast," Surgeon-General Candy recorded in his "Note of Gandhi's Fast" two days later. "From the speed with which uraemic symptoms appeared and from the knowledge of old standing high blood pressure, there is reason to believe that the kidneys were below par before the fast began. . . . Mr. Gandhi also suffers from Arterio-sclerosis a concomitant of high blood pressure."[23] This report added fuel to the chorus of cries to the viceroy to release his most famous and frail prisoner.

"The great majority of Hindus of course think that Gandhi should be released unconditionally," United Provinces' Governor Hallett wrote Linlithgow.[24] Many Englishmen and Americans agreed, requesting permission to visit Gandhi. The viceroy, eager to stop focusing on Gandhi during his last months in office, rejected all such appeals and requests. The only member of the cabinet who took any creatively constructive interest in India during this time was Cripps, who kept urging Churchill, Attlee, and Amery to do more about India's economic development and social reform, which could help them break the political deadlock as well as gain support for the war effort. Amery tried before Gandhi's fast to encourage Linlithgow to think about such matters, but the only response his ideas elicited was, "All rubbish!"[25] Now that the fast was over, Amery tried again, sending Linlithgow "A Social and Economic Policy for India," which Cripps drafted with the help of cabinet Labor minister Ernest Bevin.[26] The viceroy was focused, however, only on matters of security and finding replacements for his council members who had resigned during Gandhi's fast.

Amery kept the Commons at bay during Parliament's debate on India in late March, noting to Linlithgow what a shame it was that Churchill, "in his otherwise admirable broadcast," never said a word about India's political future prospects; they were "not even mentioned."[27] Churchill was to wind up the India debate on March 30, making Amery almost as "nervous" as his cabinet Labor Party colleagues felt at what the prime minister might say "that would still further estrange them from their party in the House . . . [though] I think Gandhi has pretty thoroughly cured most of the Labour Party of their affection for Congress."[28] Churchill decided, after preparing some 1,500 words or so "of notes" for his closing debate speech, that he could not afford the time it would take him to complete it, so much to Amery's delight he decided to say nothing. To which Linlithgow minuted, *"Thank goodness!"*[29] "He [Winston] dislikes the whole subject so much that he cannot bring himself to strike the note of sympathy which is as much needed as the note of firmness," Amery wisely added.

Amery reminded Churchill in April of Linlithgow's eagerness to leave India, strongly suggesting Anthony Eden for his successor.

> To keep India within the Commonwealth during the next ten years is much the biggest thing before us. If we can keep her for ten years I am convinced we can keep her for good . . . almost everything will depend on the personality of the next Viceroy and his successor. The job is the biggest one in the whole Empire and intrinsically more important than any in the Government here. Next to winning the war, keeping India in the Empire should be the supreme goal of British policy.[30]

Churchill nevertheless refused to even consider sending Eden off to India, viewing him as his right hand man both in the war cabinet and in his party.

A "STRICTLY SECRET" report to the viceroy on the proceedings of the Muslim League's April 1943 meetings in Delhi emphasized the "unusual lustre" that had been added to "Jinnah's leadership" since the recent death of Punjab's Muslim premier Sir Sikander Hyat Khan and the "deterioration" of the Congress Party, all of whose top leaders were in prison.[31] Linlithgow's secret informant went on to report Jinnah's presidential address at length, explaining that the League's leader now viewed the British Raj as his League's "second enemy," the Hindu Congress Party having long been the "first." As the leaders were imprisoned, Congress was no longer capable of "harming us," and Jinnah urged Muslims to focus their energies on defeating the British enemy. He rightly anticipated that the war would last another three years or so, and predicted that Allied victory would leave the British so powerful that they could easily "defy" world opinion and ignore the Muslim League's demand for the creation of Pakistan. By war's end, however, the British Raj will be "in a state of exhaustion and unwilling to face a new ordeal," he predicted, adding that "her pleasure-loving people would allow no new wars to be fought."[32] All that his followers would then have to do was "to wrest our ideal" [Pakistan] from the second enemy's "unwilling hands" by creating enough trouble to "compel him to surrender."

After reading this secret report, Linlithgow and his successors grew increasingly suspicious of anything Jinnah told them and fearful of his League's power to disturb the peace in the final years of the Raj. Linlithgow and Amery both felt particularly nervous that if Gandhi was allowed to meet with Jinnah again during the war, they might well reach agreement and launch a joint movement to accelerate the demise of the Raj. In his opening speech to his League on April 24, Jinnah unexpectedly announced, "Nobody would welcome it more than myself if Mr. Gandhi is even now really willing to come to a settlement . . . on the basis of Pakistan. . . . It will be the greatest day both for the Hindus and the Mussulmans. . . . Why does he not write to me direct? Who is there that can prevent him from doing so?"[33] Gandhi read this speech in one of the newspapers he was permitted and he immediately wrote to "Dear Qaid-e-Azam . . . I welcome your invitation. I suggest our meeting face to face."[34] The Mahatma's letter, however, was ordered by Churchill never to be delivered.[35] "Jinnah is evidently too big for his boots," Amery felt, by "daring" the government of India "to stop his corresponding with Gandhi."[36] Amery thought that keeping Jinnah from meeting Gandhi would deflate Jinnah's "undue vanity and self-importance." Linlithgow, who probably understood Jinnah better, however, noted at that remark in the margin, "On the contrary—he's more than delighted."[37]

Churchill refused to allow Gandhi to send any political letters during his incarceration, and his war cabinet timidly agreed. His egotistical arrogance in so doggedly refusing to allow India's two most popular and powerful leaders to meet served only to harden the political positions that divided their parties, widening the distance between them and deepening their mutual distrust. Churchill was not going to permit his most hated Indian "enemy" to upstage his forthcoming summit with Roosevelt in global press coverage. The prime minister took Harriman to Washington with him aboard the *Queen Mary*,[38] as well as Field Marshal Wavell, then commander-in-chief of Indian forces. The Washington "Trident" summit started on May 12, 1943, with Churchill basking in the glow of Field Marshal Alexander's stunning victory in Tunisia, which elicited the warmest congratulations from Roosevelt and his cabinet. Wavell spoke very well during that conference and reassured Churchill enough to invite him, after the summit ended, to succeed Linlithgow as India's viceroy. Both Eden and Attlee had been more highly recommended for the job by Leo Amery, but Churchill could spare neither from his war cabinet. Good soldier that he was, Wavell accepted that highest post of Indian imperial power, proud to be asked.

Unaware that Churchill had already chosen the new viceroy, Amery wrote to him on 8 June 1943 to put himself forward for that job. But first he did his best to convince the prime minister of how conscious he was of the

> very special difficulties of the task which a new Viceroy will have to handle. The whole situation in India to-day depends on the Viceroy's ability from the outset to manage and impose his personality upon a Council com-

posed mainly of Indians, men of individual ability and goodwill, but easily rattled or turned sour by hesitant or clumsy handling. They are like the Indian elephant who, with a good mahout, will face a charging tiger; if the mahout is stupid, or loses his nerve for a second, nothing can stop the beast stampeding in terror . . . a stampede may wreck the whole fabric of government in India.[39]

Leo Amery hoped that Churchill might turn to him to rule India. He modestly noted that since the very best men could not be spared, "As a last resort I have already offered you myself." But Churchill had never seriously considered Amery for the job, fearing perhaps that he was too wise. He wired Linlithgow to request his views of Wavell to be "your successor as viceroy" before proposing his name to the King.[40] Every Indian political leader, whether in or out of prison, understood Churchill's selection of the commander-in-chief of India's army for viceroy to mean "full ahead on the war front. No more waste of time on constitutional proposals." Wavell, who stayed briefly in London after his appointment to attend war cabinet meetings on India, understood as well that he was not expected during the war to play at politics or release any of his Congress Party prisoners. After hearing Churchill at his first cabinet session he noted in his diary, "He hates India and everything to do with it," agreeing with Amery that "[Winston] knows as much of the Indian problem as George III did of the American colonies."[41]

Much to Churchill's chagrin and frustration, and to the amazement of many Indians, Field Marshal Wavell hoped, as viceroy, to break the Congress-League deadlock and was eager to launch a political initiative that might lead to some form of postwar agreement among India's major parties. Amery prepared a laudatory note on Wavell for the press, stressing his martial virtue as a consummate strategist, as well as his "liberal outlook . . . and intellectual sympathies."[42] He wired his note to Halifax adding, for the American press, that "Washington, Jackson, Harrison and Grant" had all been military leaders.

Wavell was radical enough to consider inviting "an Indian" to be his assistant private secretary, until he asked Linlithgow what he thought of that idea. "To take on an Indian may annoy the communities from which [the] choice has not been made," Linlithgow replied, "and it may be difficult for you or your successor to revert to a European if [the] experiment is not a success."[43] Wavell took Linlithgow's advice and retained his predecessor's private secretary, Evan Jenkins, and his deputy private secretary, George Abell. "I have no racial feeling in the matter," Linlithgow assured Amery, "and am merely concerned with the best interests of the work and with protecting the highly confidential stuff which you and I and our successors have to handle."[44] In his seven and a half years as viceroy,

Linlithgow had never touched an Indian rupee until the day he left office, nor did he ever trust an Indian to handle any "highly confidential stuff."

The gravest problem that awaited Wavell when he returned to India as viceroy was famine. Its deadly shadow had begun to spread across Bengal early in 1943, claiming more than a million and a half lives in the province that tragic year. India's total annual food grain harvest was fifty tons at this time, which should have sufficed to feed its 400 million people. But the war disrupted transportation and most peasants and landlords were so anxious about their precarious future that they preferred to keep the crops they harvested rather than marketing them for sale. Wheat and rice became more precious than silver or gold. On the eve of the third All-India Food Conference, convened in Delhi on July 5, 1943, Governor Herbert of Bengal anxiously wrote the viceroy to report that since December 1942, when Bengal's neighboring provinces had all agreed to supply its anticipated urgent need of at least 370,000 tons of rice to avert famine, only 44,000 tons had arrived.[45] The Delhi Food Conference underscored the dire urgency of the problem, so the government of India's food department wired the secretary of state's office to request that 500,000 tons of food be shipped to India over the next six months. Half of that was needed to feed the troops.[46] Madras Governor Hope reported "much corruption" among junior officials dealing with the rice shipments that had been promised to Bengal but were never sent, describing train wagons filled with food "disappearing," and "selfish" middle classes buying up rice at highly inflated prices and "hoarding as much as they can."[47]

Trying to rush food shipments, Bengal's Governor Herbert sent a more urgent report on July 21 of "starvation in the districts . . . masses of beggars are boarding trains without tickets in the search for places where food may be available. They are a particular nuisance . . . and, apart from being insanitary, constitute a danger to security."[48] The shipping committee of the war cabinet rejected the government of India's urgent request for 500,000 tons of food, despite letters of "personal support" from the viceroy and commander-in-chief, insisting that "the real problem in India was one of inflation, of which food hoarding and the consequent shortage were symptomatic."[49] Baron Frederick James Leathers, Britain's minister of war transport, who was accountable only to Churchill, kept his fleet filled with six million tons of wheat, earmarked for "emergency" British home consumption or military use stored on ships floating in undisclosed locations in the middle of the Indian Ocean.

By early September the food crisis in Bengal was so critical that General Auchinleck wired General Brooke, chief of the imperial general staff, to urge him to use his "influence" with Churchill to get more food shipped to Bengal. "The import of food is to my mind just as if not more important than the import of munitions . . . the internal situation particularly in Bengal and

Assam may deteriorate so much as inevitably to have a . . . disastrous effect on coming operations . . . the general situation is growing worse."[50] Auchinleck had read the army's August 20 intelligence report, noting

> In Chittagong, A.R.P. personnel have had to take over the daily removal of corpses from streets and houses. In Dacca, the poor are . . . unable to obtain rice. Cholera, small-pox and starvation are causing hundreds of deaths daily. . . . Similar conditions prevail over a large area of East Bengal. . . . Suicides and child-selling have been reported . . . in Mysore . . . thousands of Indian workers are starving. . . . In planting districts in Coorg coolies die by the wayside of starvation. . . . Many Indian soldiers serving in East India have seen the famine conditions prevailing there . . . and Indian soldiers in general are already apprehensive of the effects of food shortages upon their families.[51]

The chiefs of staff support of Auchinleck's appeal moved the war cabinet to meet again on September 24 to review India's food requirements. They decided to instruct the minister of war transport to "aim at shipping a total of 200,000 tons of food grains to India by the end of 1943."[52] Wavell requested a million tons a year, to which the cabinet's response was "out of the question." Wavell flew from Delhi to Calcutta on October 26 to inspect the situation of "destitutes" there, finding about 150,000 living on pavements and in open spaces and railway premises. "The sanitary conditions are shocking," Wavell reported to Amery. "Most of the people . . . were women and children, and the condition of all was poor. . . . I saw no sign of any action. . . . The death-rate among the destitutes is high . . . as those who are ill and cannot go to the kitchens have no guarantee that they will be fed, and there is no organised medical attention."[53] He then flew to the rural Contai subdivision of Midnapore district, finding conditions much worse than in Calcutta. Everywhere he saw dead bodies and starving and exhausted people. Before leaving Bengal, Wavell told Auchinleck that they would "probably have to call in the Army" to help in the rural districts, since he found most Bengali civil officials unconscious of the "disgrace brought upon the administration" by famine conditions, and thus acting with "little sense of urgency." A million and a half tons of food grains were now needed, Wavell concluded, to make Bengal "secure," or at least 50,000 tons more per month.[54] Even though the minimal amount was approved, it took too long to reach Bengal, arriving too late to help the destitutes Wavell had seen. By mid-November an epidemic of cholera struck the province, and many villagers started to panic, abandoning their homes in despair and collapsing in death before they managed to reach any town or source of sustenance. In November, malaria took its highest death toll in Bengal.[55]

By year's end, so many Labor Party members of Parliament demanded answers in the Commons concerning the tragic "mishandling" of India's food situation that Amery wired India's food department, requesting detailed factual ammunition to meet such "attacks," especially to counter the "constantly repeated allegation that there are two million dead."[56] The food department first replied on the afternoon of January 6 : it was "unlikely" that the total number of Bengali deaths "due to famine and disease has yet exceeded one million."[57] But three hours later, at 7 p.m., the Department admitted to Whitehall: "There are no accurate data from which to compile the number of deaths that may be ascribed to famine but . . . [i]t is probable that the total deaths over the five months in 1943 did amount to about two millions but this figure included the normal deaths and also the deaths due to malaria epidemic."[58]

Wavell informed Amery that the 1943 famine in Bengal was "largely due to ministerial incompetence," and he feared that it might be repeated "on an even larger scale in 1944," unless swift action was taken to attack the problem efficiently with a sound procurement plan and effective enforcement to control stocks of food and prices.

Calling the Bengal famine "one of the greatest disasters that has befallen any people under British rule," Wavell warned "His Majesty's Government with all seriousness that if they refuse our demands they are risking a catastrophe of far greater dimensions than Bengal famine that will have irretrievable effect on their position. . . . They must either trust the opinion of the man they have appointed to advise them on Indian affairs or replace him."[59] Amery failed, however, to persuade Leathers or Churchill to change their minds." We have given a great deal of thought to your difficulties but we simply cannot find the shipping," Churchill replied a week later. "Every good wish amid your anxieties."[60]

Churchill could not focus on Bengal at this time. He was preoccupied with top secret plans for "OVERLORD"—code name for the Normandy invasion that would open Europe's second front in June 1944, and wanted to keep all available shipping ready for the transport of troops to the beaches of France and to have enough food to feed them. Trying to console the new viceroy, Amery rationalized, "I suppose the best that can be said for it is that war is a gamble and that it is better to take the risk of a second famine in India than to risk the failure of the Second Front."[61] Wavell pressed on, however, until he got a promise of 50,000 tons of wheat to be shipped to India from Australia. It was hardly the million and a half tons he so strongly urged the cabinet to ship to India.

Gandhi appealed to Wavell, "Since I regard myself as a friend and servant of humanity including the British, [and] in token of my good will I call you . . . my 'friend.'"[62] It was "no pleasure for me," Gandhi informed the viceroy, "to be in this camp, where all my creature comforts are supplied . . . when I know that millions outside are starving for want of food." Gandhi asked why Wavell kept him alone in this Pune palace-prison instead of moving him to Ahmednagar Fort "to put me in touch with the Working Committee members so as to enable me to know their minds and reactions?" He had read of Wavell's visit to "the skeletons of Bengal. May I suggest . . . a descent upon Ahmednagar and the Aga Khan's Palace in order to probe the hearts of your captives? We are all friends of the British, however much we may criticise their British Government and system in India. If you can but trust, you will find us to be the greatest helpers in the fight against Nazism, Fascism, Japanism."[63]

Gandhi was not alone in thinking of this plan. The new governor of Bombay, Lieutenant-Colonel Sir John Colville, suggested to Wavell that it might be "desirable" to move Gandhi to the fort in Ahmednagar, where he could be in touch with the Congress Party Working Committee. "This could, no doubt, be done on humanitarian grounds . . . [and could] result in an early move to modify the August Resolution and . . . come to terms with Government." Colville had been thinking about the impact on Bombay Province, which was "Congress-minded, and highly developed politically, if a Congress Ministry came in here now." They might possibly "interfere with the war effort, either in matters of production of munitions or the fulfilment of Military requirements," he realized, confessing he would rather be left with his current "Section 93" [governor's rule] government. But he was enlightened enough to understand that "the detenus must come out some day, and Congress as a political party cannot be conjured away . . . if we wait till the end of the war before allowing the leaders to reconsider their position together . . . committed as we are, to allowing India, one day, a free choice whether she will remain in the Empire or not, we stand a good chance of losing her."[64] That was why he opted to move Gandhi to Ahmednagar Fort.

Wavell acknowledged Colville's letter, but referred the entire issue to his home department, knowing how negatively Churchill would feel about any show of leniency toward Gandhi. He reported to Amery that Gandhi had of late become more active in writing letters, complaining to the home department about the poor treatment received by his wife before her death. So Wavell replied to Gandhi's last letter:

> I regret that I must view the present policy of the Congress party as hindering and not forwarding Indian progress to self-government and development. During a war in which the success of the United Nations against the Axis powers is vital both to India and to the world . . . Congress declined to co-operate, ordered Congress ministries to resign, and decided to take no part in the administration of the country or in the war effort . . . calling on the British to leave India. . . . India's problems cannot be solved by an immediate and complete withdrawal of the British.[65]

"You have sent me a frank reply," Gandhi responded on April 9.

I propose to reciprocate your courtesy by being perfectly frank. . . . Government distrust of the Congress can be seen at every turn. The result is that suspicion of Government is universal. Add to this the fact that Congressmen have no faith in the competence of the Government to ensure India's future good. . . . Unfortunately . . . the Government are pursuing a policy of suppression of liberty and truth. I have studied the latest ordinance [Ordinance III of 1944] about the detenus, and I recall the Rowlatt Act of 1919 . . . popularly called the Black Act. As you know it gave rise to an unprecedented agitation. That Act pales into insignificance before the series of ordinances that are being showered from the Viceregal throne. Martial Law in effect governs not one province as in 1919, but the whole of India. Things are moving from bad to worse. . . . As I visualise India today, it is one vast prison containing four hundred million souls. You are its sole custodian.[66]

On April 14, 1944, a disastrous series of explosions and fires in Bombay's huge Victoria Dock sank or seriously damaged sixteen ships and burned between 50,000 and 60,000 tons of food grains stored there. The first explosion was ignited by fire on a ship carrying cotton and ammunition.[67] Suspecting Indian sabotage, Wavell asked General Auchinleck to investigate the loss of precious ships and food at a time when neither could be spared. The next day "unprecedented rain with thunderstorms and hail" covered much of India, damaging thousands of tons of wheat. There was a "growing state of nervousness in India," Wavell reported and not enough food on hand to "meet Service requirements."[68] A week later, he calculated the toll both events had on Bombay—some 500 people killed in the explosions, 2,000 injured, 20,000 left homeless, 70,000 tons of shipping and 40,000 tons of food lost, as well as millions of pounds' worth of stores destroyed.[69]

While he was in Bombay, Wavell discussed Gandhi's transfer to Ahmednagar with Colville and agreed it would do more good than harm, urging Amery not to let the cabinet be "frightened by the Gandhi bogey." Gandhi's health had deteriorated seriously from the after-effects of malaria, which remained rampant in the Pune Palace-prison. Surgeon-General Candy felt that Gandhi was "on a slippery slope," suffering from anemia and high blood pressure.[70] Wavell now believed that Gandhi's health had become so poor that it was improbable he would ever again actively participate in politics. He agreed with the medical opinion of doctors who saw Gandhi that his immediate release would be best, since his "death in custody" would only intensify antigovernment feeling. Amery convinced Churchill to approve "Gandhi's release on medical grounds."[71] Instead of dying, Gandhi showed remarkable resilience, soon enjoying substantial recovery at a friend's house on Bombay's Juhu Beach, where he greeted old friends and young admirers. Churchill sent Wavell a "peevish telegram to ask why Gandhi hadn't died yet!"[72]

Gandhi had, in fact, enough energy to visit Bombay's fire area. Bombay's Indian mayor asked the governor to convey his "high appreciation" to Lord Wavell for releasing the Mahatma. Colville thought that Gandhi would soon try "to get into touch with Jinnah."[73] Nationalist newspapers were talking of possible negotiations between Gandhi and Jinnah, Wavell told Amery a few days later, but since Jinnah was in Kashmir and not expected to return to Bombay until the end of June, the viceroy was not worried about any prospect of an imminent break in the current Congress-League "deadlock." Wavell agreed, in fact, with Amery's conviction that "as long as Gandhi and Jinnah are in the lead there is little likelihood of a settlement."[74] He considered both men "intransigents," and later added Churchill's name to the Aged Trinity (Gandhi nearly 75, Churchill almost 70, and Jinnah 68) of obstacles to any resolution of India's political problems.

Meanwhile, Allied forces were cheered in Italy, Amery reported to Wavell in late May, battles there going so well that it looked as if "we might be on the outskirts of Rome in a very few days."[75] He hoped India's newspapers were adequately publicizing what "an effective part in it all" India's "Tiger" troops of the Eighth Army had played in that softening up of western Europe's underbelly on the eve of the Normandy invasion. Wavell and his wife flew to Assam to visit the Allied troops there, one of whom was their son, who lost his left hand to "a grenade or an explosive bullet while leading an attack near Mogaung."[76] Gandhi asked Wavell to meet with him and also to allow him to meet with the Congress Party Working Committee in prison, but the viceroy refused both requests, now considering the Mahatma "rather impudent."

A "more important development" Wavell noted in July was that Rajagopalachari devised a new formula to break the deadlock, hoping to bring Gandhi and Jinnah to agreement. Wavell sent the text of that formula, carried in India's press, to Amery, explaining that Rajagopalachari said "Gandhi was prepared to accept it" if Jinnah would. "It appears to accept the principle of Pakistan, but does so by providing for the demarcation of 'contiguous districts' in the North-West and East of India in which the Muslims are in an absolute majority."[77] If "district" was being used in the current British Indian cartographic sense, Wavell added, that would mean dividing Punjab and Bengal, relegating eleven districts of each of those provinces to "Hindustan," the rest to Pakistan. In Assam, only one district had a Muslim majority. Thus, "at first reading it seems that the 'formula' might leave Pakistan with Karachi as its only port, with the Punjab partitioned in an unsatisfactory way, and with a block of rural districts (including, however, the city of Dacca) in Bengal. One can hardly blame Jinnah for thinking twice before swallowing this whole . . . [though] I think Jinnah made a tactical blunder in rejecting the 'formula' so brusquely. He could have suggested alterations. . . . Much of his strength is, however, due to the Muslims . . . feeling that he is the only one of them who can stand up to Gandhi."[78] The League's newspaper, *Dawn,* insisted, however, that Jinnah did not reject the formula, only saying he could not accept it on "his own responsibility," and being in Kashmir could not meet with his Muslim League's working committee until after he returned to Bombay.

Thus, the stage was set for a new round in the political end-game struggle that was to keep the top Congress and League leaders as well as Britain's martial viceroy intensely engaged for the next year, staking out incompatible claims to the most valuable real spoils of British India's Raj.

4

Summit Failures and Cabinet Obstacles, August 1944–July 1945

AS THE UNITED STATES took upon itself the lion's share of the Allied war against Japan, Roosevelt's frustration at Churchill's intransigence over India grew stronger. FDR's personal envoy, Ambassador Phillips, reported, after returning to Washington, that when he talked to Churchill about India, "Churchill banged the table and said 'I have always been right about Hitler and everyone else in Europe. I am also right about Indian policy, any change in Indian policy now will mean a blood bath.'"[1] Whenever Roosevelt himself tried to discuss India with Churchill he received "a blunt cold shoulder." By late summer of 1944 he entirely agreed with Phillips's forthright report of what needed to be done about British policy in India.

Since India would have to become a major base of future operations against Burma and Japan, "We should have around us a sympathetic India rather than an indifferent and possibly hostile India," Phillips wrote. Indians currently felt that "they have no voice in the Government and therefore no responsibility in the conduct of the war. They feel that they have nothing to fight for as they are convinced that the professed war aims of the United Nations do not apply to them. The British Prime Minister in fact has stated that the provisions of the Atlantic Charter are not applicable to India." The Indian Army was "purely mercenary," Phillips told FDR, adding that General Stilwell was quite worried about "the poor morale" of Indian officers.

> The attitude of the general public is even worse. . . . While India is broken politically . . . all have one object in common, eventual freedom and independence from British domination. . . . Even though the British should fail

again it is high time they should make an effort to improve conditions and re-establish confidence among the Indian people. . . . It is not right for the British to say this is none of your business when we alone presumably will have the major part to play in the struggle with Japan.[2]

The British Embassy in Washington was quick to telegraph this letter back to Whitehall and on to India, but careful to keep it out of London and Indian newspapers.

Labor Members of Britain's House of Commons continued, moreover, not simply to ask probing questions about India, but to demand a full "debate" on the government's India policy, which finally came up for discussion in the Commons early in August of 1944. Amery was relieved to report that "all the speeches were moderate and responsible in tone," but in light of American feeling, agreed with Wavell to start "talking" to Gandhi and encouraging him to meet with Jinnah. On both of those points Churchill expressed "grave uneasiness," insisting it was "most undesirable that the viceroy should find himself in correspondence with Mr. Gandhi . . . [who] had consistently been a bitter enemy of this country."[3] The thought that "immediate independence" after the war ended and a "National Government" prior to its end might even be mentioned to Gandhi by Wavell outraged Churchill to the point of demanding that the war cabinet devote no fewer than three meetings to redrafting that letter. "We are much concerned at the negotiations which you have got into with Gandhi who was released on the medical advice that he would not again be able to take part in active politics," Churchill wired Wavell.[4]

"There is no question of negotiations," Wavell replied.

I am merely informing Gandhi of the position repeatedly stated by His Majesty's Government in the Cripps offer. . . . It was not possible to ignore medical opinions. . . . I think you must admit that I have done my best. . . . I have borne constantly in mind the necessity to compose the differences between Hindus and Muslims. I do not think meeting between Gandhi and Jinnah will produce settlement but it will at least clear up position between two principle [sic] parties. I am naturally keeping rights and interests of other minorities in view.[5]

A weary Amery replied the next day: "I am afraid the Cabinet have introduced a good many amendments to your draft, but they felt that it was essential to recapitulate clearly the main points. . . . On the whole I hope you will think that the revised draft . . . changes nothing of substance."[6] After a week of telegraphic revisions and uncounted hours of war cabinet ministers' time they finally agreed on the wording of a letter to Gandhi, in which the viceroy should state: "I see no reason why preliminary work on the new Constitution should not begin as soon as the Indian leaders are prepared to co-operate to that end. If they can arrive now at a genuine agreement as to the method of framing new Constitution as suggested above I see no reason why any very long time need be spent after the war in reaching final conclusions and in negotiating a treaty with His Majesty's Government."[7]

"I do not like the War Cabinet's draft of the reply to Gandhi," Wavell wired Amery. "It does not differ greatly . . . from the draft I proposed, but seems to me much more unfriendly. As I explained . . . our immediate object should be to get as good a press as we can without giving anything away. Politeness costs nothing and is likely to pay a dividend not only here, but at home and in the United States."[8] Some twenty-five of Gandhi's Congress Party followers had been arrested in Bombay a day earlier, August 9, 1944, for attempting to read aloud in public the 'Quit India' resolution adopted by the Congress Party two years before. "It is disappointing," the not insensitive viceroy confessed to Amery, "to be unable to do anything . . . more palatable to educated Indians."

The good news Wavell reported was that the RAF had just recently flown enough of its planes into Manipur's capital of Imphal to smash *Netaji* ("Leader") Subhas Chandra Bose's Indian National Army (INA) that had advanced to its outskirts before the monsoon began. Bose's INA consisted of about 20,000 of the British Indian soldiers captured by the Japanese in Singapore, who had volunteered to serve under *Netaji* Bose when he offered them "Freedom" if they were willing to risk their "Blood" to liberate India a year earlier. The British considered Bose and his "army of traitors" no better than their Japanese sponsors, but to most of Bengal's 50 million Indians, Bose was a great national hero and potential "Liberator." The INA was stopped before entering Bengal, first by monsoon rains and then by the RAF, and forced to retreat, back through Burma and down its coast to the Malay peninsula. (In May 1945, Bose would fly out of Saigon on an overloaded Japanese plane, headed for Taiwan, which crash-landed and burned. Bose suffered third-degree burns and died in the hospital on Formosa.) Wavell's bad news was that the general food situation was "unchanged," with serious scarcity suffered throughout south India's Travancore and Cochin states, where the monsoon had failed, and food grain harvests were less than "one-third of normal."

Wavell tried to keep himself informed not only of Gandhi's activities, but also of his political plans and objectives. In a SECRET report on Gandhi since his return to his ashram, Governor Twynam of the Central Provinces told the viceroy that Gandhi had drafted a statement containing bitter criticism of government but Rajagopalachari managed to dissuade him from publishing it. It was also said that Gandhi had no faith in the Pakistan scheme and no hope of a successful outcome of the discussions with Jinnah but that "his objective is to place both Government and Jinnah in the wrong in the eyes of the world."[9] Press reports indicated that Gandhi was to meet with Jinnah in Bombay on August 16, but by August 11 the war cabinet still refused to give the viceroy approval to send his encouraging letter to Gandhi, awaiting Churchill's permission. "I feel strongly on this matter," Wavell wired Amery. "I cannot understand why War Cabinet should not approve my revised draft. . . . I suggest you put this to Attlee . . . and [omission] Winston's displeasure."[10] Precisely which of Lord Wavell's possible expletives was omitted from that telegram is uncertain, but even thirty years after it was written, Her Majesty's Stationery Office censor felt obliged to delete it. Amery's private reply that same day assured Wavell, "I entirely agree with you over this silly business."[11]

But Churchill, heartened by rapid American advances in Normandy and by Alexander's victories in Italy, wired his cabinet via Allied Forces Headquarters in Italy: "I hope the Cabinet will stand firm and not be disturbed by the attitude of the Viceroy. He thinks that because Gandhi wrote a letter to him he is entitled to reply. . . . As a matter of fact he has no right to negotiate with Gandhi at all . . . after what Wavell said about Gandhi's state of health he has no right to enter upon correspondence with . . . newly released invalid."[12] So the war cabinet met again on August 14, and Amery had to dissent from the majority's rebuff to the viceroy, whose opinion, he argued, "should not be overridden." To Wavell, Leo Amery wired, "Cabinet . . . differ from you with reluctance and only because of their strong sense of importance of the issue."[13] Then he added five paragraphs, each one attempting to explain to Field Marshal Lord Wavell why the same British cabinet that had appointed him to be viceroy of India little more than a year earlier now refused to allow him to send Mahatma Gandhi the polite letter he had drafted, insisting on their harsher, colder version. Obedient soldier that he was, Wavell did as ordered. But when Amery was informed that Deputy Prime Minister Clement Attlee refused to allow his dissent at the war cabinet's August 14 meeting to be "added to the minutes," since "your agreement with the previous Cabinet decisions makes it impossible for you to take that ground now,"[14] Leo Amery wrote, "My dear Clem,

> I really cannot accept your argument. . . . My objection throughout has been not so much to the wording of the drafts as to the overriding of the earnest and repeated protests of the Viceroy. A Minister is put in an impossible position if he has to register his formal protest at every stage of a negotiation about which he is not entirely happy or otherwise forfeit his normal right of registering his dissent from a conclusion whose character can only be appreciated when the negotiations have been completed.[15]

To Wavell, Amery wrote his PRIVATE AND SECRET assurance that "it would have been a great mistake at this juncture to have invited a direct collision with the Prime Minister . . . on an issue, not of real substance, but of tone and wording, the full importance of which would never have been recognised by the public."[16]

The real trouble, as we both know well," Leo Amery continued,

is that you and I both genuinely mean to implement the Government's pledges . . . to enable India to start off at peace within herself and in conditions which are likely to have some reasonable stability. The Prime Minister passionately hopes that any solution involving the fulfilment of our pledges can still somehow or other be prevented, and . . . makes difficulties at every stage. In between come the Cabinet, most of whom agree with us in their hearts. . . . But when in the Cabinet room . . . they are overborne by the Prime Minister's vehemence and are glad to find an escape against a particular matter . . . whether it be an Indian Finance Member . . . or the terms of an answer to Gandhi. We have just to be patient and carry on as best we can.

Wavell's marginal comment next to that paragraph was "*Quite true, and yet the S. of S. is vilified in the Hindu Press even more than the P.M.*" W.[17]

Amery's "hope" was that Churchill's actions would not stimulate "some unholy alliance" between Gandhi and Jinnah "for the purpose of embarrassing us." Wavell marginally noted his own fears that a lot of harm had already been done and support Gandhi had been losing was now rallying back to his side. Amery wrote of Jinnah as "the future Emperor of Pakistan" and of "Pakistan" itself as "essentially a negation."[18] He and Wavell both understood, of course, how strongly Churchill favored Jinnah over Gandhi, and how much he favored the idea of Pakistan, as well as "Princestan." On August 18, 1944, Bombay's Governor Colville wrote to Wavell on what was to have been the eve of Gandhi's meeting with Jinnah at his Malabar hilltop home, but that summit was postponed because violent extremist demonstrations threatened to disrupt the meeting. Colville reported that Gandhi still held "unchallenged leadership" over the Congress Party and that his Muslim League followers were "solidly behind Jinnah and think they are on a good wicket."[19]

Wavell felt bitterly disappointed at the defeat he had suffered at the hands of his own prime minister, who obliged him to omit any suggestion in his letter to Gandhi that "we hoped for the success of the discussion . . . and were prepared to consider any proposals" that might emerge from Gandhi's talks with Jinnah. "In fact, what I told His Majesty's Government was entirely correct," the viceroy wrote Amery in his PRIVATE AND SECRET reply. "My own letter would have achieved the same purpose without arousing nearly the same bitterness. I feel very sore about this. Some day we have got to negotiate with these people . . . and this letter has destroyed at one blow a reputation that had been accorded me in the Congress press of being at least straightforward and courteous. . . . The Hindu line will now be that the British are the common enemy, and that the Hindus and Muslims must join to secure independence."[20]

Wavell agreed with Amery that "Winston . . . did not realise the importance of sympathetic allowance for the Indian point of view" on the sterling balances issue, on which Churchill continued to attack, as well as on matters like appointing Indian civil servants to positions of real power. "I suppose it is just part of Winston's general hate against India."[21]

Punjab's governor Sir Bertrand Glancy wrote to Wavell that August day about Gandhi's possible motives for agreeing to meet with Jinnah.

> Some believe that his main idea is to extract from Jinnah a definition of Pakistan and thus expose the hollowness of "vivisection." If this is his object, it seems scarcely conceivable that Jinnah will fall into the trap. If the C.R. [Rajagopalachari] formula were accepted, this would mean that twelve districts of the Punjab (the whole of the Ambala and Jullundur divisions plus the district of Amritsar) would be excluded from Pakistan, and such a dismemberment of the Province would find few supporters amongst Punjabi Muslims. There are some faint indications that Muslim intelligentsia might be satisfied with a united India provided that Muslim representation at the Centre were . . . increased. This would certainly be a saner solution than crude Pakistan, which has every appearance of being the direct route to civil war in the Punjab.[22]

Precisely three years and eight days before Punjab's partition, Glancy thus accurately predicted the result of the misguided division: civil war. Glancy thought Jinnah's power had begun to wane before Gandhi approached him, but that, thanks to Gandhi's invitation to talk, "Jinnah's importance has now revived." He also warned that Punjab's Sikhs "loudly condemned the approaching negotiations," for several million Sikh farmers lived on the richly watered central heartland of Punjab's wheat-basket, spread across those Ambala and Jullundur divisions. He feared that if Jinnah was able to win his "Pakistan," then their rich and beautiful Punjab might be cut through its mid-section, leaving millions of Sikhs forced to live under Muslim rule, which they found intolerable, or to abandon their fields and homes to seek refuge in Hindu-majority India. The option many Sikh leaders now hoped for and wanted was an independent Sikh nation-state of Sikhistan.

At the end of August 1944, Jinnah "graciously condescended," Amery noted in his "TOP SECRET" letter to Wavell, to meet with Gandhi in Bombay after September 7, but "like you, I don't think much will come of it."[23] The liberation of Paris at this time brought the joyful prospect of the war's end much closer, and Wavell believed Pakistan would emerge soon after the war ended. He thought that Muslim state would come to life as much "the creation of Congress" for having stubbornly refused "to establish Coalition Governments" [in 1937] in provinces with substantial Muslim minorities as because of Jinnah's insistent demand for it.[24] The viceroy felt that it would be best after Germany surrendered to invite leaders of the Congress Party and the League to assist him in running a transitional government of India in Delhi. He asked his governors how they felt about restoring popular ministries to their provinces and some of them liked the idea, though several others were happier to continue to govern under Section 93 (governor's autocratic rule) and saw no hope of trying to run a popular transitional government at the center until Indian leaders settled their communal disputes. Wavell was eager to invite the key leaders to a summit conference but would first see if anything came of the Gandhi-Jinnah meetings rescheduled to begin on September 9.

Gandhi was driven to Jinnah's elegant Bombay hilltop home, where they conferred for over three hours on that first day. "A test of my patience," Gandhi called his meeting with the League's "Great Leader," but "a friendly talk." He reported to Rajagopalachari that "[Jinnah's] contempt for your Formula and his contempt for you is staggering."[25] From his prison cell in Ahmadnagar, Jawaharlal Nehru was even more "put out" by C. R. Rajagopalachari's proposal to accept Jinnah's Pakistan demand, viewing it as a "devil's dance." In his prison diary, Nehru wrote of that Bombay meeting: "I feel stifled and unable to breathe normally. . . . I have a sensation of blankness and sinking of heart."[26] All members of the Congress Party's working committee were to remain behind British bars until the war with Germany ended.

Gandhi and Jinnah agreed to take the weekend off, meeting again on September 12 in the morning and in the evening. The two charismatic leaders of Congress and the League were old enough and wise enough to know how much depended upon the success of their summit, how many lives might be lost and ruined if they failed, or happily saved if only they could agree upon a peaceful postwar plan for South Asia's polity. Jinnah knew by this time, moreover, that he had lung cancer from his decades of heavy cigarette and cigar smoking. The firmness of his will and his tenacious desire to win a sovereign independent state of Pakistan for his Muslim League followers were keeping him alive.

"He said I should concede Pakistan and he would go the whole length [in any future struggle for independence] with me," Gandhi reported after their meeting. "He would go to jail, he would even face bullets."[27] Gandhi also knew that his own frail body had all but expired during his last fast, yet he refused to agree to what he considered the "Vivisection" of his sacred Mother-India. "My constant prayer these days," Gandhi told his disciples at a prayer meeting after the second day, "is that He may so guide my speech that not a word might escape these lips to hurt the feelings of Jinnah Saheb or damage the cause that is dear to us both."[28]

Yet the cause most dear to Gandhi—to preserve at all costs the unity of India—was the antithesis to the cause equally dear to Jinnah's heart and mind: to preside over the birth of a sovereign Pakistan, carved out of the northwest and eastern wings of India. At the end of the second day of their summit, Gandhi reported, "He [Jinnah] told me today, 'If we part without coming to an agreement, we shall proclaim bankruptcy of wisdom on our part.' What is more, the hopes of millions of our countrymen will be dashed to pieces."

A week later they did proclaim bankruptcy. "[Can] you not appreciate our point of view," Jinnah wrote to Gandhi, "that we claim the right of self-determination as a nation and not as a territorial unit, and that we are entitled to exercise our inherent right as a Muslim nation, which is our birth-right?"[29] Yet Gandhi was "unable to accept the proposition that the Muslims of India are a nation, distinct from the rest of the inhabitants of India. . . . The consequences of accepting such a proposition are dangerous in the extreme. Once the principle is admitted there would be no limit to claims for cutting up India . . . which would spell India's ruin."[30] Gandhi was convinced that although Jinnah was a "good man," he suffered from "hallucination when he imagines that an unnatural division of India could bring either happiness or prosperity to the people."[31]

No member of Britain's war cabinet was surprised at the swift demise of that Gandhi-Jinnah summit. A few years earlier Cripps might have been shocked, but he well understood now how antipathetical to one another these two greatest political leaders of India had become. Though both were trained as British barristers, it almost seemed at times that they now presided over totally distant universes. Jinnah's was far more familiar and congenial to Englishmen, especially those like Churchill, Amery, and Wavell, who loved the British Indian Army and its Punjabi or frontier Muslim soldiers, always true to their salt. As Wavell wired Amery on October 2:

> Breakdown reveals complete absence of common ground between Gandhi and Jinnah. . . . Gandhi wants transfer of full power to some nebulous national . . . government and later settlement of Hindu-Moslem differences. His belief in unity of India is sincere but he is also profoundly Hindu, and if his interim government materialised he would hope for Hindu domination subject to some degree of self-determination for Moslem provinces. Jinnah is determined to get division of India into Pakistan and Hindustan cut and dried before the British leave. . . . Breakdown makes settlement between the parties even more difficult than before. . . . Sikhs and many Congressmen are relieved at the breakdown. But there is also much disappointment.[32]

Wavell also viewed that mini-summit breakdown as a personal challenge on how best to bring Jinnah and Gandhi together. He had a number of creative ideas and hoped to use his experience and position of power to help India solve its thorniest problem before he was obliged to quit his viceregal job after the war ended. He would try to square the circle of Congress-

League conflict by inviting a number of responsible moderate leaders of Indian opinion to meet with him at a Himalayan summit in British India's summer capital, Simla. He told Amery that he thought of inviting Gandhi and one "other" member of the Congress Party, Jinnah and one other member of the Muslim League, Ambedkar to represent the "depressed classes," Tara Singh to represent the Sikhs, M. N. Roy to represent Labor, and a few others to represent non-Congress and non-League Hindus and Muslims. He decided not to invite any Indian princes to his summit, first seeking only representative Indian advice as to how best to bring harmony to British India, opening constitutional doors to a postwar era of truly responsible government.

Wavell soon learned, however, that the most formidable obstacle to holding such a summit was his own prime minister's cabinet. "Apart from my doubts as to your proposals on merits," Amery wrote on October 10, "the Cabinet have always hitherto deferred to the Prime Minister's passionate feelings about India. They are bound to do so all the more in the present delicate situation. Moreover, . . . Labour Ministers would I am sure prefer to keep their hands free to advocate their own solutions of Indian difficulties."[33] Nor did Amery himself believe that either Gandhi or Jinnah would now budge from their recent breakdown positions. Wavell was left once more to simmer silently. He decided before the end of October to write directly to Churchill.

"I will begin by saying that . . . I feel very strongly that the future of India is the problem on which the British Commonwealth and the British reputation will stand or fall in the post-war period. . . . Our prestige and prospects in Burma, Malaya, China and the Far East generally are entirely subject to what happens in India. If we can secure India as a friendly partner in the British Commonwealth our predominant influence in these countries will . . . be assured; with a lost and hostile India, we are likely to be reduced in the east to the position of commercial bag-men."[34] After the war ended, Wavell warned that India could fall into a state of "chaos" and become a "running sore," sapping the strength and fortune of Great Britain, if it were possible to hold "down uneasily for some years."[35] Nonetheless, he observed, vital problems of India were now being treated by His Majesty's government with "neglect . . . hostility and contempt." He pulled no punches, reminding Churchill how fiercely he was obliged to fight to secure enough food for Bengal to avoid as bad a famine this year as it had suffered in 1943. He cautioned that the present government of India "cannot continue indefinitely, or even for long," and the British civil services, so long proud of their administrative virtues, were now virtually "moribund, the senior members tired and disheartened."[36] Wavell reminded Churchill that neither the Congress Party nor the League could be ignored, for though "We have every reason to mistrust and dislike Gandhi and Jinnah," they control India's press, electoral machines, and "money bags."

He then spelled out to Churchill a plan for what he felt must be done. First of all, a provisional government had to be established along lines Cripps had originally proposed, including all of India's best and most talented political leaders. Most important of all, Wavell insisted, was the need for "a change of spirit," to convince educated Indians that the British government was "sincere in its intentions" and truly "friendly" toward India. He knew how easy it was to condemn his plan on grounds of potential "risk" but was brave enough and wise enough to argue that to make any "progress" risks had to be taken and possible "failure" anticipated. Wavell believed that his plan would "do good" if only it was generously and honestly tried.

For six weeks, Churchill ignored Wavell's letter, passing it on to his cabinet for their "reactions," confining his personal response to "earnestly consider before I reply . . . at leisure and best of all in victorious peace." He said nothing about Wavell's plan but sent him "all good wishes for Christmas and the New Year."[37] Frustrated, Wavell proposed to Amery on December 1 that he should fly to London to make his case personally to the cabinet. Churchill, who would soon start to prepare for his own summit with Roosevelt and Stalin at Yalta in February 1945, told Amery he couldn't possibly think of seeing Wavell before March. Churchill was hardly eager to see him at any time now, expecting that "he [Wavell] is going to make trouble and stage a scene for resignation."[38]

Still, Wavell tried his best to advance his own plan, inviting Jinnah to meet with him on December 6. They talked for an hour, Jinnah insisting that "Indian unity was only a British creation," Wavell noting South Asia's "geographical unity, with very defensible frontiers; and, from the point of view both of security and economics, [it] should certainly remain as one."[39] Jinnah admitted that though Indian unity might be an "ideal," it was an impracticable one. Wavell argued that in the Army Hindus and Muslims had worked together closely, and for the last seven years at least they had cooperated in the Unionist Coalition Government of Punjab. He urged Jinnah to consider how "a strong and united India would make a very great contribution to the peace of the East and of the whole world, while a disunited India, possibly engaged in an internal struggle, would be a menace to the whole peace of the world."[40] But Jinnah only "reiterated his conviction that Pakistan was . . . both necessary and desirable." To Amery, Wavell optimistically reported of the conversation: "Jinnah was friendly and forthcoming. . . . I think he meant what he said."[41]

The astute governor of Bengal, Richard Casey, had even more misgivings than Wavell about the potential problems and dangers of Pakistan. Casey feared that neither Jinnah nor any of his Muslim followers had taken into account the lack of economic and financial security of a bifurcated

Muslim state that had hardly advanced "beyond the stage of political wishful thinking." He considered it no more than a "valuable bargaining counter" for Jinnah to use in negotiations and only hoped he would "compromise before Pakistan turns into a tiger that he is riding." Casey knew enough about recent Congress-League relations to rightly inform Wavell that "the Congress is basically responsible for the growth of the Pakistan idea, by the way they have treated the Muslims," especially in refusing to allow them into coalition provincial governments. But "unless the Pakistan idea is squashed," he warned, it was likely to "delay . . . independence for India."[42] If Wavell wished, Casey volunteered to try to influence Bengal's leading Muslims "away from the Pakistan idea." He believed it would take him at least six months of "discreet conversations" to do so. He would start by debunking Jinnah's idea of holding a plebiscite on the Pakistan question only among the Muslims of Bengal, as opposed to its general population, since that position could not be defended on any democratic or other grounds. He would also do whatever he could to convince Muslims that Calcutta could never be included in "Eastern Pakistan," since it was more than a provincial capital and rather, was an "All-India city that happens to be in Bengal."

Wavell agreed with everything Casey said about Pakistan, concluding in his reply "I do not believe that Pakistan will work, . . . but like all emotional ideas that have not been properly thought out, it thrives on opposition." It had a strong sentimental appeal for the Muslim masses, so the British government "cannot openly denounce Pakistan until we have something attractive to offer in its place."[43] He then pointed out how successful the former chief ministers of Punjab, Sikandar Hayat Khan and Fazl-i-Husain, had been in using the local patriotism of that province's common language to unite its political parties and the common economic interests of Punjab's Hindus, Sikhs, and Muslims, rather than dividing them on their communal differences. Wavell suggested that Casey might try to do the same thing in Bengal, urging him "to exploit this local patriotism." That could only be done, however, by Bengali leaders of strong character themselves, and would only happen with the emergence of "Bangladeshi" nationalism, based on the common Bengali language that unified the population of "Bangladesh" ("Bengali-speaking Nation") in 1971.

Churchill chaired his war cabinet meeting on December 18 that reviewed and rejected Wavell's proposals for constitutional change, finding them essentially the same as Linlithgow's and Wavell's from a year before. Despite their rejection of Wavell's ideas, however, the cabinet invited him to fly to London to discuss future options for India. "I think even Winston realises that we cannot . . . say nothing indefinitely," Amery reported on December 21.[44] Wavell requested minutes of the cabinet meeting that rejected his proposals, but Deputy Prime Minister Attlee judged that request completely out of line. "I am quite certain it would be wrong to send the Viceroy the minutes. . . . The reason, of course, is . . . the collective responsibility of the Cabinet for policy. The Viceroy may properly be given an indication of how the collective mind of the Cabinet is working . . . [not] of the line taken by individual members. . . . The making of this request is, I fear, only another example of the disadvantage of having a Viceroy with no political experience."[45]

Amery now focused his attention on trying to develop a proposal to solve India's complex constitutional problem that was more sophisticated than Wavell's, convinced that Britain's cabinet must reconsider and resolve this matter soon. "It is becoming increasingly more obvious that Indian politicians are neither able nor willing to come to terms as to the future constitution," Amery informed his cabinet colleagues on January 5. "Logically, we are, of course, in an unassailable position if we say we have offered all that we can . . . [and] sit back and wait for Indians to do their share. But good logic is not always good . . . statesmanship." The failure of Indian political leaders to agree among themselves, Amery argued, only made them more bitter against the British government, which they accuse of setting an impossible task for them so that the Raj can "sit tight and postpone any further advance." He feared that as soon the war ended and emergency powers were removed, general unrest would break out, "likely to be accompanied by fierce communal rioting."[46]

Amery informed his cabinet colleagues that "the root" of India's political deadlock was based, first of all, in "the prepossession, in Indian minds and in our own, with our own peculiar British conception of parliamentary government, and secondly, in our failure to realise that what India most passionately desires is not a particular constitution, whether of the British type or otherwise, but freedom from a status of subordination to an outside authority."[47] Indian discontent with British imperial rule, Amery argued, was much the "same emotion" that caused the revolt of American colonies, precisely why Gandhi's "Quit India" movement met with so "wide a measure of acceptance." So Leo Amery advised in his memorandum on "The Indian Problem" that as soon as the war ended, Great Britain "declare that India . . . pending agreement on a new constitution" was " independent of the United Kingdom under her existing constitution." He was thus recommending termination of his own India Office at Whitehall, as well as his job. Though "that would be . . . a provisional arrangement, pending agreement on a future constitution which could then be discussed by Indians at their leisure." Amery's idea would require no more than "a declaration of intention," which he suggested should be made directly by the king, as emperor of India, in Delhi immediately after the war ended. "The effect on India would, I believe, be profound." Congress Party leaders could all be released and provincial self-governments restored to their prewar powers. It was Leo Amery's swan song, which Wavell later read and ignored, and had less chance of being accepted by Churchill than Wavell's own less radical proposal.

Wavell met with the India Committee of the war cabinet on March 26, right after he arrived in London. Attlee chaired that meeting and asked the viceroy to give his "general appreciation" of the Indian position. Wavell began by praising British Indian troops in India and in Burma, where they were "more than a match" for the Japanese. The inflationary strain on India's economy was very great, but the food position had improved with rationing working well in most towns and food prices now under control. Grain imports, he advised, must continue. There was urgency about reaching a political settlement, in view of the current general deterioration. The Indian civil service was "almost moribund," its men overburdened and in need of leave. Wavell requested authority to reform his executive council, choosing some Indian political leaders to work under the present constitution. He wanted to broadcast his proposals and would invite the smallest possible number of important leaders (not more than eight or nine) "to meet him in a conference and try to form a Government."[48] In assessing Gandhi, he told the cabinet that he was not only seventy-five but also "fairly sick." Of Jinnah, he said, he would "never commit himself . . . was now getting on in years and was not very fit, though his brain was as active as ever."

Wavell dined alone with Churchill, who launched into "a long jeremiad about India" that lasted forty minutes, including dire predictions of South Asia's breakdown into "Pakistan, Hindustan, Princestan, etc." in the wake of any British withdrawal. He saw, Wavell concluded, "no ray of hope."[49] A few days later Wavell dined with Amery and Attlee, who were ready to hold elections throughout India, which would have meant first releasing all Congress Party political prisoners. Wavell was, however, reluctant to take that "radical" a step, revealing not only his lack of political experience but also his deep distrust of the democratic political process. Nothing Leo Amery or Clem Attlee said to him sufficed to bolster his courage enough for him to release Nehru and his Congress Party's working committee colleagues until after Germany surrendered.

Wavell heard the announcement of Germany's unconditional surrender little more than a month later, on May 8, 1945, from his own seat in the House of Lords, noting in his diary that the momentous Allied victory in Europe had come "too soon for my plans in India."[50] He impatiently urged the cabinet to approve his plan for Indian Council reform, but Churchill angrily reminded him that " your visit to this country was [not] necessary at the present time, but as you wanted to come and discuss matters here every effort has been made to meet your wishes."[51] To Amery, Churchill wrote of Wavell's proposed changes: "No action or negotiation until the election has shown which party is in power."[52]

Despite England's euphoria over its victory in Europe, Winston Churchill well knew how unpopular his Tory Party had become at home. The India Committee of the cabinet met twice on May 30, 1945, Churchill insisting that nothing should be said or done by Wavell after he returned home until the British electorate had spoken. Amery, however, felt "gravely apprehensive of the effect that would be produced in India were the viceroy to return empty-handed at a time when Indian nationalism was passing through an acute phase."[53] So Churchill agreed to invite Wavell to meet one more time with his cabinet on May 31. He then told Wavell that the cabinet "were not satisfied as to the wisdom of making a fresh offer to India on the lines proposed."[54] Wavell replied earnestly at length, insisting that "he did not under-rate the difficulties of carrying through the proposals which he had put forward," but that "making no move would be more dangerous. . . . [I]f the experiment succeeded, it would, in his judgment, be accepted as a substantial step forward by opinion in India and outside. If it failed, we should have the advantage of having made the most generous offer . . . to secure a Council which would not be inferior in intellectual quality to the present Council and would conduct itself in a reasonable manner, though admittedly it would be more difficult to handle and more nationalist in temperament." Churchill was sufficiently impressed to ask the cabinet to meet again on that matter in the late afternoon, and Wavell was allowed to fly back to India in June, using his discretion to release Congress Party Working Committee prisoners, some of whom could be invited to the Simla summit he had in mind, and then, if they agreed, to join a reorganized representative government of India council.

After reaching New Delhi in early June, Wavell convened his old council, facing immediate opposition from all of its previously pliable Indian members to the cabinet's new offer of cautious change. Those members demanded an immediate declaration of "complete dominion status forthwith" as a prerequisite to any "national government." They also called for general elections before any new council was chosen, to be certain that its members were truly representative, and urged the release of political prisoners.

Wavell showed Dr. Ambedkar, the "untouchable" member of his current council, his proposed list of political party numbers he hoped to add to his new council, inviting Ambedkar to join the forthcoming Simla summit. "Five seats to 90 millions of Muslims, one seat to 50 millions of Untouchables," Ambedkar irately remarked, refusing to join either the summit or the new council, and labeling Wavell's proposal "a strange and sinister kind of political arithmetic which is revolting to my ideas of justice."[55] Despite his "special caution about secrecy," Wavell wired Amery on June 7, "Associated Press this afternoon carried accurate summary of this morning's Council proceedings. . . . It is almost impossible to transact business when course of discussions in Council is public property."[56] It hardly proved the happy "homecoming" reception the viceroy had anticipated. But he staunchly pushed forward with his summit plan, ordering the release of Nehru and other members of Congress's working committee from prison, inviting Gandhi as well as Azad, and Jinnah as well as Liaquat Ali Khan, and Tara Singh, to join him at the grand viceroy's palace in the Himalayan foothills on June 25. Though more optimistic about his summit's chances than either Churchill or Amery, Wavell rightly suspected just before it started that "either Gandhi or Jinnah may decide to wreck it."[57]

"I have been authorised by His Majesty's Government to place before Indian political leaders proposals designed to ease the present political situation and to advance India towards her goal of full self-government," Wavell broadcast from New Delhi on June 14.

> This is not an attempt to obtain or impose a constitutional settlement. His Majesty's Government had hoped that the leaders of the Indian parties would agree amongst themselves on a settlement of the communal issue, which is the main stumbling-block. . . . India has great opportunities to be taken and great problems to be solved, which require a common effort by the leading men of all parties. I therefore propose . . . to invite Indian leaders . . . to take counsel with me with a view to the formation of a new Executive Council more representative of . . . political opinion.[58]

Gandhi accepted Wavell's invitation, though he explained that he had no official position in the Congress and strongly objected to the viceroy's distinction between "Caste Hindus" and "so-called Untouchables," which, as the Mahatma had always insisted, were as truly "Hindu" as any Brahman or Bania. Three days before the Simla summit, Gandhi met with Sardar Vallabhbhai Patel in Panchgani hill-station, both of them going together to Bombay, where they joined other members of Congress's working committee, convened there by Congress president Azad to consider the viceroy's proposals. Nehru did not think that merely changing the viceroy's council could solve India's basic problems. "India needs a surgical operation," Nehru noted after considering Wavell's idea. "We have to get rid of our preoccupation with petty problems and concentrate on the fundamental problem of slavery and poverty."[59]

Jinnah accepted Wavell's invitation, but only if he could meet alone with him first on June 24, the eve of the conference. Then he telegraphed Wavell on June 18 to say that he could not "decide" whether to summon the working committee of his Muslim League to meet earlier. "Jinnah is evidently waiting until Congress attitude is known," Wavell told Amery.[60] Wavell also invited Amery to join him at Simla, but Leo regretfully had to campaign back in Britain, trying to defend his hotly contested seat in the Commons, which he lost in a "mud bath" battle against Bengal-born British communist R. Palme Dutt.

Though that sudden dramatic change in Britain's home government dominated headlines throughout India as well as England, the Simla summit went ahead as planned. On the eve of the first day's round table, Wavell met alone with Congress Party president Azad prior to his private meeting with League president Jinnah, thus giving both major parties equal time. He reported to Amery that

> Azad . . . appeared to accept the main principles underlying the proposals . . . but hoped that closer relations could be established between Indian Government and public and Indian Army. Congress would regard India as even more closely concerned with Japanese War than Britain and could not be a party to illiberal treatment of liberated areas. I told him I saw no difficulty under either of these heads. . . . On the parity issue he said that Congress would accept equality of Caste Hindus and Muslims but would not compromise on the method of selection. Congress must have a voice in the selection of non-Hindus; and Muslims . . . must not be selected by an exclusively communal body [Muslim League].[61]

Gandhi came in to see Wavell alone immediately after Azad left and made "a long and tortuous statement largely historical lasting over half an hour and ending with a sort of general blessing on the proposals." He then went on to ask for the release of all political prisoners, not just the working committee, and to repeat how objectionable he found the terms "caste Hindu" and "non-Scheduled Hindus." He also "dilated on non-communal character of Congress and said that from the political point of view caste did not exist."[62]

Jinnah came in just after Gandhi left.

> He began by saying that the Muslims would always be in a minority in the new Council because the other minorities . . . Sikhs and Scheduled Castes would always vote with Hindus. . . . I said I doubted his assumption and pointed out that Viceroy and Commander-in-Chief would see fair play for Muslims. He then proposed that if majority of Muslims were opposed to any decision, it should not go by vote. I said I certainly could not accept this. . . . He then claimed that Muslim League had the right to nominate all Muslim Members to the new Council. I said I could not accept this. He then asserted that the League . . . represented all the Muslims of India. He suggested that I was thinking of the nomination of Muslims by Congress. I replied that I also had in mind the nomination of a Muslim by the Punjab Unionist Party. Jinnah retorted that Unionist Party were traitors to Muslim interests and that Punjab Coalition Ministry existed only by his sufferance. I refused to accept this and said that Unionist Party had done a very good job of work in Punjab. . . . I would not . . . pledge . . . that all Muslims should be nominated by the League.[63]

The Simla conference opened on the morning of June 25, Wavell giving a short introductory speech, followed by Azad for the Congress Party, then by Jinnah for the League, Tara Singh for the Sikhs, and Siva Raj, who represented "untouchables." By noon of that first day it became clear from what each of those leaders demanded that there would be no meeting of minds at this Simla conference. No attempts at mediation or political bridge-building had been made prior to the general meeting, either by British officials or apolitical Indians. Next morning Azad stated that members of the council should all be appointed on a political, not a "communal basis." Jinnah retorted "sharply" that if necessary "he could deliver a lecture on Pakistan." Rajagopalachari then suggested, and Jinnah agreed, that private discussions were essential before reconvening the conference as a whole. Jinnah met with Congress Party leader Pundit Pant alone, insisting that Congress should not propose any Muslim member for council. Jinnah refused to meet with Azad, calling him a "show-case Muslim." Khizr Hayat Khan Tiwana, the Punjab's young Unionist Party premier who was also at Simla, told Wavell it would be "disastrous for Punjab" if one of his Unionist Party Muslims was not selected for membership on the new council. Wavell informed the conference of how he proposed to choose his new council, after which Jinnah announced that "no progress" had been made in his discussions with Pant. So Wavell suggested more "private meetings," and Jinnah asked to see him that evening.

"My discussion with Jinnah yesterday," Wavell reported to Amery,

> was inconclusive. I began by saying that while I appreciated his difficulties, I had to consider Provinces as well as Parties, and in view of importance of Punjab both to the Army and to food supply, I thought the inclusion of a Punjabi Muslim . . . essential. . . . Jinnah made rambling and prolix reply . . . attacking the Unionist Party, and working up to the conclusion that he really commanded the allegiance of practically all the Muslims in the Punjab. I then asked him about his conversations with Pant. He said they had been completely negative. . . . I then asked what his position was regarding the selection of Muslim Members. He said they must all be nominated by the League. I replied that this was entirely unacceptable to me and asked whether he intended to wreck the conference. . . . After considerable discussion I gathered . . . he would be prepared to consult his Working Committee. . . . He was more polite and less businesslike than usual.[64]

The next day, Jinnah said that any proposals made at the conference which he was prepared to accept would have to be ratified by his League, and he could not go to them until he had a complete scheme before him. He "asked me to send him a statement of it in writing. I agreed. . . . He also asked to what he was being committed. I replied that . . . he should submit a list [of proposed Members' names]."[65] Jinnah wanted a fourteen-member council, with the viceroy and commander-in-chief both remaining, adding five Hindus, five Muslims, one Sikh, and one untouchable, all Muslims nominated only by his League.

Wavell adjourned the conference after its fourth meeting, until Saturday July 14, fearing by now that neither the Congress Party nor the League would give any ground. He wrote to all provincial governors to explain the stalemate, and asked them to advise "what course you recommend if Muslim League decline to co-operate." On July 2 he met with Nehru for the first time, finding "little bitterness," and his charming manners and "reasonable good sense" unaffected by his long lonely years in prison.[66] Wavell knew that if Jinnah continued to refuse to accept a non-League Muslim on a new multiparty council that he would have to turn primarily to the Congress Party, asking Nehru for an appropriate list of names.

Most provincial governors responded to Wavell's inquiry by suggesting that he should form a council without Jinnah's support if he proved unreasonable. Governor Glancy thought his demands

> outrageously unreasonable. If he is given three nominations out of, say, five Muslim seats he should account himself fortunate indeed. . . . Jinnah is evidently nervous . . . but . . . I agree with you that it would be inadvisable . . . to attempt forming Council without League representation. This would place Congress in unduly dominating position. . . . Jinnah would pose as Islamic hero and though after some interval the falseness and untenability of his position might be appreciated and his power for mischief broken, it seems not unlikely that meanwhile the central machine would collapse.[67]

Governor Casey reported that he had learned from Khwaja Nazim-ud-Din, one of Bengal's Muslim League leaders, that Jinnah would not agree to a Congress Muslim on the council and "Conference would break."[68]

Maulana Azad sent Wavell his Congress list of fifteen names for the new council on July 7, starting with his own, followed by Nehru, Patel, Rajendra Prasad, Jinnah, Liaquat Ali Khan, and others, and concluding with Tara Singh. Jinnah refused to submit a list, after consulting his working committee, insisting that his list would be presented in a "confidential discussion" with the viceroy. "Further the Working Committee is emphatically of the opinion that all the Muslim Members of the proposed Executive Council should be chosen from the Muslim League."[69]

Wavell reported to Amery on July 9 that "Azad is deeply hurt at Jinnah's refusal to treat with him [*sic*] and I have seen an Intelligence report of attempts by Azad to consolidate the minor parties with the Congress against the Muslim League. He is said to have offered Tara Singh full Congress support for the Sikhs. . . . He believed that on this basis Jinnah and the League could be broken. The Sikhs have not accepted the Congress offer and Tara Singh's list was sent in separately."[70] Wavell then reported on his meeting with Jinnah again, of his refusing to accept League vetoes. He found Jinnah "obviously wrought up and . . . afraid of being made [the] scapegoat for failure of the Conference . . . many of his followers . . . anxious to accept offer and office."

Wavell tried his best to persuade Jinnah, but could not budge him, and on July 11, 1945, he wrote again to all provincial governors to report that the Simla summit conference had "failed." That very day, Amery lost his own "dreary and sordid" reelection bid, some 10,000 of "my old supporters having been driven out by the blitz, while . . . many thousand immigrants had come in who knew nothing about me . . . [other than Dutt's] campaign of vilification against me as 'the gaoler of India', the murderer who was directly responsible for a million-and-a-half deaths in Bengal, etc."[71]

The final plenary session of the Simla conference was addressed by Wavell on July 14. He sadly summarized the outcome of the meetings.

> Unfortunately, the Conference was unable to agree about the strength and composition of the Executive Council. . . . I asked the parties to let me have lists of names, and said I would do what I could to produce a solution acceptable to the leaders. . . . I received lists from all parties . . . except from the Muslim League. . . . I therefore made my provisional selections including certain Muslim League names, and . . . believe that if these selections had been acceptable here they would have been acceptable to His Majesty's Government. . . . When I explained my solution to Mr. Jinnah he told me that it was not acceptable. . . . The Conference has therefore failed. Nobody can regret this more than I do myself. I wish to make it clear that the responsibility for the failure is mine. . . . I cannot place the blame for its failure upon any of the parties.[72]

Wavell's insistence upon taking all the blame for his conference's failure on his own broad shoulders was either a generous act of diplomacy or utterly misguided duplicity, designed to save Jinnah from having to leave Simla in disgrace as the spoiler of India's "best chance" of immediately achieving representative, responsible rule on the revived viceroy's executive council. This could have been the dawn of Britain's true transfer of power to a unified independent India, on the eve of the very end of World War II. Instead, it augured a dismal frustrating return to the pre-conference political deadlock and continued communal antipathy that would soon erupt into a state of intermittent arson, murder, and hatred.

No Congress Party member at Simla, however, was deceived by Wavell's claim that he alone was responsible for its failure. Azad rightly insisted that the blame "rested on other shoulders. . . . The Muslim League wanted all Muslims . . . nominated by them. . . . If the Congress had accepted this position, it would be reduced to a communal organisation." Yet Azad also viewed the viceroy's protection of Jinnah's pride and position more as the work of "perfidious Albion" rather than an act of gracious diplomacy, adding "that the British Government could not absolve itself of the blame for the present communal problem. So long as there was a third power, the two parties were like pawns which could be moved one way or the other. The question could only be solved on the basis of justice, equity and fairplay and not of expediency."[73]

Rajagopalachari believed

> that the solution which His Excellency had attempted was entirely an interim one. . . . The communal problem required a long-term solution based on agreement for a permanent constitution. . . . The Congress had shown itself willing to co-operate. Mr. Jinnah's claim that he represented the Muslim community, which was not tested by a general election, could not be accepted and His Excellency was right in rejecting it. On that basis the Conference stood defeated.

Jinnah agreed that Wavell had done his best, but insisted that both Azad and Rajagopalachari "forgot the fundamental principles underlying the Muslim League attitude. . . . The Congress stood for a united India whereas the Muslim League stood for Pakistan and these two were entirely incompatible."[74] That was the rock on which Wavell's Simla conference was shattered.

Wavell invited Nehru to meet with him after the conference ended, to sound him out as to whether Congress might be ready now to join the executive council. "He was quite friendly. . . . His main theme was that Congress represented a modern Nationalist tendency—the League a mediaeval and separatist one. He showed no special bitterness against Jinnah and the League, admitted that there was a psychological fear of Hindu domination, but claimed that it was unreal and unwarranted. . . . He did not put forward any special solution of the problem. He is more of a theorist than a practical politician but earnest and I am sure honest."[75]

Wavell wrote his own report on his failed Simla summit to King George VI, with whom, as viceroy, he kept periodically in touch:

> The Congress members sat on my left, led by Maulana Azad . . . one of the few Congress Muslims of any distinction, an elderly scholar, with good manners, but with no administrative experience and not much political wisdom. . . . Jinnah . . . treated him as a Muslim traitor in the pay of Congress. Azad understands English quite well, but will not speak it. . . . On my right was Jinnah and the League members. Jinnah is a very clever advocate from Bombay, a very bad Muslim as far as religion goes, but a man of considerable courage . . . and quite incorruptible. . . . I had about five or six hours with him . . . but we never really got on . . . he was continually trying to entrap me into some concession or admission that he could use. His manners are bad. . . . Next to him sat his principal lieutenant, Nawabzada Liaqat Ali Khan . . . a big heavy man, reputed to be able, but I do not know. . . . I wanted to have a talk with him after the Conference to make his acquaintance, but Jinnah refused him permission to come. . . . The root cause of the failure was Jinnah's intransigence and obstinacy. But it represents a real fear on the part of the Muslims . . . of Congress domination, which they regard as . . . a Hindu Raj. . . . It shows more

openly than ever before the great rift between Hindu and Muslim, which events of the last few years have accentuated. . . . Outside the Conference I had two meetings with Gandhi, [and] two with Nehru. . . . I found Gandhi pleasant to talk to, with a sense of humour and good manners, but I am quite sure he is an old humbug in many ways, and I should never trust him very far. Nehru was friendly, and is interesting and well read; he is sincere and courageous, but more of a doctrinaire and theorist than a practical politician.[76]

After Simla, Wavell's fond dream of forging a viable solution to India's communal division and political deadlock all but died. He returned to Delhi, a quieter and sadder man, knowing that his interlude as viceroy, during which he briefly imagined that he might accomplish more than merely holding down Fortress India, would soon be over. Leo Amery wrote his last letter as secretary of state for India to Lord Wavell late in July: "The avalanche has carried me away with all the rest and I dare say it may take some little while before I can flounder up . . . to daylight again. Anyhow, that is the end . . . of our happy partnership."[77] Wavell replied: "I regret that our partnership has been broken . . . but I still hope that what we have done together may bear some fruit in the end; and anyway we did our best in the face of some difficulty."[78]

5

From the End of World War II
through the Cabinet Mission,
August 1945–June 1946

CHURCHILL WAS IN BERLIN for the "terminal" Allied Potsdam Summit Conference in mid-July of 1945, when the election avalanche that removed him and Amery from high office struck. He had sensed two weeks earlier from loud heckling he elicited during electioneering appearances around London that Labor had made inroads into his own constituency. But on July 5, when Britain went to the polls he still expected to win, just as he had won the European war. Most British soldiers were eager to stop fighting and go home and opted for a new Labor government, as Churchill realized with a jolt when he and Attlee, each in his own jeep, reviewed British troops in Berlin on July 21, Deputy Prime Minister Attlee getting more "vociferous cheers" from the soldiers than weary old Churchill did.[1] Churchill learned from Truman at Potsdam that the United States had successfully tested the atom bomb it would drop on Japan in early August. The night before that last Allied summit ended, Churchill dined alone with Mountbatten, who flew in from his Southeast Asia Colombo Headquarters at Churchill's invitation, and announced "I have great plans . . . about your future." That confident promise of India's viceroyalty gave Mountbatten an "eerie feeling," he later recorded, since "I felt equally confident that he would be out of office within 24 hours."[2]

Two days later, when all the votes had been counted, Labour won by a landslide, its first absolute majority in the House of Commons, with 393 seats to only 213 for Churchill's Conservatives. Churchill tendered his resignation to King George on the night of July 26. Prime Minister Attlee's new government brought Cripps back into the cabinet as president of the board of trade, and Gandhi's old admirer, socialist Lord Pethick-Lawrence, to Whitehall as secretary of state for India and Burma.

After his appointment, Pethick-Lawrence told the Indian press on August 8, 1945:

> All my life I have been greatly attracted to . . . India. . . . I spent several months with my wife [suffragette leader Emmeline Pethick-Lawrence] in India in 1926–7 and . . . I was a member of the Indian Round Table Conference. . . . The ideal which I set before myself as the goal to be reached . . . is none other than Equal Partnership between Britain and both India and Burma. This is passionately desired, I am confident not only by myself and His Majesty's Government, but by the vast majority of all our peoples.[3]

His first telegram to Wavell advised commuting imminent executions of four Indians on death row, scheduled for that month. Wavell "most reluctantly" agreed on "humanitarian [not political] grounds" to commute their death sentences to transportation for life.[4] Pethick-Lawrence's faith in the efficacy of nonviolence to solve India's problems was thus introduced at Whitehall the same month that the United States bombed Hiroshima and Nagasaki, convincing the Japanese to surrender unconditionally.

Wavell now met with his provincial governors, all of whom agreed that it would be best to hold elections throughout India in December 1945. India's commander-in-chief, General Auchinleck, expected Jinnah's League to win "almost all" the Muslim seats, with the Congress Party winning most of the rest. "Nehru has continued his injudicious speeches," Wavell informed Pethick-Lawrence. "Congress leaders are difficult people to deal with . . . outwardly very reasonable when one meets them, but in dealing with their followers they have no balance. . . . I think Nehru is trustworthy . . . but he is unbalanced and unreliable. . . . I am not surprised that Jinnah is apprehensive of them."[5]

Attlee chaired his cabinet's first India committee meeting on August 17, noting that the end of the Japanese war "materially altered" the situation, overtaking any interim solutions, requiring a general review of Britain's future policy toward India. The cabinet invited Wavell to London to discuss the situation, urging him to go ahead with his plans for holding elections. Secretary of State Pethick-Lawrence was to prepare a paper of possible options for the cabinet to consider.

Wavell warned Pethick-Lawrence on August 19 that Jinnah "seriously demands immediate grant to Moslems of . . . separation of Moslem majority provinces from rest of India by plebiscite of Moslems only. . . . Governor of Punjab says, 'If Pakistan becomes an imminent reality, we shall be heading straight for bloodshed on a wide scale. . . . Sikhs are not bluffing, they will not submit peacefully to . . . Muhammadan Raj.' "[6] Wavell noted two days later that the "Pakistan idea" was stronger in Muslim minority provinces than in those where Muslims "are already well on top," since there they would generally gain nothing from Pakistan. "In Bengal the Muslims, though numerically dominant, are inferior to Hindus in wealth and education."[7] He urged the importance of quickly exposing the "crudity of Jinnah's ideas" by launching a high-level inquiry into Pakistan, even though Jinnah would probably "boycott" it. The total population of Punjab in 1941 was 28.4 million, 16.2 million of whom were Muslims, the rest Hindus and Sikhs.

Azad wrote to Wavell on August 22 to "protest" the early call for elections, explaining that "Congress is still under ban, political prisoners and detenus in prisons, . . . funds and properties confiscated, civil liberties drastically reduced under war-time Ordinances . . . still in operation."[8]

Wavell reached London before the end of August, and Pethick-Lawrence expected him to remain at least two or three weeks for consultations on major issues affecting India's present and future. Attlee welcomed Wavell to the cabinet on the afternoon of August 29 and the viceroy told them of the "hardening" of communal feeling in India in the aftermath of the failure of his Simla conference. Jinnah now spoke "for 99 per cent of the Muslim population . . . in their apprehension of Hindu domination."[9] Wavell felt that the Congress Party had been unwise in handling their provincial governments from 1937 to 1939, intensifying Muslim anxiety concerning dangers they faced from a "Hindu Raj," thus bolstering Pakistan. The "wholly impracticable" idea of Pakistan had to be exposed to the Muslim electorate, Wavell argued, in order to undermine support for it. He recognized that Jinnah might not submit his case to any commission, whether British or Indian, but thought that the cabinet should now declare such an examination of the Pakistan issue "necessary." He also called their attention to the importance of considering Britain's future policy toward the princely states, which would require "very careful handling."

Pethick-Lawrence then informed his cabinet colleagues that he had asked the viceroy if he could suggest any modifications of Cripps's 1942 offer that might conduce to "acceptance in India of our scheme." The viceroy and secretary of state agreed that after the elections, Indian political leaders should be invited to London to reconsider how to resolve their communal concerns, Wavell warning that "if we forced the pace," the risk of serious communal outbreaks was great. Most members of the cabinet saw no advantage in having India's political leaders return to London, which would effectively mean just a restaging of the round table conference and the more recent Simla summit. Attlee agreed and asked Pethick-Lawrence and Wavell to reconsider the matter.

Wavell wired Acting Viceroy Colville for his suggestions as to possible ways of improving the Cripps offer. Wavell trusted Colville's political judgment, tempered by two decades of experience in Parliament, prior to his appointment as governor of Bombay in 1943. Colville believed that the

Congress Party would now accept the original Cripps offer they had rejected and that if the Muslim League abstained, Sikhs would support the Congress Party. Like Wavell and Punjab's Governor Glancy, however, he thought Jinnah's League would now reject the offer. He feared that if His Majesty's Government announced its intention of reviving Cripps's offer, immediately to convene a constituent assembly after elections, that Jinnah would win the great majority of Muslim votes, and order his followers to abstain from attending an electoral college controlled by the Congress Party. "His Majesty's Government would then be faced with the alternatives of breaking their pledge or coercing the Muslims in the provinces in which they have a majority . . . increasing communal tension especially in Punjab. We might be obliged to employ British troops on large scale."[10]

Wavell warned Pethick-Lawrence, who agreed and informed the cabinet that it would be too dangerous to announce a single constituent assembly to follow provincial elections in the spring of 1946. Better to wait until after all elections were concluded, giving the viceroy time for further discussions with political leaders at the center and in provinces to see how they felt about reviving Cripps's offer. Princely states' representatives would also be invited to join those deliberations. Wavell hoped to convert his executive council into a politically representative one soon after the first round of elections ended in December.

Attlee and Cripps disagreed with Wavell, finding him too anxious and fearful about holding elections, sensing that Pethick-Lawrence was only agreeing with his viceregal partner as any good secretary of state would. Cripps argued that unless his original offer was now reaffirmed, the "world would think . . . we would be going back on it." He added that the advent of Labor's new government "created great expectations in India, and if the policy of the Government were to appear to be less favourable to India . . . the effect on Indian opinion would be disastrous."[11] Cripps wanted political leaders appointed immediately to the viceroy's council, believing that the "psychological effect" of Indians filling key appointments would make a profound impression. Wavell was willing to accept those suggestions and to incorporate them into a statement he could make after flying back to Delhi in mid-September.

The working committee of the Congress Party met for the first time in three years in mid-September, conveying "its greetings and congratulations to the nation [India] for the courage and endurance with which it withstood the fierce and violent onslaught of the British power." Congress feared that with the atom bomb unleashed, civilization itself was in danger of destruction from the acquisitive "imperialist tendencies" that had launched the last war, the end of which brought no freedom to colonial countries. "The independence of India must be unequivocally recognised and the status among the United Nations must be that of an independent nation."[12] Wavell enclosed that report in his letter to Pethick-Lawrence to illustrate some of the "difficulties with which we are likely to be faced."

On September 19 the viceroy broadcast his message to all of India from New Delhi:

> It is the intention of His Majesty's Government to convene as soon as possible a Constitution-making body. . . . The task . . . for India is a complex and difficult one. . . . We must hold elections so that the will of the Indian electorate may be known. . . . After elections, I propose to hold discussions with representatives of those elected . . . to determine the form which the Constitution-making Body should take. . . . I can certainly assure you that the Government and all sections of the British people are anxious to help . . . the people of India . . . arrive at their goal. . . . It is now for Indians to show that they have the wisdom, faith and courage to determine in what way they can best reconcile their differences and how their country can be governed by Indians for Indians.[13]

Jinnah's *Dawn* carried his response to Wavell's speech, that "no attempt will succeed except on the basis of Pakistan. . . . The division of India is the only solution . . . and this is the road to happiness, prosperity, welfare and freedom of 400 millions inhabiting this sub-continent."[14] Wavell also told Pethick-Lawrence that in their resolutions,

> Congress leaders are no doubt relying on ignorance. . . . They know . . . they can say almost anything and be believed by a very large number of people. . . . The Congress has always included people who prefer revolution to reform, violence to passive resistance, and non-co-operation to co-operation with the British. . . . [M]uch will depend on the final attitude of men like Vallabhbhai Patel and Nehru who though hitherto subservient to Gandhi do not in their hearts believe in his ideas.

Near the end of October, Wavell warned that "Reports from Governors . . . confirm my view that the Congress may intend a violent mass movement after the elections, and that we must expect a steady deterioration in communal feeling and in the general attitude to constituted authority. You must be prepared for very stormy weather ahead."[15] One factor adding turbulence to India's political weather was the trial of several officers of Subhas Chandra Bose's Indian National Army, which had begun in old Delhi's Red Fort. Bose himself had died, but his INA, composed of about 20,000 men out of some 60,000 Indian troops captured by the Japanese in Singapore, had fought against the British in Burma and Malaya before surrendering with the Japanese and were viewed by Wavell and Auchinleck as traitors. Most Indians, however, considered them nationalist heroes, who followed former Indian National Congress President Netaji Subhas Bose out of patriotic fervor, eager to liberate India from imperial rule. Several Congress Party judges and barristers, including Nehru, volunteered to defend those INA officers under trial. Even Mahatma Gandhi wrote to Wavell, appealing for their release, noting that they were "loved" and "admired" by all Indians. By November Wavell was uncertain of how many INA officers should be tried, but Auchinleck's estimate was that out of a total of 125 offenders, "not more than 45 persons will be sentenced to death" for "waging war against the King." Of those, Wavell informed Pethick-Lawrence, he "guessed" no more than "20 death sentences will be confirmed."[16] Before those trials ended Indian opposition rose to such a fever pitch of patriotic fury that Auchinleck feared it would undermine the loyalty of the entire British Indian Army. Though three INA officers were found "guilty" of treason, their sentences were all commuted by the viceroy at the recommendation of the commander-in-chief.

During his recent visit to London, Wavell had learned that the British Labour government's party was co-chaired by Nehru's closest comrade, V. K. Krishna Menon, so in early November the viceroy invited Nehru to meet with him, hoping to convince him to adopt a more friendly attitude toward British officers, appealing to him to stop "incitement to violence or threats to . . . officials" in his campaign speeches, and to "compromise" with the Muslim League. But Nehru insisted that "Congress could make no terms whatever with the Muslim League under its present leadership and policy, that it was a reactionary body with entirely unacceptable ideas . . . Hitlerian in its leadership and policy, and tried to bully everyone."[17] Nehru "practically admitted that he was preaching violence," Wavell reported, and though he could not "help liking him," feared he had become "a fanatic" and that "his mood is dangerous to peace."[18]

A few days later Wavell sent Pethick-Lawrence a memo, reporting that Nehru, Pant, and Patel had been making speeches "intended to provoke or pave the way for mass disorder . . . asserting that the British could be turned out of India within a very short time; denying the possibility of a compromise with the Muslim League; glorifying the I. N. A.; and threatening the officials who took part in the suppression of the 1942 disturbances with trial and punishment as 'war criminals.'"[19] Wavell now believed the Congress Party was preparing to serve an ultimatum on the British government after elections, organizing a mass movement on a much larger scale than in 1942.

> I do not imagine that His Majesty's Government will wish to yield to force or threats of force; nor can we lightly divest ourselves of our obligations to the minorities. . . . [W]e must be prepared to suppress the movement, and to suppress it this time with . . . the use of considerable force of British troops . . . the declaration of martial law; the detention of a large number of persons without trial . . . and the suppression for an indefinite period of the Congress Party. . . . [T]he alternative is to hand India over to a single

party . . . consisting mainly of caste Hindus. . . . If we handed over British India, it would be impossible for us to fulfil our obligations to the States, the rulers of which have loyally supported us.[20]

Wavell felt he would be "justified" to move against the Congress immediately, but did not recommend such action, unless forced to do so by violent disorders.

Pethick-Lawrence was not surprised by Wavell's warnings. "I would have thought myself, however, that some of this violent talk by Congress leaders is due to their anxiety to keep their organisation together in the stress of the election. . . . But . . . I entirely agree that the speeches of the Congress leaders do not make very pleasant reading."[21] What worried Pethick-Lawrence more than inflammatory Congress rhetoric, however, was the prospect of Jinnah's refusing after elections were held to budge from the inflexible position he had taken in Simla. He could not "see any satisfactory way out through Pakistan," but asked Wavell if he thought Jinnah could be induced to accept a modified form of it which it might be possible to concede?"[22]

Wavell doubted whether any new frontier solution would be acceptable both to the Congress Party and the League. The former would never agree to handing over all of Punjab and Bengal to the League, and "Jinnah can hardly accept anything less than the present provincial boundaries on an option to be exercised by Muslims alone . . . [since] there is certainly something in the Muslim view that they cannot reduce their demands without depriving themselves of the only possible safeguards against Hindu domination."[23]

Pethick-Lawrence put Wavell's warning about Nehru's call for "revolution" before the cabinet, but the tough questions raised by the viceroy as to how best to deal with inflammatory Congress opposition had to await the prime minister's return from the United States. Cripps chaired the India and Burma committee while the prime minister was away, and he reported on what Gandhi's trusted friend Rajkumari Amrit Kaur advised: that the viceroy should see Gandhi, and the secretary of state should invite Nehru and Jinnah to London as soon as elections were over and announce Britain's intention to implement proposed changes immediately.[24] Pethick-Lawrence wired Wavell, asking him to do all of those things, and reporting as well on the imminent visit to India of a parliamentary delegation of leading Commons members of the Labor Party to help "bridge the gap between political opinion in India and here, to demonstrate the sympathy of Parliament with Indian aspirations."[25] Wavell was happy to receive the parliamentary delegation, but did not think it "advisable" to invite Gandhi to meet with him, nor for the secretary of state to invite Nehru and Jinnah to London, convinced they would only decline and publicize such invitations to enhance their political capital.

On November 28 the India committee of the cabinet met again, with Cripps "most uneasy" about Wavell's refusal to see Gandhi and rejection of their idea of inviting Nehru and Jinnah to London. He feared the "steadily widening breach between ourselves and the Indian leaders," insisting "it was very desirable to resume and improve the personal contacts which have been interrupted by the war. . . . [T]here would be great advantage in having the leaders over here and giving them an opportunity to talk."[26] Attlee disagreed, however, thinking "very little would be gained by inviting the leaders. . . . There might, however, be something to be said for a representative of His Majesty's Government going out to India and talking to the leaders on the spot." Cripps said he would be "satisfied" with that, and in six months, he would be asked by Attlee to fly back to India, though not alone.

As the Labor government's cabinet grew more anxious about the political concerns and eagerness for independence of its Congress Party friends, hoping swiftly and effectively to reassure them, Wavell's own mind hardened in its conviction that "the only possible solution is for H. M. G. [His Majesty's Government] to take charge; to give up further consultations with political leaders, and to lay down a programme of its own which will . . . be acceptable at least to the more sensible and moderate."[27] The viceroy confessed to his private secretary George Abell at the end of November, "I am not sure whether this is still possible," but he wanted to invite the "best" men of moderate Indian opinion, princes as well as political leaders, to join his new executive council, something like a national defense council, and they would work together to keep things quiet, while HMG could draft a suitable treaty between Great Britain and India. Wavell now believed that was the "only possible way of arriving at a solution without an internal struggle."

Abell doubted that HMG "would accept a change of policy in advance of an actual breakdown, especially if the proposed new policy were undemocratic in form."[28] He advised instead that Private Secretary Evan Jenkins's idea, which he called "a reserve plan," to set up a federation of Hindu provinces, might be acceptable to the Congress Party and could work rather well. A "constitution for Hindustan" would be framed by representatives of the Hindu-majority provinces; when ready it would be submitted to the provincial legislatures. Those that accepted would enter the federation at once. For the "Pakistan provinces" an attempt would be made to avoid deciding whether territorial adjustments should be permitted in these provinces before they exercised their options and by what procedure that option should be exercised. Those provinces would instead be offered to continue for the time being under their present constitution with British support. They could watch the "formation of Hindustan" and decide later whether to join the federation or stay out, Abell explained. "H. M. G. would be ready to grant Dominion Status as under the Cripps Plan to the Pakistan

Provinces if they wanted it."[29] That brilliant idea would have avoided the bloodshed of Partition, but it was never tried. The "main difficulty," as Abell noted, would be to keep the Congress Party and the Muslim League from "forcing an immediate decision on the issue of accession or non-accession," thereby preventing the Hindu and Sikh districts of east Punjab from immediately breaking off to join India, and Hindu-majority portions of west Bengal from doing the same. It would allow enough time to test the all-India constitution first, and then to decide how best to divide the major provinces of Pakistan, if that proved the wish of their respective electorates, after waiting years enough to test alternative options, or hold impartial plebiscites.

"If we cannot bring pressure to bear on the Muslims to go beyond a certain point, and if the Hindus will not meet them at that point, we must, I think, be prepared to throw in a new proposal," Pethick-Lawrence cautioned Wavell at the end of November. "If we do not we may be faced with a Congress ultimatum such as you have forecast."[30] Wavell then invited Gandhi to see him in early December, but reported: "He had nothing special to say . . . admitted danger of violence and indicated that he was trying to reduce temperature. . . . He was friendly and seemed in good health. . . . Congress obviously do not want trouble at present."[31]

Wavell sent home his "Breakdown Plan" four days before 1945 ended. If Jinnah refused to agree to join the new council or to allow his League to attend the constitution-making body, he would be informed that at least two divisions of the Punjab and all of west Bengal, including Calcutta, would be allowed to join the union, and all that would remain for his Pakistan would be the "husk" he denigrated as inadequate. "It has been suggested that the principle of Pakistan should be conceded, without defining its area," Wavell noted, but "I think this would be embarrassing and not really honest, and that we should be better advised to face the problem when the breakdown occurs . . . [though] the result might be serious communal conflict."[32]

Francis F. Turnbull, private secretary to the secretary of state, wrote a cogent minute of Wavell's plan, which Pethick-Lawrence forwarded to Attlee.

> The Viceroy contemplates that if a deadlock arises . . . H. M. G. will give a decision on the Pakistan issue and will, if necessary, define Pakistan geographically. This raises the question whether the British Government ought to make itself responsible at all or at any rate until it is absolutely the last resort, for a decision that there shall be Pakistan. . . . No-one believes that Pakistan is in the best interests of India . . . and no-one knows where the partition of India, once it starts, will end short of Balkanisation. Moreover, if there were a deadlock in the preliminary stages, to give a decision that there shall be a Pakistan greatly weakens any possibility of compromise on the basis of a very loose federation.[33]

On January 14, 1946, Pethick-Lawrence proposed that a mission of three members of the cabinet be sent to India to pursue negotiations with India's political leaders as to how best to resolve India's constitutional problems. The mission, which would be led by the secretary of state, included Stafford Cripps and First Lord of the Admiralty Albert Victor Alexander. They would fly to India before the end of March, after provincial elections there ended. The cabinet discussed the extent to which the British government could "legitimately divest itself of responsibility for the future conduct of affairs in India."[34] They agreed that if India and/or India and Pakistan could not "stand on their own feet economically" or for defense purposes, then Great Britain had "a moral responsibility" not to hand over the country until satisfied that India's people would face up to those problems with appropriate plans to solve them. "We should not, therefore, in fact be able to divest ourselves of our . . . responsibilities, however much we might appear to do so. . . . If no solution was reached . . . we should continue governing India even if it involved rebellion which would have to be suppressed by British troops."

Pethick-Lawrence was eager to learn as much as possible about how best to resolve India's problems before flying out there. So he asked one of his old friends, Carl Heath, chairman of the India Conciliation Group of Quakers, who had spent a good deal of time in India, "What is to be done with the 'Pakistan' problem?" Heath replied: "Pakistan is the expression of a reasonable Moslem fear of being submerged in what may prove to be an all-powerful unitary State of India dominated by the . . . majority of Hindus. . . . The Government should recognise this sympathetically . . . and endeavour to meet it frankly. . . . But it must not in doing so ignore the equally reasonable claim of the 3 to 1 majority (Hindus plus Sikhs, Christians, Buddhists, Parsees) that Indian unity, built up under the British, must remain unimpaired."[35] Heath recommended that each of British India's eleven provinces be turned into "autonomous States" after the elections, given self-government in all but five areas reserved to the central federal government, which would briefly remain under Britain, controlling foreign affairs, defense, customs, communications, and common finance. The latter three "utility services" should raise no disputes among states, though the first two could pose communal conflicts, and if they did in the case of defense, a state might opt out of the central federal part of Heath's plan.

"This provisional settlement," Heath concluded, "had in mind, and in sympathy, both the fears of the Moslems and the democratic claims of all the others. The settlement implemented would be on the basis of fundamental State right, and agreed devolutions to a federal body of limited powers, to be determined by a representative Assembly of the now free and autonomous States."[36] It was a singularly creative, sympathetic scheme, never tried. Had Heath been India's last viceroy, he could have negotiated wisely with its political leaders, of every faith and party, and would have taken a decade or more to reach final agreement, yet this plan might well have saved a million lives and could perhaps have established an enduring solution to South Asia's most intractable problems. But obviously Britain's cabinet and India's political leaders would all have had to agree that Heath's "solution" for India was worth supporting.

Krishna Menon was much closer to Cripps than to Pethick-Lawrence and helped to convince Cripps that Nehru would be the best man to become free India's prime minister. So Cripps had written to Nehru to ask what he should do after the elections if he "happened to be the viceroy." On January 27, Nehru responded:

> My dear Stafford . . . British policy, in order to maintain British rule, was inevitably one of balance and counterpoise, of preventing unity and encouraging fissiparous tendencies, and one of protecting and strengthening the reactionary elements in the country. . . . Pakistan as such is hardly understood. . . . [T]he Muslim League still commands the great majority of Muslim votes. . . . Jinnah threatens bloodshed. . . . I do not think there is much in Jinnah's threat. The Muslim League leadership is far too reactionary . . . to dare to indulge in any form of direct action. They are incapable of it, having spent their lives in soft jobs. . . . The British Government has to decide once [and] for all its policy. . . . It cannot force Pakistan on India, in the form demanded by Jinnah, for that certainly will lead to civil war.[37]

Wavell met with Azad and Asaf Ali again and rejected a proposal they made on behalf of Congress, for fear that Jinnah would find it "unacceptable, innocent though it looks. . . . The Congress are difficult people, and I am a little unhappy about the growing influence of Patel," Wavell moaned. "Fortunately Gandhi's influence is still paramount, and I think he is likely to be more reasonable in these matters than Patel."[38] The viceroy also saw Liaquat Ali Khan, Jinnah's right-hand man, "much easier to talk to than Jinnah. He said that the British would have to face the Pakistan issue and settle it before any progress could be made. . . . He said at the end that the British would have to stop in India for many years yet."[39] Liaquat was clearly expressing Jinnah's hope as well as his own, for no rational leader at this time, knowing the communal complexity and explosive feelings of so many millions of Indians, dreamed that Great Britain would remove all its martial and administrative cover from India in less than two years.

India's commander-in-chief, General Sir Claude Auchinleck, in January requested an additional three British brigade groups from London's war office to provide a "steadying effect" throughout India, to cope with communal fires ignited by Congress and League campaign rhetoric. Field Marshal Viscount Alanbrooke replied in early February 1946 that he could not oblige, postwar demobilization having pared Britain's armed forces down to "an irreducible minimum in all areas" of Britain's worldwide commitments.[40] British troops were now quietly but steadily leaving India, every officer and soldier eager to sail home as soon as a vacant berth could be found aboard any Peninsula & Orient liner or troop ship out of Bombay, Madras, or Calcutta.

Then on February 18 Indian sailors aboard the Royal Indian Navy's signal school ship *Talwar* ("Sword") in the port of Bombay mutinied. They jumped ship, seized several military trucks in the harbor, driving them around to the more than twenty nearby Indian navy vessels, and incited their crews to join the mutiny. Commercial activity in Bombay stopped for a week as thousands of protesting sailors marched through the streets, denouncing their British officers. The Royal Marines were called out to quell the violence and opened fire, leaving 228 dead and over a thousand wounded. The Royal Navy's heavy cruiser *Glasgow* was sent to the harbor to threaten the *Talwar*, and, if required, to sink it. Sardar Vallabhbhai Patel personally went on board the mutinous vessel, firmly ordering the rebel Indian sailors to turn themselves in to the Royal Navy. They finally did so, thus ending Bombay's worst crisis of the century after one week of raucous rioting. A week later another mutinous crew of Indian sailors seized the HMIS *Hindustan* in Karachi's harbor and opened fire with its four-inch guns at Sind's capital, hitting Grindlay's bank and two post offices. Police returned fire, killing eight sailors and injuring eighteen. "A number of vehicles were also stoned including some belonging to the U.S. Army," Governor Mudie reported to Wavell. "The rioters consisted mostly of Hindu students with a few Muslims. They would listen to nobody."[41]

The last weekend of February 1946, Pethick-Lawrence, Cripps, and Alexander met with Attlee at Chequers, the prime minister's country house, to discuss the Indian problems their mission would soon have to face. They agreed to spend their first week in India in conversations with the viceroy, governors, and political leaders, as well as with some princes. If they saw any hope of agreement among party leaders they would follow up with further meetings. If not, they would have to gauge "what kind of arrangement would have most prospect of being generally acquiesced in if enunciated by us," Pethick-Lawrence wrote to Wavell.[42] They were not going to make the same mistake of Cripps's earlier mission, flying out with one offer neither party would accept.

On March 23 the cabinet mission reached Karachi. "India is on the threshold of a very great future," Lord Pethick-Lawrence told reporters there. "The British Government and the British people desire, without reservation, to consummate the promises and pledges that have been made. . . . The precise road towards the final structure of India's independence is not yet clear, but let the vision of it inspire us all in our renewed efforts to find a path of cooperation."[43] When asked about his views on Pakistan, Cripps equivocated, "We have not come with any set views. We are here to investigate and inquire."[44] They flew on to New Delhi and met two days later with Wavell and his executive council.

Central election results clearly established the popularity of Jinnah's Muslim League among most Muslims, and of the Congress Party among all others. Wavell's council focused on the primary issue of how best to "allay" Muslim fears, advising the mission to invite one of its members to chair a small committee of two Hindus and two Muslims to try to resolve the Hindu-Muslim "issue." Untouchable Dr. Ambedkar cautioned them not to forget the smaller minorities, warning against "dangers" posed by "dictation by Congress to the minorities."[45]

The council was unanimous in feeling that whatever happened, India should remain within the British Commonwealth, to "resist" possible future "foreign invasion." Sikh Sardar Jogendra Singh felt that the "British connection should be retained until India knows how to use its power." He feared that if India were divided, Hindus and Muslims "will fight one another." Muslim Sir Azizul Huque felt that "nothing can be done until the principle of Pakistan is accepted." The council's other Muslim member, Sir Akbar Hydari, however, said it would not be "wise . . . to concede the principle of Pakistan until Mr. Jinnah had put down in black and white what was the content of Pakistan."[46]

Cripps met with Jinnah on March 30, finding him "calm and reasonable but completely firm on Pakistan."[47] Jinnah agreed to ask Gandhi to meet with him again as soon as Gandhi reached Delhi and thought it "possible" that he and Gandhi might be able to reach a point at which their differences were so "narrow" that the cabinet delegation could "bridge" them, though he feared that Gandhi might later try to "slip out." As for any change in the interim government, Jinnah was "very nervous" that the Congress Party might get power, one way or the other, and was anxious that "antagonism and public vituperation" from all parties should cease.

On April 3 Gandhi came to meet with the delegation and told them that he had spent eighteen days over the past several years with Jinnah, who had "never in concrete terms given a definition of Pakistan," which Gandhi considered "a sin."[48] He believed that Jinnah, like himself, was possessed by "a kind of mania," and he advised the delegation to ask Jinnah to form the first representative government and to "choose its personnel from elected representatives."[49] The secretary of state pointed out that since most of the newly elected representatives were from the Congress Party, Jinnah would have to choose members from parties other than his own. Gandhi said in that case, if he was not prepared to choose, then Congress should be invited to do so. He did not "underrate the difficulties of the situation" facing the delegation and would despair of any solution if he were not an "irresponsible optimist."

The next day, Jinnah arrived for his first meeting with the cabinet delegation. He explained to them the fundamental differences between Hindus and Muslims, insisting that

> Muslims have a different conception of life from the Hindus. . . . [T]hey have a different culture based on Arabic and Persian instead of on Sanskrit origins. Their social customs are entirely different. . . . Hindus worship the cow and even today in certain States a 10-year sentence is imposed for killing a cow. This means nothing to the Muslims. . . . How are you to put 100 millions of Muslims together with 250 millions whose way of life is so different? No Government can ever work on such a basis and if this is forced upon India it must lead to disaster.[50]

Cripps asked if Jinnah thought the difference between a Hindu and Muslim in Bengal was greater than that between a Pathan and Muslim of Sind. Jinnah insisted that all Muslims "believed in one God" and in " equality of men and in human brotherhood," while Hindus believed in none of those things. The secretary of state explained that the cabinet mission came as representatives of "one of the world's great powers," which had "a vital interest in the preservation of peace" in South Asia, and did not wish to leave India's main communities "faced with a major head-on collision."[51] Jinnah said that his Pakistan could have a "sovereign State's" treaty relations with Hindustan on matters related to defense, much the way Great Britain did with its dominions. The cabinet mission must assume, he added, that they would be handing over power to "responsible people."

Wavell asked Jinnah what he conceived of as the boundaries of Pakistan. Jinnah wanted "a viable Pakistan," not a "mutilated" one. He was willing to consider "mutual adjustments" of provincial boundaries, but his Pakistan must be "a live State economically." He insisted that Calcutta must be part of Pakistan, arguing that "Pakistan without Calcutta would be like asking a man to live without his heart."[52] Congress was equally determined to retain control of Calcutta, which for over a century had been British India's capital.

The cabinet delegation also met in early April with leaders of the chamber of princes, all of whom were anxious to know what the British planned to do about its treaty obligations of the last century to protect and, if necessary, defend princely states against foreign or domestic enemies. Attlee, Pethick-Lawrence, and Cripps had agreed before the mission left London that all treaties with princely states would lapse once the British decided to which successor Indian government or governments it would hand over its powers. States would then enter into "political relations" with one or the other successor government. They were not, however, quite ready as yet to inform the princes of this decision and its full implications.

The delegation then heard from the Sikhs, three of whom, led by Master Tara Singh, warned that to "divide India would be a very . . . risky game." If there was to be any "division," the "Sikhs could not . . . remain either in Hindustan or in Pakistan."[53] Sikhs were content to remain within united India, but if Pakistan were granted to the Muslims, then Sikhs wanted a nation-state of their own, a Sikhistan or Khalistan carved out of central Punjab, where four million Sikhs lived. Not even one district of Punjab had its own Sikh majority, however. When this was pointed out by the cabinet delegation, the Sikhs suggested the transfer of Sikhs from other districts to those in which Sikhs owned more of the land than Muslims, between Lahore and the sacred Sikh city of Amritsar. If Punjab was divided, that region should become "Sikhistan," Tara Singh insisted; otherwise the Sikhs would not feel secure, and Sikhs had always been loyal soldier-officers in the British Indian Army.

The delegation continued to meet daily with leaders of most of India's parties from all of its provinces through April 10, feeling by then that they had to draft their own scheme to present to the Congress Party and to the League, hoping to bridge the communal gap between the distant visions of South Asia's future they had heard. On April 11 they wrote to Attlee to report that there seemed only two "possible bases of agreement": Scheme A, which would be "a unitary India with a loose federation at the Centre charged primarily with control of Defence and Foreign Affairs," and Scheme B, "a divided India, the Pakistan element consisting only of the majority Muslim Districts that is roughly Baluchistan, Sind, North-West Frontier Province and Western Punjab . . . and Eastern Bengal without Calcutta but with the Sylhet District of Assam."[54] They feared that unless they could get both Congress and the League to agree to either of those schemes, "we risk chaos in India." The viceroy and commander-in-chief both "fully" agreed.

Two days later, Attlee wired that the cabinet agreed that, while Scheme A was "preferable," Scheme B would be acceptable, if it seemed to hold the only chance of reaching agreement.

Delhi's summer heat had begun to take its toll on the members of the mission, so they planned to fly up to Kashmir's cooler climate for a brief Easter holiday break, from April 19 to the 24. Before leaving, they met again with Jinnah and put their two schemes to him, asking which he preferred. He insisted that the principle of Pakistan must be granted and that it must have six provinces, though he was willing to "discuss the area," only he insisted upon Calcutta, despite its Muslim minority. Pethick-Lawrence explained that they weren't sure the Congress Party would accept either scheme, but knew they wouldn't concede Calcutta. He warned Jinnah that a transfer of British power without any agreement between Congress and the League would lead to "chaos and starvation," since another dreadful famine seemed imminent, with drought threatening the grain crops in many provinces. Jinnah promised to "try his very best to reach agreement with the Congress," but insisted he could never do so if they "struck at the heart of Pakistan."[55] Cripps met with Jinnah again privately the next evening, but then felt the delegation would first have to "get out its own basis of settlement" and show it to both parties "confidentially."[56]

Wavell feared "great danger" in announcing the delegation's own proposal before the Congress and League leaders agreed, otherwise the Congress Party might issue "an ultimatum . . . about the interim Government."[57] The delegation agreed. Cripps emphasized the importance of publicity, and they agreed to put out the announcements, once they were ready, in two segments on consecutive "auspicious days," which meant first of all consulting several astrologers. Then they met with Azad again, and Cripps saw Gandhi and Nehru alone. Those meetings all confirmed what they had previously concluded, that there was "no basis for agreement."

During their Easter holiday in Kashmir, the mission refined its schemes, turning Scheme A into a three-tier all-India federation, with a powerful middle tier of three "Groups of Provinces": Group A: the Muslim-majority provinces of Sind, Punjab, Baluchistan, and the North-West Frontier; Group B, all the Hindu-majority provinces of most of the rest of India; and Group C, Bengal and Assam. The upper central government tier would be much less important than the groups, responsible basically only for defense, foreign affairs, and communications. Each group would have its own bicameral legislature to raise taxes and maintain order among its predominantly Muslim or Hindu populace, enjoying the virtual autonomy of a sovereign state. Provinces would enjoy traditional local powers over education and law and order but remained dependent on their own group legislature for most of their funding. After ten or fifteen years, moreover, any group or any one of its provinces could opt out, to reconsider its constitutional position. Cripps hoped these options would appeal sufficiently to Jinnah to agree to try that loosely integrated federation. Pethick-Lawrence believed that by retaining the unitary character of India's government, the federation would win the support and approval of the Congress Party.

Soon after they returned to sweltering Delhi, the delegation decided to move back up to a cooler climate, shifting their mission's venue to the viceroy's palace in Simla, where they stayed for the first two weeks of May. Jinnah was asked to travel to meet with them there and to bring three of his Muslim League members, choosing Liaquat Ali Khan, Sardar Nishtar, and Nawab Ismail Khan. Azad was invited to bring three other members of the Congress working committee to Simla, and asked Nehru, Sardar Patel, and "Frontier Gandhi" Abdul Ghaffar Khan to join him. Starting on May 5 they met daily, for two hours each morning and in the afternoon. Pethick-Lawrence reported to Attlee that first day: "Our talks started well this morning apart from the refusal of Jinnah to shake hands with Azad! Both sides have shown themselves ready to take the three-tier basis seriously and to discuss it reasonably. . . . I am happy to tell you that my confidence in the Viceroy has grown all through my visit here. . . . But I realise that when we go he is likely to have a most difficult time in front of him."[58]

The Congress delegation was not happy, however, as Azad informed Pethick-Lawrence after the first day's meetings in Simla. "My colleagues and I . . . stand for the independence of the whole of India now. . . . Other matters are subsidiary to this and can be fitly discussed and decided by the Constituent Assembly. . . . In our discussions yesterday repeated references were made to 'groups' of Provinces functioning together. . . . [W]e are entirely opposed to any executive or legislative machinery for a group of Provinces."[59] Pethick-Lawrence seems to have misjudged the intensity of Congress Party members' feeling on this point, which remained the strongest objection of all the Congress leaders throughout their talks with the cabinet mission.

The next day, Jinnah raised the question of how best to "change the Constitution," whether after ten or fifteen years, either by 75 percent of the union legislature or the constituent assembly, or by a plain majority on any but sensitive communal issues. Nehru then spoke against the groups, insisting that provinces "tended to hold on to power." The viceroy replied that the reason for those groups was "to get over the communal difficulty." Nehru shot back that "in the view of the Congress the first thing was to dispose in practice of the problem of the Indo-British relationship. The communal problem could be dealt with afterwards."[60] Jinnah countered that "If the Congress would accept the Groups, the Muslim League would accept the Union." Nehru replied that it was "difficult for him to accept grouping" since he felt that most decisions must be made by provinces. Jinnah offered to "sit together" with Nehru, "for whom he had a great regard" to try to convince him of the value of grouping, since he "had no desire to ask the British to stay in India."[61] A day later, Nehru insisted on the need for one constitution-making body, but Jinnah was adamant about the need for two, as the "only way" to prevent "complete partition." Jinnah then said he thought that in "the first instance" the "right of secession" from the union should come after five years. Sardar Patel grew irate at that, shouting it "clearly indicated the reality behind the grouping proposal."[62] Cripps then redrafted the proposal and showed it to Gandhi, while the viceroy met with Jinnah and Azad and Nehru.

Jinnah was willing to accept the three-tier scheme only if there were definite, virtually autonomous Muslim groups of provinces that would have separate constituent assemblies, but the Congress Party was unwilling to commit what it insisted must be India's one constituent assembly to anything, since it should be a sovereign constitution-drafting body. Gandhi told his Congress friends that the cabinet mission's "suggestions" would be "binding on no one. The Constituent Assembly would be free to throw out any of

the items and the members of the two delegations were equally free to add
to or amend the suggestions . . . meant only as a scaffolding . . . brought to
the Constituent Assembly."[63] Each party thus retained its own view of the
union's future constitution, and neither was ultimately willing to back off
or move its position close enough to the other's to permit India in the aftermath of Britain's departure to live in cooperative harmony as a peaceful
South Asian federation.

They adjourned for several days, Nehru and Jinnah trying to agree upon
an arbitrator, who might meet with them to help resolve disagreements on
the cabinet mission's proposal, but nothing came of their attempt at reconciliation. There was no trust, no faith on either side of the other party's
good intentions. Still, the cabinet mission's delegation soldiered on in Simla,
while thirty battalions of British troops gathered in the port cities, quietly
leaving India on every available ship under the cover of night. Wavell and
Auchinleck had developed a top secret "Bedlam" contingency plan of secure forts and bases in which to keep all European civilians secure until they
could be evacuated, should chaos erupt before Congress and the League
agreed to an amicable transfer of power. There were almost 100,000 such
civilians, many of them women and children, still living in India.

Abell had drafted a note for the mission, which included another top
secret plan in the event of chaos following the second Simla summit's failure. That "scuttle" contingency plan was also never used. It basically proposed the evacuation of all British forces from most of India's provinces,
moving up from the south to the northwest and northeast, securing those
"Pakistan" wings of British India's north, "scuttling" the Hindu-majority
subcontinent, which would be left to defend and protect itself. Auchinleck
considered that plan potentially "disastrous."[64] It would have required as
large a British army, the commander-in-chief felt, to defend both distant
wings of Pakistan as it took to defend all of India, but with insufficient
resources and insufficient depth. The Hindu and Sikh minorities in Pakistan's
wings, moreover, would become potential "fifth columns" against British
troops, especially if "Hindustan" appealed to Russia for an alliance that
could arouse every communist in Bengal and Sind and all along the north-
west frontier to emerge as actively subversive enemies. The cabinet mission
also judged that plan impracticable, the viceroy anticipating "widespread
rioting" led by Congress extremists as soon as British forces started moving
out. No "Hindu officer" would remain in the British Army if it moved
north to defend only Muslim-majority regions claimed by "Pakistan."

The cabinet mission left Simla in mid-May, failing to secure any agreement between Congress and the League before returning to New Delhi.
Pethick-Lawrence broadcast his farewell message to the people of India from
the capital. "There is a passionate desire in the hearts of Indians . . . for
independence. His Majesty's Government and the British people as a whole

are fully ready to accord this independence . . . and friendly association between our two peoples on a footing of complete equality. . . . During our stay in India we have tried by every means to secure such an accommodation between the parties as would enable constitution-making to proceed . . . but . . . it was not found possible to reach complete agreement."[65] He outlined the three-tier federation that his delegation had recommended to both parties in Simla, explaining how it would make it possible for Muslims to secure "the advantages of a Pakistan without incurring the dangers inherent in the division of India."[66]

Since no agreement was reached between the Congress Party and the League, the mission had recommended, and Britain's cabinet agreed, to authorize the viceroy to invite newly elected Indian representatives to join his council as India's interim government. The only British members of the council who would remain were the viceroy and the commander-in-chief. The new provincial legislatures would soon send their own representatives to Delhi to meet as a constitution-making body of an all-India union. "The future of India and how that future is inaugurated are matters of vital importance . . . to the whole world," Pethick-Lawrence informed them. "But the constitution for India has to be framed by Indians and worked by Indians . . . the responsibility and the opportunity is theirs and in their fulfilment of it we wish them godspeed."[67] Wavell addressed India the next day "at the most critical hour of India's history," urging all who heard him to accept the cabinet delegation's proposed "blue-print for freedom" as a workable basis for India's future constitution.[68] He explained how hard they had all worked and stressed the necessity of getting on with the job of launching a representative interim government as soon as possible to tackle such urgent matters as the current food crisis and the launching of a constituent assembly. For India the choice was "between peaceful construction or the disorder of civil strife, between co-operation or disunity, between ordered progress or confusion." Mahatma Gandhi's reaction, published in his *Harijan,* was quite positive: "Whatever the wrong done to India by British rule . . . the statement of the Mission was . . . in discharge of an obligation they had declared the British owed to India, namely, to get off India's back. It contained the seed to convert this land of sorrow into one without sorrow and suffering."[69]

Jinnah, however, had remained in Simla and phoned Abell to inform him that he could not "come to a decision" on the mission's statement without first consulting his working committee, which would take another month.[70] Gandhi then wrote to Pethick-Lawrence raising a number of questions against the "grouping clause," which he had earlier expressed in Simla. Nehru agreed with Gandhi that a sovereign constituent assembly could not be constrained by any prior agreements. Azad wrote on May 20 that

Congress's working committee agreed that a "sovereign body for the purpose of drafting the Constitution . . . [must be] unhindered by any external authority."[71]

"I am feeling stale and over-worked," Wavell confided to his journal. "Indian politicians are disheartening to deal with; and we British seem to have lost faith in ourselves and the courage to govern."[72] Most British Indian civil servants were now keen to retire as soon as possible and to book passage home. Europeans in cool hill stations began to feel trapped, and feared they might soon be cut off from its sea ports, their only escape route. "In the end, we are really faced with repression or withdrawal," Wavell noted to himself, "a complete and immediate withdrawal from all India, which is unthinkable."[73] He knew all too well how bitter and pervasive India's religious communal fears and hatreds had grown, fed by political differences and competing personal as well as party ambitions.

6

The Interim Government, June–December 1946

T HE CABINET MISSION'S FAILURE to bridge the gap between India's National Congress Party and the Muslim League left Wavell and the cabinet no option but to try to patch together a representative political council to work in harness with the viceroy as New Delhi's interim government. Wavell informed Azad that he had been assured by His Majesty's Government that it would treat the new interim government of India with the "same close consultation and consideration as a Dominion Government."[1] This meant it would have virtually total freedom to carry out its desired plans, without viceregal interference or inhibition. That same information was conveyed to Jinnah by the viceroy, and on the evening of June 7 Jinnah told Wavell that his League's council had accepted the cabinet mission's plan of the previous month.

Jinnah reported, however, that he "must insist on the 5/5/2 ratio in the Interim Government," Wavell noted after they met. "As regards himself he . . . said the only portfolio he would consider was that of Defence."[2] Congress would not agree to the latter, nor would it accept the idea of joining a council of five Muslim Leaguers, only five members of the Congress, and two representatives of lesser minorities, one a Sikh, the other a Christian or Anglo-Indian. On June 10, the cabinet delegation and Wavell met with Azad and Nehru to try to allay their fears about Muslim League "parity." Wavell explained that it was the only way he could persuade Jinnah's League to enter the government, but that he would not regard that "as in any way a precedent establishing a claim to parity but simply as an expedient for the interim period."[3] Pethick-Lawrence added that coalition cabinets in the United Kingdom never decided matters by "majority voting" but by general agreement. He told the Congress Party leaders that the only way their coalition would survive was to accept parity as a "temporary expedient." Nehru protested that the League was appointing people to their provincial governments who were "neither competent nor honest. They had an entirely different outlook to the Congress and did not care for nationalist ideals."[4]

First Lord of the Admiralty A. V. Alexander suggested that since Jinnah had "to swallow a bitter pill" in finally accepting his delegation's proposals, Congress should now be willing to "rub off the corners" of problems that caused "friction" and work together with the League to help "assimilate into a United India nearly 100 million Muslims." Avuncular Alexander had been a successful labor union negotiator before entering the cabinet, his good nature as valuable an asset as his good sense in practical problem solving. But Nehru insisted it was "beyond the power of Congress to agree to parity."[5] In his autobiography, Azad later sadly reflected that "Jawaharlal's [Nehru] mistake in 1937 had been bad enough. The mistake of 1946 proved even more costly."[6] In 1937 it had been Nehru's refusal to permit the Muslim League to join the Congress Party in forming a provincial coalition government in the United Provinces that led to Jinnah's firm resolve to prove that his League commanded a Muslim majority and then to demand a separate nation-state of Pakistan. Now, nine years later, Nehru was still opposed to doing the little it might have taken to encourage Jinnah and his League to work with the Congress rather than fighting it.

Nehru was not alone among the leaders of Congress who rejected cooperating with the League. Sardar Patel, with whom Wavell also met, told him that "no-one" in Congress's working committee favored accepting the cabinet mission's proposal, and that all opposed parity with the League in an interim government. Patel believed that "Jinnah would only use his position in the Interim Government for purely communal and disruptive purposes and to break up India."[7] Before mid-June Nehru gave Wavell his Congress-approved list of names for a new council of the interim government, seven members from the Congress Party, four from the Muslim League, and one non-League Muslim. The cabinet delegation agreed that Wavell should see Jinnah again and try to get a preferred League list from him. Gandhi then urged Wavell to "make your choice of one horse or the other. . . . [Y]ou will never succeed in riding two at the same time. Choose the names submitted either by Congress or the League."[8] The Mahatma warned the viceroy that an "incompatible mixture" of both lists could "produce a fearful explosion."

By June 14 a "critical phase" in the negotiations had been reached, Pethick-Lawrence informed Attlee, explaining that Jinnah was now willing to agree to join a thirteen-member new government of five Muslim Leaguers, five Hindu upper-caste Congress members, one scheduled caste ("un-

touchable") member from the Congress (Jagjivan Ram), and two other minorities (one Sikh, and one Christian or Parsi). Wavell had drawn up a list
with all but one of the chosen members' names, which was being submitted
to King George the next day in London for his "informal approval." The
cabinet delegation planned to fly home on June 15 and wanted to make an
uplifting announcement of their success at least in negotiating agreements
with both major parties as to the names of members of the new representative interim government.

The Congress Party, however, insisted on a council of fifteen, with five
Congress members and only four League members, though they were willing to allow one more non-League Muslim, yet also demanded a Congress
scheduled caste member, a Sikh, a Christian man, and a Congress Christian
woman, Rajkumari Amrit Kaur. "The situation is worsening through the
prolonged delay," an exhausted Pethick-Lawrence noted in his "secret" wire
to Attlee.[9] The unbridgeable gap was thus narrowed to a single member of
the viceroy's new council. Each party would insist that, though the gap was
small, the principle was great, as indeed it was, reflecting basic distrusts,
compounded by fears and hatreds rooted deep in the hearts and minds of
the leaders of each party for those of the other.

The cabinet's defense committee met that day in London to discuss the
grave danger that every English person remaining in India might have to
face in the very near future and the best military action to take. The chiefs
of staff concluded that their wisest policy was to remain in the whole of
India, "firmly" accepting responsibility for law and order. It was "difficult"
to be certain whether the Indian armed forces would remain "totally loyal,"
yet the chiefs felt that the best way to ensure their loyalty was to stand
firm.[10] The secretary of state for foreign affairs agreed, arguing that "everything possible should be done to keep affairs in India as stable as possible"
and that not to adopt such a policy would undoubtedly lead to Britain's loss
of "considerable prestige in the Far East and in Europe." General Sir Mosley
Mayne believed that despite a breakdown in negotiations, neither party had
"any justification for blaming us," so any "disturbances which broke out
would not . . . be anti-British." The prime minister agreed, stressing the
importance of safeguarding against any "leakage" that they had even been
discussing such plans. The war office, inaccurately, reported that there were
44,537 European civilians still left in India, though there were actually
100,000. The cabinet agreed that no British women or children should be
permitted to book passage to India, but this must be kept strictly secret to
avoid panic.

At 4 p.m. on June 16 the cabinet delegation and the viceroy issued a
statement announcing that the viceroy had sent invitations to fourteen leading political figures, including Nehru and Patel, Jinnah and Liaquat Ali Khan,

Rajagopalachari and Rajendra Prasad, to join his new interim government council. If any of those invited declined to accept, the viceroy would invite some other person to take his place. He would distribute portfolios to each of his new council's members "in consultation with the leaders of the two major parties."[11]

Should either of the two major parties be "unwilling" to join the interim government, then the viceroy would turn to the other for help in forming his new council. The viceroy would also direct all the governors of provinces to summon their legislative assemblies to proceed with elections of representatives to a constitution-making body that would be assembled in New Delhi as soon as possible. Those invited from the Congress Party responded that their decisions would have to await that reached by the Congress Party Working Committee, which was being convened by Azad. On June 17, Pethick-Lawrence and Cripps, having postponed their departure for home a third time, decided to meet with Azad to discuss Congress concerns and criticisms of the viceroy's choices. George Abell informed Jinnah of that intended meeting and invited him, on behalf of the viceroy, to meet with Wavell if he had any questions. Jinnah instead chose on the evening of June 17 to meet with Pethick-Lawrence and A. V. Alexander.

Jinnah gave them a "long" disquisition on the "question of parity," going back to the first Simla summit in 1945. Jinnah argued that though the Congress Party then "took exception in writing to a large number of matters" they had "never questioned the matter of parity" in the interim government. Pethick-Lawrence assured him that he "knew for a fact" that Congress had from the start disagreed with the idea of parity. Jinnah insisted, however, that the mission was being "pushed" hard by the Congress Party and had yielded too much to them, but was told that Congress argued precisely the opposite. Jinnah also wanted to know when the allocation of council portfolios would be decided, fearing that the Congress Party would make "unreasonable demands" in that matter as well. He also wanted reassurance that on any question involving a major communal problem there would have to be agreement by members of both major parties, to which Pethick-Lawrence told him that was "the essence of a coalition."

Wavell met the next day with Azad and Nehru, with whom he discussed several alternative names to their potential interim government list and possible portfolios for each. That evening he met with Jinnah for a difficult hour and a half, finding him "rather depressed and tired" and feeling "rather let down."[12] All three parties to this process were losing patience. If Nehru and Jinnah could have risen above their mutual distrust at this eleventh hour there might still have been time to patch together an interim government that might have emerged a few years later as united India's cabinet. Nehru remained as revolted by the thought of Congress having to share power equally with a "reactionary" Muslim League as Jinnah was by the thought of serving on a council dominated by "caste" Hindus and "Quisling" Muslims. The cabinet mission was more than ready to fly home but did not wish to do so before both parties agreed to join Wavell's interim government. Cripps tried his best, at this last desperate hour, to persuade Azad and Gandhi of the importance of helping Jinnah to bring his League into the new council, by not insisting on Congress's nominating any Muslim member. Azad begged off, however, urging Cripps to see Gandhi, who said it was not for him but for Congress president Azad to decide. After a futile hour and a half of arguing, Gandhi insisted that a Congress-League coalition was "the wrong way of forming a government," reiterating that it should be left to one party or the other.[13] So Cripps gave up, seeing once again that there was no way for him to reconcile these irreconcilable parties.

The cabinet mission met with Wavell on June 22 and informed him that they must fly home before the end of that week because Attlee was leaving for Australia shortly and they needed to meet with him to discuss what further steps must be taken for India. They urged Wavell to approach Jinnah "as soon as the Congress rejected the proposals," which they expected Congress to do.[14] If Jinnah refused to submit his own list for an interim government, then the viceroy should appoint a caretaker government of his own choosing. Wavell prepared a secret list of non-Congress Hindus he planned to invite, if Congress and the League both failed him.

Pethick-Lawrence made one last appeal to his Congress Party friends, explaining that he had come out "with the intention of transferring power from his country to India, but . . . the greatest obstacle to India going forward towards independence was the inability to get started. The value of getting a start made was so great as to be worth not the sacrifice of a principle but abstinence from enforcing it for the time being."[15] He felt certain that if Congress insisted upon nominating a Muslim, Jinnah would refuse to join the interim government. "If the Congress did not give him the easements necessary to enable him to get Mr. Jinnah to come in, they defeated not his purpose but their own." Sardar Patel then argued that if the Congress Party gave in and failed to nominate a Muslim they would "force all the Muslims out of the Congress." Nehru agreed.

On June 24, the delegation and viceroy met with Gandhi and Patel one last time. Cripps said that Gandhi was anxious to have an interview with the entire delegation to explain his views on how the interim government should be formed. Alexander was angered now by Congress "maneuvers," saying that "He had come out to India quite unbiased and in the early stages had been somewhat exasperated with Mr. Jinnah's attitude. But . . . the behaviour of the Congress in the last six weeks seemed to him the most deplorable exhibition that he had witnessed in his political career."[16] The viceroy warned the delegation that "we should lose Mr. Jinnah's support" if they continued much longer to see Congress leaders around the clock, nor did they convince the Congress to change its mind. On June 25, the Congress Party Working Committee adopted a resolution rejecting the proposed interim government of June 16, but agreeing to join the constituent assembly proposed a month earlier by the delegation. "The kind of independence which Congress has aimed at is the establishment of a united democratic Indian Federation with a Central authority which would command respect from the nations of the world, maximum provincial autonomy and equal rights for all men and women," that resolution noted.[17]

The delegation and Wavell met that evening with Jinnah to show him the Congress Party resolution. Jinnah argued that Congress had expressed "reservations" about the cabinet mission's proposed groups of provinces, which his League considered the heart of their May 16 statement, and which "broke the whole thing."[18] Pethick-Lawrence disagreed, insisting that the delegation viewed the Congress letter as a definite "acceptance" of the Mission's long-term plan. Jinnah said the groups were "essential" and Congress wanted "to smash" them and would do so as soon as they had their majority in the constituent assembly. Virtually independent groups of provinces were the only thing that had kept the Muslim League from bolting the discussions months earlier. "He begged the Delegation to make it clear that they did not accept the Congress interpretation. He had with great difficulty made substantial concessions in these negotiations because he felt that if we succeeded in making a settlement we should be blessed by 400 million people."[19] It was Jinnah's most poignant appeal to the delegation, and it would be his last attempt to persuade them.

The viceroy said it would not be possible now for him to appoint an interim government of political leaders, since the Congress Party had rejected the proposals of June 16. When Jinnah pointed out that his League had accepted them and should, therefore, be invited to propose its members for that government, the viceroy would not agree, unless Jinnah was ready to accept a Congress Muslim member. That would mean starting all over, Jinnah said, berating the delegation, and warning that to postpone the interim government was "bad for the prestige of the Delegation and also for his own prestige."[20] Pethick-Lawrence was offended by that rebuke and snapped that they "were not asking for Mr. Jinnah's opinion of their conduct." Alexander tried to lower the temperature, jumping in to say that he accepted "100 per cent" what Jinnah earlier said about "the sacrifices" he had made to help India's millions, "begging" him to use his "influence" to help the viceroy form an interim government "later." For now they were all much too weary to continue arguing. Wavell flew up to Simla's cooler clime. The members of the cabinet mission flew home to England.

Indian leaders. Members of the Indian National Congress (left to right) Mahatma Gandhi, Congress President Subhas Chandra Bose, and Sardar Vallabhbhai Patel at the March 1938 Indian National Congress. Dr. Rajendra Prasad, India's first president (1950), is seated behind them.
Getty Images/Keystone.

Jawaharlal Nehru, G. D. Birla, Gandhi, and Patel, 9 June 1939. Outside Birla House, Bombay. Getty Images/Keystone.

Soon-to-be Prime Minister Jawaharlal Nehru and Sir Stafford Cripps, Labour
Party Leader of Britain's House of Commons, on his mission to New Delhi,
1942. Getty Images/Keystone.

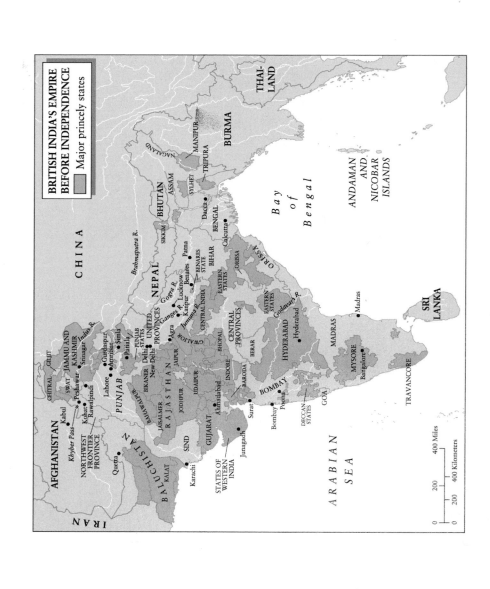

BRITISH INDIA'S EMPIRE
BEFORE INDEPENDENCE

Major princely states

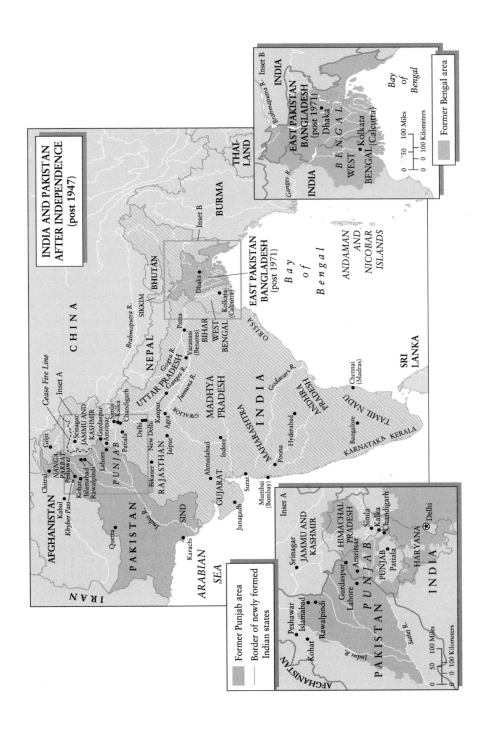

INDIA AND PAKISTAN
AFTER INDEPENDENCE
(post 1947)

Lord Linlithgow (1887–1952), Viceroy of India, 1936–October
1943, with Lady Linlithgow. Getty Images/Keystone.

Indian National Congress leaders:
Sardar Vallabhbhai Patel (1875–
1950) with Maulana Abul Kalam
Azad (1885–1958) in Simla, 1946.
India Office Library and Records.

Lord Willingdon (1866–1941),
Viceroy of India, 1934–36.
Getty Images/Keystone.

Field Marshal Claude Auchinleck
(1884–1981), Commander-in-
Chief, India, 1943–47.
Getty Images/Fox Photos.

Viceroy Lord Wavell, with Lady
Wavell and their daughter
Felicity, October 18, 1943.
Getty Images/PNA_Rota.

Jammu and Kashmir State's Maharaja Hari
Singh in London as one of two Indians
invited by Churchill's War Cabinet during
World War II. Getty Images/Keystone.

H.H. The Nizam of Hyderabad (1911–67), once the "richest man on earth" and considered a loyal ally of the British Raj until Indian Independence; his state was taken over by Indian troops in 1948. Getty Images.

Netaji ("Leader") Subhas Chandra Bose (1897–1945), President of the Indian National Congress and Japan's puppet leader of the Indian National Army during World War II, ca. 1940. Getty Images/Keystone.

Lord Pethick-Lawrence (1871–1961), Secretary of State for India,
1945–1947, with Mahatma Gandhi. India Office Library and Records.

Top: The Viceroy's house,
Simla, where Wavell and
Mountbatten both held
summits with the political
leaders of India's major
parties, 1945–47.
Getty Images/Keystone.

Right: Pandit Jawaharlal
Nehru with Quaid-i-Azam
Jinnah. Simla, 1946. Getty
Images/Topical Press Agency.

Maharaja Jam Saheb of Nawanagar welcomed to London by the Secretary
of State for India Leo Amery during the war. Getty Images/Keystone.

India conference, 1947. Front row, left:
C. Rajagopalachari, Governor-General
of India, 1948–50, leading Indian
National Congress figure of South India
until his death. Getty Images/Hardy.

Prime Minister Nehru, Lord ("Pug")
Ismay, Viceroy Lord Mountbatten, and
Governor-General Jinnah of Pakistan on
the eve of British India's Partition and the
birth of the independent Dominions of
India and Pakistan. June 1947.
Getty Images/Keystone.

"The depressing thing is that one should have to hand over the control of India to such small men," Wavell wrote as he summed up the mission's labors from Simla for King George. He distrusted Gandhi most, considering him a "shrewd, malevolent, old politician."[21] Jinnah he found "straighter . . . more sincere than most of the Congress leaders. . . . He is a curious character, a lonely, unhappy, arbitrary, self-centered man, fighting with much resolution what I fear is a losing battle." Nehru he thought "sincere, intelligent, and personally courageous. But he is unbalanced." For Sardar Patel, "the recognised 'tough' of the Congress . . . I have a good deal more respect for him than for most of the Congress leaders." As for the "immediate future," Wavell was hardly sanguine. "I am left with one rather sickly infant, the Constituent Assembly, and one still-born babe, the Interim Government. . . . The Sikhs, who have . . . more conceit than political sense, are threatening to make trouble. . . . [T]he Congress left-wing will certainly do so if they see a chance; the Services, on whom the good government of India depends, are tired and discouraged; the loyalty of the Police and Indian Army in face of a really serious challenge to British rule is problematical. . . . Outside politics . . . it looks as if we may just scrape through 1946 without famine."[22]

That week the All-India Congress Committee reelected Jawaharlal Nehru as its president, and on July 10 Nehru told the press that Congress had made "no commitment" to the cabinet mission and the viceroy, other than to go into the constituent assembly, which was to be a "Sovereign body." Asked about "grouping of provinces," Nehru commented that there was "a big probability" that "there will be no grouping."[23] He insisted that everybody but the Muslim League was "entirely opposed to grouping." Even along the North-West Frontier and in Muslim Sind, he argued, most people were against any grouping, for fear they would be swamped by the Punjab.

Jinnah, simmering from what he viewed as the cabinet delegation's "betrayal" of its promises, viewed Nehru's July presidential press conference as proof of the "Tyranny" and "betrayal" his Muslim League could expect of any "Hindu [Congress] Raj." Jinnah wrote to Attlee "not without deep regret" that the delegation had

> impaired the honour of the British Government and have shaken the confidence of Muslim India and shattered their hopes for an honourable and peaceful settlement. They allowed themselves to play into the hands of the Congress, who all along held out the threat of non-cooperation and . . . adopted an aggressive and dictatorial attitude, pistol in their hand. They are determined to seize power and try to establish Caste-Hindu domination over Muslim India. . . . It has become a disease with the Congress. . . . I therefore trust that the British Government will still avoid compelling the Muslims to shed their blood, for, your surrender to the Congress at the sacrifice of the Muslims can only result in that direction.[24]

Jinnah sent a copy of that letter to Churchill. Attlee thanked Jinnah for his "very real contribution" to the general effort to reach a settlement, but insisted that the Congress Party had also made a contribution. The present differences, he added, must be resolved by "argument and compromise," appealing personally to Jinnah to "use your great influence in India's cause, and . . . do your utmost to assist the Viceroy in the formation of an Interim Government."[25]

Nehru wrote to Wavell that same day to inform him that it "would not be possible to pick up again the old threads" left by the departure of the cabinet delegation. A new working committee of his Congress had been formed, and there was "little hope of a successful issue along the old line of approach. . . . [W]e have all along attached the greatest importance to . . . 'independence in action' of a Provisional Government. Anything else would be more or less a copy of the Executive Council."[26] The Congress Party wanted assurance that it would enjoy the status and full power of an independent cabinet before joining any interim government. Wavell was so alarmed by Nehru's letter that he wired Pethick-Lawrence it seemed "almost certain . . . Congress have decided to challenge HMG [His Majesty's Government] and to become the only effective power in India." He reminded the secretary of state that "we have obligations in honour not to hand over the Muslims and other minorities to the unchecked domination of Congress and our own interests demand that we should not surrender tamely."[27]

Pethick-Lawrence did not, however, regard Nehru's letter as "a final challenge" to HMG but rather as a Congress political ploy to "squeeze some further concessions" from the viceroy. "Nehru was faced with a strong left wing element in Congress and . . . found it necessary to put at least two representatives of left wing on the Working Committee."[28] Socialist radical that he was, Pethick-Lawrence found it easier to empathize with the Congress radicals than did Wavell. Unions were threatening to strike in Bombay and Calcutta, as food scarcity was growing and the price of grain rising in all major cities. "We regard it as quite vital," Pethick cautioned Wavell, "that your conversation with Nehru on the 29th [July] should not end in complete rupture with Congress. . . . If no progress towards agreement results from your conversation . . . we think it may be desirable to ask Congress and Muslim League each to send representatives to London."[29] The Labor cabinet had little faith in Wavell's political acuity, especially in dealing with Indian Socialists, and knew how costly and dangerous any explosions in India could prove to be.

Attlee tried to teach Wavell how to cope more effectively with political problems, writing to assuage his disappointment in having "come so near to complete success," reminding him "but one needs infinite patience in dealing with Indians."[30] The prime minister recalled his own experience on the Indian Statutory Commission when

I was always struck by the fact that our Indian friends though politically minded and fully acquainted with the theory of democratic government had little or no understanding of its actual working. . . . I was equally impressed by the fact that our admirable civil service . . . was almost equally devoid of practical experience of the working of democratic institutions. . . . It has often occurred to me that you must find a great lack of the kind of experience on which it is necessary to draw in political matters. . . . I have felt that we have perhaps put you in an unfair position in not having provided you with someone of experience in these things. You as a soldier without political advisers must be somewhat in the same position as a Prime Minister would be without the advice of the Chiefs of Staff on military matters.

Attlee suggested that retired Chief Justice Sir Maurice Gwyer, who had considerable political as well as legal experience, might be a useful special "adviser" to the viceroy. Wavell, who was after all Churchill's appointee, was too thin-skinned about his own weaknesses to accept such sound advice, however, or perhaps he was too proud to take criticism from Labor's prime minister, "Major" (his rank during World War I) Attlee.

Nor was Wavell pleased with Pethick-Lawrence's advice, replying to his cautionary warning, "I have no more desire or intention to break with Congress, if it can possibly be avoided, than you have. But Nehru's letter is more challenging than anything which was put up while the Mission was out here, and we cannot go on being perpetually subject to these squeezes."[31] George Abell, Wavell's able private secretary, better understood the cabinet's anxieties, briefing his viceroy very carefully before meeting with Nehru:

You have considered his letter . . . and you would like to discuss its implications. At first sight it would seem to close the door firmly on any possibility of an Interim Government but you cannot believe that is the intention. Everyone acknowledges that it will be hard for the Constituent Assembly to succeed if there is no *coalition* Interim Government. . . . What is wanted is an Interim Government *at once.* . . . You are sure that the Congress and Nehru himself want a peaceful transition and realise the danger that the country may lapse into chaos from which recovery may take a very long time. There is a clear choice before Congress and in spite of some things that have been said which would suggest the contrary you believe Congress intend to take the statesmanlike view. A conflict could undoubtedly lead to chaos in India, and . . . opposition to His Majesty's Government could only in the end be disastrous. . . . You would like your proposal put to the Working Committee at Wardha and you very much hope Nehru will . . . support it.[32]

Studying that brief, the viceroy felt better prepared to meet with Nehru.

But just before Wavell met Nehru, the Muslim League Council met in Bombay and resolved to withdraw its previous support of the cabinet mission's proposals, because the "Congress have made it clear that they do not accept any of the terms or the fundamentals of the Scheme but that they have agreed only to go into the Constituent Assembly. . . . This fact, taken together with the policy of the British Government of sacrificing the interests of the Muslim Nation . . . leaves no doubt that . . . participation of the Muslims in the proposed constitution-making machinery is fraught with danger."[33] So the League resolved that "Whereas the Congress is bent upon setting up Caste-Hindu Raj in India with the connivance of the British . . . the time has come for the Muslim Nation to resort to Direct Action to achieve Pakistan." This "Direct Action" resolution was Jinnah's angry response to Nehru's "treachery" and the cabinet delegation's "betrayal" of his Muslim League. He said "Goodbye to Constitutionalism and passive cooperation," and welcomed violent "Action" instead.

Wavell met with Nehru the next day, July 30, telling him that his "intemperate statements" and "unguarded language" to the press had in part provoked the League to pass their "most unfortunate" resolution. "I said that Congress now had a chance of showing real statesmanship and of giving the Muslim League assurances that would bring them into the Constituent Assembly."[34] But Nehru "did not quite see" what assurances he could give them. He asked Wavell what was going to be done about the constituent assembly, and "I said that obviously it was impossible to make a Constitution for India without the participation of the Muslims." Nehru replied that as soon as the British left, the League would "be forced to come in and take part," that it would be "fatal" to hold things up "indefinitely." As for the interim government, Wavell said he was "most anxious" to form one as soon as possible, but there could be no question of an "independent Government." Nehru "made no comment on this."[35] Nehru left the viceroy's office as angry and disillusioned about his intentions toward granting the Congress power, as Wavell felt about the Congress president's willingness to cooperate with him and the Muslim League.

The cabinet's India Committee met the next day with Cripps in the chair to discuss the political situation. Looming threats of an Indian postal and railway strike helped them to decide to go ahead with the constituent assembly and also to urge the viceroy to try to form an interim government as quickly as possible. The viceroy should see Jinnah at once and ask if his League would participate or not. He should next see Nehru again and ask him for his list of Congress Party representatives. Wavell did not think it advisable to send immediately for Jinnah, warning Pethick-Lawrence it would be "regarded as a panicky reaction to a threat and will put up Jinnah's stock and increase his intransigence."[36] Pethick-Lawrence agreed with that point, but cautioned Wavell that it would be "wise to endeavour to get a more friendly reaction" from Jinnah soon, "and we must . . . not let it slip."[37]

Jinnah, who had devoted his life to the law and never before lost faith in British justice, had now suddenly turned his League into a lethal weapon of direct action. Friday, August 16, 1946, was announced by the League to be "Direct Action Day," when all Muslims should stop work and meet in every town and village to read and "discuss" the League's most ominous resolution. With so many idle Muslims on the streets, enraged by feelings of Hindu-British betrayal, the chances of keeping Jinnah's Direct Action Day from exploding into deadly communal rioting were hardly negligible.

United Provinces governor Sir Francis Wylie warned Wavell a week before Direct Action Day that "Muslims are now in a thoroughly truculent mood," convinced that "the British have totally ceased to matter in India and that it is a suitable time for the Muslims to clear themselves of the damaging Congress accusation that they are all toadies of the British. . . . We would seem in fact now to have got nearly every body against us."[38] So Wavell decided now to invite Nehru, as president of the Congress Party, to submit "proposals for the formation of an Interim Government."[39] The Congress Party Working Committee met at Wardha to seek Mahatma Gandhi's advice on how they should respond to the viceroy's invitation. Gandhi urged them to accept it, which they did after considerable discussion and debate, on August 10.

Two days earlier, Wavell met with his governors of Bengal, Uttar Pradesh, Punjab, Sind, and the North-West Frontier Province. Governor Sir Frederick Burrows of Bengal then informed the viceroy that Muslim League Prime Minister H. S. Suhrawardy had "asked" for a public holiday on August 16 "to avoid trouble on that day," and he had approved that request.[40] Thus all of Bengal's police were given a holiday on what became Calcutta's darkest day of mass murder and arson. Shockingly enough, neither Wavell nor Burrows had the good sense to anticipate the violent horrors that would engulf Calcutta on that Direct Action Day.

On August 13, the chiefs of staff committee of the British cabinet invited India's commander-in-chief Auchinleck to give them his "views" of an intelligence staff note they had received, concluding that "civil war" might break out in India in the "near future," in which event "the Indian Armed Forces as a whole cannot be relied on."[41] Field Marshal Auchinleck "did not think the situation was any more dangerous to-day than it had been six weeks ago, indeed, it was perhaps a little better." Three days later, all hell broke loose in Calcutta's "Great Killing," while Bengal's police enjoyed their holiday, and British troops and armored Dragoon tanks remained useless, locked inside their barracks.

Congress President Nehru, now having accepted the viceroy's invitation to form an interim government, wrote to Jinnah, inviting him to join in organizing a coalition government. "It is naturally our desire to have as representative a Government as possible," Nehru sensibly informed Jinnah. "Should you wish to discuss this matter further with me . . . I shall gladly see you in Bombay."[42] He planned to reach Bombay from Wardha on August 15. Jinnah replied that day: "I know nothing as to what has transpired between the Viceroy and you, nor have I any idea what agreement has been arrived at between you two except what you say in your letter . . . If this means the Viceroy has commissioned you to form an Executive Council . . . and has already agreed to accept and act upon your advice . . . it is not possible for me to accept such a position. . . . However, if you care to meet me, on behalf of Congress, to settle the Hindu-Muslim question and resolve the serious deadlock, I shall be glad to see you today at 6 p.m."[43] They met late that afternoon, but failed to reach any reconciliation or agreement, for Jinnah felt as betrayed by Wavell as he had previously felt by Pethick-Lawrence and Cripps. He refused so much as to consider joining any interim government that could include a Congress or other non-League Muslim, and Nehru refused to promise him veto power. So their stalemate continued as day turned to twilight in Bombay and to "Dreadful Night" in Kipling's old quarter of Calcutta, its underworld sharpening all their razors and rusty knives.

For three days and nights, British India's former capital, still its most populous city, became a free killing field for thugs and thieves, first Muslims, then retaliating Hindus, murdering, plundering, butchering whatever attracted their eyes. Thousands of dead bodies were hauled off Calcutta's blood-stained streets by martial patrols, only belatedly brought into action by the stink of decaying flesh. "It was unbridled savagery and homicidal maniacs let loose to kill and . . . main and burn," reported General Francis Tuker, who finally ordered out his British troops and tanks to put an end to the butchery.[44] By then over 4,000 were dead and some 16,000 wounded. Bengal's deadly communal fever then spread to neighboring Bihar, where the Muslim minority was most vulnerable, some ten thousand murdered by their long-friendly Hindu neighbors in remote rural villages.

Before that week of brutal communal mayhem ended, on August 22, Wavell met with Nehru to review his list of Congress names proposed for the interim government, almost all of whom were appointed. Wavell had hoped for a coalition, and offered to speak to Jinnah, but Nehru was so outraged by what Jinnah's League had unleashed that he preferred "a strong, virile, active and stable Government which knows its mind and has the courage to go ahead, not a weak, disjointed, apologetic Government which can be easily bullied or frightened. . . . To give an impression to the country and our people that we are merely a casual and temporary Government waiting for the favour of the Muslim League is to undermine the prestige and authority of the Government."[45] Two days later the viceroy broadcast his announcement of the new interim government's appointment. "The recent terrible occurrences in Calcutta have been a sobering reminder that a much greater measure of toleration is essential if India is to survive the transition to freedom. . . . No conceivable good . . . can come either from violent words or from violent deeds."[46]

Escalating communal killing convinced Wavell that only a coalition interim government would be able to avert civil war, so he tried again to explain to Nehru and Gandhi the importance of reopening negotiations with the Muslim League in order to lower communal temperatures and have a coalition at the center. The "crux of the whole matter," he told them was the League's concern about Congress's opposition to grouping for the constituent assembly, which had been at the heart of the cabinet mission's scheme.[47] Wavell informed them that he could not "undertake the responsibility" of convening the constituent assembly until the Congress working committee agreed to a written statement accepting the mission's idea of grouping. Nehru "got very heated" at that, calling it "bullying" by the Muslim League. Gandhi went off "into long legalistic arguments" about how to interpret the mission's statement, until Wavell interrupted him, saying "I was a plain man and not a lawyer, and I knew perfectly well, what the Mission meant, and that the compulsory Grouping was the whole crux of the Plan."[48]

Gandhi sent Wavell a "Dear Friend" letter next morning:

> We are all plain men though we may not all be soldiers. . . . Your language last evening was minatory. As representative of the King you cannot afford to be a military man only, nor to ignore the law. . . . You should be assisted, if necessary, by a legal mind. . . . If British arms are kept here for internal peace and order your Interim Government would be reduced to a farce. The Congress cannot afford to impose its will on warring elements in India through the use of British arms. Nor can the Congress be expected to bend itself and adopt what it considers a wrong course because of the brutal exhibition . . . in Bengal . . . chiefly due to the continued presence in India of a foreign power. . . . [T]he Congress claims to know both the Hindu and Muslim mind more than you or any Britisher can do.[49]

Gandhi asked that his letter be sent to the British cabinet, which Wavell did at once. That widening breach between Wavell and Congress leadership confirmed the grave misgivings Attlee, Pethick-Lawrence, and Cripps had all earlier felt about the martial viceroy's lack of political sensitivity. The more difficult question for them, however, was whether any other British viceroy could handle the increasingly incendiary, bitterly explosive situation of India, now in its last British year of growing conflict and insufferable pain, any better.

On August 31, Punjab's new governor, Evan Jenkins, warned Wavell of the feelings on the ground from Lahore.

> Muslims are frightened and angry. They believe that Jinnah has been out-witted and that they have been betrayed. They think that our refusal to put the Muslim League into power when the Congress was non-co-oper-ating, and our apparent eagerness to bring the Congress in as soon as the party positions were reversed, can be explained only by a deep-laid plot between the British and the Congress. They regard the formation of the Interim Government as an unconditional surrender of power to the Hin-dus, and are convinced that the Governor-General will be unable to pre-vent the Hindus from using their newly-acquired power for the systematic suppression of the Muslims all over India. . . . The Hindus are —they are bad winners, and will do all they can to taunt and humiliate the Muslims. They are foolish enough to believe that here in the Punjab they will be able to suppress the Muslims once for all with British aid. . . . The Sikh attitude is still . . . divided. . . . Sikh leaders are among the most violent in the Punjab. . . . We have here the material for a vast communal upheaval.[50]

In early September, Nehru told Wavell that Suhrawardy had just in-formed the press that if Bengal's Muslims took to the "war path" there would "not be a single Hindu left alive in eastern Bengal." Wavell met with politically shrewd Suhrawardy to ask if he had made that statement, and stood behind it. Suhrawardy was not afraid to admit the "truth," and in-deed, he might have presided over an independent nation-state of Bengal if Nehru and Patel had allowed Bengali Congressmen to serve under him and if Jinnah had allowed him to bring those Congressmen into his coalition cabinet. Suhrawardy informed Wavell that Jinnah would never come to him "as a suppliant."[51]

Hearing that, Wavell feared the situation had almost reached the "break-down" stage. His intelligence team had prepared a top secret plan. Their more careful count of the total number of Europeans still living in India, all of whom would have to be evacuated if communal civil war broke out, was 96,081, over twice the number presented to the British cabinet by the war office. Wavell feared that the administration of most British provinces had sunk to "an oriental standard" of incompetence and corruption, with the former substantial powers of British governors now virtually negligible.[52] Unless HMG were prepared to change their current policy and invest re-sources enough to remain in India for another fifteen to twenty years, Wavell warned Pethick-Lawrence and Attlee that "we could not govern the whole of India for more than a year and a half."[53] "In India," he told them, "one must either rule firmly or not at all. With a largely uneducated and highly excitable people . . . it is essential that . . . incitement to unbridled riot should be stopped at once." Now that all Congress political "agitators," most of whom he had kept in prison throughout the war, were free to shout whatever they liked, all Europeans, including women and children, would soon be in "grave danger." Wavell's proposal called for complete British withdrawal from India by the spring of 1948. He was sick and tired of being scolded daily by Nehru, Gandhi, or Patel and had firmly resolved never to use "British bayonets . . . to support one-party regime."[54] He was quite ready, in fact, to "dismiss the Interim Government if they refused to cooperate." His breakdown plan called for the immediate staged withdrawal of all British officers and troops from south India to the north, providing secure facilities at Bombay and Calcutta for British nationals to gather in until they could be evacuated.

On September 16 Wavell met with Jinnah and tried his best to reassure him about the grouping of provinces and to convince him of the value of bringing his League into the interim government. Jinnah protested to the viceroy that "I had made a great mistake in forming the present one-party Government; and went on to dilate on the intensity of Muslim feeling."[55] He was not ready to join the interim government, but remained "friendly" and "polite" to Wavell throughout their two-hour talk. Wavell pressed Jinnah to submit his own list of five names, but it would be another month before Jinnah finally agreed to allow those five League lieutenants to join a coalition government led by Nehru and Patel. By October 1946, when Liaquat Ali Khan took charge of the ministry of finance in the interim government, both Bombay and Bengal were aflame.

In Bombay, from late August to October, when Sir Andrew Clow became acting governor, 329 people had been murdered and 983 injured in communal "stabbings and bouts of stone-throwing."[56] Clow was also disturbed by the economic "attack" aimed at the Muslim community. Hindu owners were forcing many Muslim millhands to leave their jobs in Bombay and Ahmedabad. "Muslims are by now tired of the trouble and probably sorry they started it . . . but . . . there appear to be many Hindus of influence who are anxious to keep the fires burning . . . and Jinnah's allegation that the Hindus are out to crush the Muslims is not quite so false as it formerly was."[57]

In East Bengal, the situation was even worse by mid-October. "A vast area of Bengal has ceased to have any Government functioning, any security, and has just become the happy hunting ground of the worst elements in the community," Nehru reported. "Mass slaughter, arson, burning of human beings, rape, abduction on a large scale, forcible conversions and all manner of other horrible things are happening."[58] Those reports of rape and conversions to Islam of Hindu women in East Bengal's Noakhali District induced Mahatma Gandhi to leave his ashram and undertake his last and most arduous foot-pilgrimage of peace, walking from one burned out and torture-filled village to the next, seeking through his faith in Ahimsa to counter violent terror with the healing powers of love.

When the Muslim League's five members joined the interim government on October 15, 1946, Wavell reported that "Congress have shown no signs of enthusiasm" but the viceroy optimistically thought "a coalition will do an immense amount of good to the general condition of the country."[59] However, it did little more than to bring New Delhi's government to a virtual standstill, since the cost of everything was questioned and carefully reviewed by finance member Liaquat Ali Khan before, as a rule, being rejected or returned for review and further justification. "In recent weeks we have obviously been on the edge of a volcano," Pethick-Lawrence wrote Wavell, congratulating him on bringing in the League, hoping now for "relaxation" of communal tension.[60]

No sooner had the League joined the interim government, however, than the Congress Party regretted ever agreeing to a coalition. Nehru and Patel feared that Jinnah agreed to come in only to wreck the interim government, not to help it function more effectively. "Is the Interim Government to be the arena of party politics and intrigues and for driving in the very partition wedge which the long-term arrangement has withdrawn?" Home Minister Patel wrote to ask Wavell. "Removal of corruption . . . scarcity of food and clothing, health of the millions, their education, removal of chronic poverty . . . are the immediate needs of the country. If wrangles over partition and fomenting of trouble are to take the place of immediate work of the administration, it would be a question for the Congress to revise its attitude about shouldering the burden it has taken over in response to your invitation."[61]

Wavell's pleasure at having achieved an interim coalition was short-lived. Just a week later he reported to King George: "I am afraid that the political outlook is still most unpromising in spite of the decision of the Muslim League to enter the Interim Government. It seems impossible to get any sense of urgency into these people."[62] The viceroy confessed to the king that his attempts to get the Congress Party and the League to cooperate

reminds me of one of my childhood's puzzles—a little glass-covered box with 3 or 4 different coloured marbles which one had to manipulate into their respective pens. . . . [J]ust as the last one seemed on the point of moving in . . . all the others invariably ran out."[63] Wavell concluded that "altogether the omens are not favourable. . . . [T]he only possible chance for India has always been . . . to get the two main parties round a table and working together on the problems of administration. . . . But I am frankly sceptical about their finding the necessary good-will and spirit of compromise to hold them together. . . . As regards the food situation, a large part of India continues to live from hand to mouth, with practically nothing in the hand.[64]

In Bihar, riots took their toll of Muslims. "The first serious riot in this Province," Bihar's Governor Dow reported on November 9, "was . . . in Muzaffarpur District where 14 Moslems were killed. . . . In Bihar the rural Moslem population is comparatively small and isolated groups have been the objects of most determined attacks. Roving Hindu mobs have sought to exterminate the Moslem population. . . . Large numbers of refugees are moving into Patna. . . . Police figures of deaths from rioting so far are just over 2,000."[65]

Wavell flew to Bihar to inspect the situation personally. Nehru joined him there, but neither of them could energize the provincial Hindu government to stop or arrest rural killers, incited to madness by reports of the rapes of Hindu women in Noakhali. Soon, the butchery spread to neighboring United Provinces, where 200 Muslims were murdered near Lucknow on a single mid-November day. Congress blamed Wavell for not coming down harder on Suhrawardy after the Calcutta killings. Wavell blamed the Congress for targeting so many isolated Muslims. Jinnah felt betrayed by both, saying it was no use for the Muslim League even to consider joining the constituent assembly while so many Muslims were being "ground down." In mid-November of 1946, Jinnah told the press in Delhi that "the only solution" to India's communal situation was "Pakistan and Hindustan," adding that he meant "absolute Pakistan—anything else would be artificial and unnatural."[66] As for the interim government, he called it a "shambles" which was "forced upon us." Asked about the British Labor government, he said they were "living in a dream land . . . groping in the dark."[67] Asked about Pakistan, Jinnah said it would be "a popular, representative Government in which . . . [every one] no matter what his caste, colour or creed, will have equal rights."

Much to Nehru's chagrin and frustration Wavell kept postponing the date to convene India's constituent assembly, which was originally supposed to have met in October, and then in November, and was finally put off until December 9. "If anything comes in the way of the Constituent Assembly meeting on the 9th December, the Congress would . . . have to reconsider the whole question," Nehru warned.[68] Wavell felt certain, however, that if the assembly met without Jinnah's participation there would be "very grave and widespread disorder," and he so cautioned Pethick-Lawrence.[69] To Jinnah, he said, "the only alternative to agreement was civil war, which was likely to be disastrous for the Muslims."[70] The British could not remain in India "indefinitely," he added, which triggered Jinnah's accusation that Britain was putting Muslims "under Hindu rule." He still insisted that any "settlement" between the Congress and his League was *quite* impossible." Jinnah accused Congress leaders of having "organised . . . the massacre of Muslims" in Bihar. "They are fooling the world," he told the viceroy, who "heartily agreed"—to himself—"hardly" able to say as much aloud.[71] But Wavell was able to convey his thoughts and fears frankly to London's cabinet.

"Everything else in India is overshadowed by the savage outbreaks of communal violence in East Bengal, Bihar and the United Provinces," Wavell wrote Pethick-Lawrence. "I doubt whether anyone in England yet quite realises the extent and bestiality of the attacks on Muslims in Bihar. . . . The Muslims are undoubtedly to blame for their policy of 'direct action' which led to the Calcutta killings. . . . But the retaliations in Bihar . . . have been on the scale of numbers and degree of brutality far beyond anything that I think has yet happened in India since British rule began. And they were undoubtedly organised . . . by supporters of Congress."[72]

Jinnah claimed that 30,000 Muslims had been murdered in Bihar, but Wavell thought that was high, estimating the death toll between 5,000 and 10,000. Over 120,000 Muslim refugees, whose homes had been burned down, remained in open shelters in Bihar. "It is a tragic ending of our rule in India," Wavell noted. The cabinet was convinced by that report to take more drastic action, so Pethick-Lawrence told Wavell to bring two leaders of the Congress Party and two of the League to London for "urgent talks" with the cabinet before the constituent assembly met. Nehru's response was initially negative, but following a strong personal appeal from the secretary of state he agreed to come, bringing Congress Sikh leader Baldev Singh, who was soon to be India's minister of defense in Nehru's first cabinet. Jinnah also reluctantly agreed to fly to London, bringing Liaquat Ali with him. London was cold and bleak that first week in December, though no colder than Jinnah and Nehru remained to one another throughout a bitter, frustrating series of attempts by Attlee, Cripps, and Pethick-Lawrence to bring those hopelessly distrustful leaders of India's most powerful parties together on the eve of convening the constituent assembly.

Wavell expected nothing to come of this London summit, grimly informing the cabinet at its start that "Congress feel that H.M.G. dare not break with them. . . . Their aim is power and to get rid of British influence as soon as possible, after which they think they can deal with both Muslims and Princes; the former by bribery . . . and if necessary force; the latter by stirring up their people against them. . . . They will continue a gradual process of sapping and infiltration against the British, the Muslims, and the Princes . . . for as long and so far as they are allowed, until they consider themselves strong enough to . . . revolt against British rule." The Muslims were thoroughly alarmed, Wavell added, and many were "getting desperate." Still, they trusted the British to give them "a fair deal" and Muslim League leaders had initially raised the "cries of Pakistan and Islam in danger . . . to enhance their prestige and power." But now they had "so inflamed their ignorant . . . followers with the idea of Pakistan as a new

Prophet's Paradise on earth as their only means of protection against Hindu domination, that it will be very difficult to satisfy them with anything else."[73]

Wavell no longer believed the Labor government's cabinet had courage enough to confront the Congress and reassert the actual plan its cabinet mission had proposed to both parties the previous May. He now rightly felt that unless Congress signed an agreement to the primacy of grouping, the League would never join a constituent assembly dominated by Hindus. "To surrender to Congress as the Majority party, to acquiesce in all it does," Wavell warned, "I do not think . . . an honourable or a wise policy; it will end British rule in India in discredit and eventually an ignominious scuttle by Congress. There is no . . . generosity in Congress."[74] The only long-term plan Wavell supported was his "breakdown plan," to announce the withdrawal of all British subjects and forces by a certain date and firmly to proceed with it, leaving to provincial governments what powers of administration remained. He warned the Congress Party high command that any interference with Britain's withdrawal would be dealt with immediately and firmly as an "act of war."

By this time, Attlee, Pethick-Lawrence, and Cripps had no more faith in Wavell than the martial viceroy did in any of them. Cripps himself offered to take over Wavell's job, but Attlee said he felt it was more important to keep Cripps in charge of the board of trade in London. He had a much younger, more flamboyant candidate in mind, the same one Churchill himself, now the leader of the opposition, had been ready to pick as Great Britain's final glorious viceroy of India.

On December 3, Pethick-Lawrence met with Jinnah, who told him that "no effective compromise" with the Congress Party was possible. He and his League followers were "determined not to be submerged in the Hindu nation. . . . [I]t was better to resist now than to be gradually overwhelmed."[75] That same day, Pethick-Lawrence also met with an equally pessimistic Nehru, who "saw no hope of reconciling Mr. Jinnah and thought it would be wrong to try to appease him as a result of violence."[76] On December 4 the cabinet mission trio and Wavell all met with Nehru, who told them that "there was a great urge among the masses of India for political progress. . . . The Muslim League was a fly in the balance, compared with the vast human forces in India."[77] Nehru explained that the interim government was no coalition, but two disputing parties in one cabinet. "The Congress was a revolutionary party and its Left-Wing were still agitators. . . . The League was in the Government but was in open opposition to it. . . . He did not see how the Congress could continue in the Interim Government with this state of affairs."[78]

The last London conference meeting was held at 10 Downing Street on December 6. The prime minister found it "ironical" that after the British government had done everything and three of its ministers had spent three and a half months in India working out an "agreement," its "progress was hung up" now by the failure of Indian parties to agree as to "methods of procedure."[79] He thought "world opinion" would think this "a very curious situation. . . . The British Government had . . . secured acceptance in this country of a line of policy urged for many years by leading Indians. They were entitled now to ask for Indian cooperation."[80] But neither party trusted the other; there was no faith in the mind of Nehru or of Jinnah as to the reliability of anything promised by the other. They were no closer to agreement at the end of that London conference than they had been when it started.

Nehru and Baldev Singh flew home to Delhi the next day, meeting with their Congress colleagues at the opening session of the constituent assembly at which the chairs for all putative Muslim League "members" remained empty. Jinnah and Liaquat lingered on in London. When the British cabinet met on December 10, Attlee and Pethick-Lawrence reported the failure of their conference. Attlee confided to his cabinet that "Nehru's present policy seemed to be to secure complete domination by Congress throughout the government of India . . . [and] there would certainly be strong reactions from the Muslims. Provinces with a Muslim majority might refuse to join a central Government on such terms at all; and the ultimate result of Congress policy might be the establishment of that Pakistan which they so much disliked. . . . [T]he situation might so develop as to result in civil war in India, with all the bloodshed which that would entail."[81]

The cabinet felt that Indian politicians were deluding themselves if they thought that the British Indian Army was still powerful enough to prevent such bloodshed. For they all knew that "the strength of British forces in India was not great. And the Indian Army . . . could not fairly be expected to prove a reliable instrument for maintaining public order. . . . One thing was quite certain . . . that we [Great Britain] could not put back the clock and introduce a period of firm British rule. Neither the military nor the administrative machine in India was any longer capable of this."[82] Most ministers felt that the only thing left for them to do was to evacuate all British subjects as swiftly as possible. Only a few idealists objected, feeling that would be "an inglorious end to our long association with India. World opinion would regard it as a policy of scuttle unworthy of a great Power."[83]

The cabinet's most difficult challenge now was how to evacuate India as quickly as possible while making it look like a simply glorious liberation rather than a shameful flight. All of them understood as 1946 came to a close that Wavell's briefly hoped for coalition interim government was dead.

7

Lord Mountbatten's Last Chukka, December 1946–June 1947

W AVELL STAYED ON in London, pressing the cabinet for a "defi-
nite policy" on his breakdown plan, unaware that Attlee had
already decided on his replacement. Rear-Admiral Lord Louis
Mountbatten, called "Dickie" by his favorite cousin "Bertie," King George
VI, and by dear friends like Noel Coward, Alan Campbell-Johnson, and
Winston Churchill, had served as Supreme Allied Commander of South East
Asia since 1943. He and his wife, Lady Edwina Mountbatten, had met and
befriended Nehru in Singapore in March 1946. The Labor Party's Indian
Chair Krishna Menon, Nehru's closest comrade, had tirelessly urged Attlee
to send Mountbatten out to India to replace Wavell as Britain's last viceroy.
Mountbatten's royal blood appealed as much to India's princes as his radi-
cal views and social charms did to Nehru.

On December 18, Attlee offered Mountbatten the viceroyalty of India.
He claimed to be "staggered" by the offer, so Cripps, who was at 10 Downing Street when Attlee proffered it, volunteered to return to India as his
chief of staff. Mountbatten shuddered at that prospect, insisting it would be
"too great an honour."[1] Cripps knew much more about India than
Mountbatten, yet had struck out twice in his recent diplomatic missions.
The last thing Mountbatten wanted was a dour elder statesman telling him
what to do. His ego demanded constant adulation and unquestioning support from a team of acolytes. He knew he needed someone who understood
India, so he decided to keep George Abell as private secretary. And he needed
someone close enough to Churchill and the Tory Party back home to keep
them from vetoing all he intended to do, so he invited General Hastings
Lionel ("Pug") Ismay, Churchill's wartime aide, to be his chief of viceroy's

staff. The rest of his team were wardroom buddies like Captain Ronald Vernon Brockman, his personal secretary, and his press attache, Alan Campbell-Johnson, and cousin Bertie's royal assistant private secretary, Sir Eric Charles Mieville, lured on board as principal secretary to the viceroy. Mountbatten viewed the prospect of ruling India during the Raj's sunset year as challenging as a hard-fought polo game, as he put it to the King— "The last Chukka in India—12 goals down."[2]

Attlee agreed to leave Rear Admiral Mountbatten's name on the active flag list of the Royal Navy, since it was his intention to rush back to the fleet as soon as he could extricate himself from India and to vindicate his father's reputation. First Sea Lord of the Royal Navy Prince Louis of Battenberg, was forced by London's fierce anti-German prejudice during World War I to abandon the fleet over which he had once so proudly presided. His then fourteen-year-old son resolved to join the navy himself and remain in it until he became first sea lord. Being India's viceroy would sidetrack his naval career, forcing him to give up the senior officers technical course he had just begun. "I do regret your time lost in the Navy," Cousin Bertie wrote, commiserating with Dickie, "just as you were going back to it. As you say you can go back now but can you in say 2 years, which will be more difficult."[3] So Mountbatten resolved to make fast work of his India job. Though the cabinet gave him eighteen months to complete it, he never had any intention of taking so long to finish off his last chukka.

In negotiating with Attlee, Mountbatten insisted on keeping his fast York plane that had come with his job as supreme allied commander of South East Asia. "I feel it is essential that I should be allowed to fly home as often as I feel it really necessary to do so (say every 3 or 4 months) for personal discussions with you," he told Attlee. "I would ask you to be so kind as to make it clear, in the announcement of my appointment that I am on loan [from the Royal Navy] for this short period."[4] He also requested that he and Edwina be allowed to "visit Indian Leaders" in their own homes, unaccompanied by staff, allowing them both more quickly to get to know Nehru intimately.

"An unexpected appointment but a clever one," Wavell noted in his diary, when he heard the news. "Dickie's personality may perhaps accomplish what I have failed to do."[5] Noel Coward, one of Mountbatten's intimate friends, put it this way: "The position having become impossible, they call on Dickie."[6] Mountbatten remained quite relaxed before embarking on his singularly challenging, if not daunting, task. "He was chiefly concerned with what he should wear on arrival," Woodrow Wyatt recalled. "'They're all a bit left wing, aren't they? Hadn't I better land in ordinary day clothes?' He was delighted when I said, 'No, you are the last Viceroy. You are royal. You must wear your grandest uniform and all your decorations and be met in full panoply and with all the works. Otherwise they will feel slighted.' And that is what he did, to everyone's pleasure." Mountbatten looked best in his full dress whites and relished the adulation of India's cheering crowds.

On February 20, 1947, prime minister Attlee's government issued a solemn statement in London promising to hand over its "powers" and "great responsibilities" in India, either to one central Indian government or, in some areas, to provincial governments by no later than June of 1948. His majesty's government's statement concluded, "expressing on behalf of the people of this country their goodwill and good wishes towards the people of India as they go forward to this final stage in their achievement of self-government."[7]

"The process of transfer can now begin in an atmosphere of goodwill and cordiality," noted India's *Hindustan Times* lead article next day. "The desire of H. M. G. that India should have continued peace and security so that the full possibilities of economic development may be realized and a higher standard of life attained by the Indian people will be appreciated for its sincerity and goodwill. . . . This is what the Congress has been asking for all these twenty-five years. . . . The Muslim League and Mr. Jinnah are now face to face with reality."[8] A day later, Liaquat met with Wavell and told him that "he did not see how the two parties could ever really agree."[9]

Rioting broke out in Punjab in early March. Governor Jenkins reported twenty dead in Multan on March 5 and more in Lahore, where incendiarism was "widespread." There had also been incidents of arson in Rawalpindi and Amritsar, and "We shall be lucky if we escape communal rioting throughout Punjab on an unprecedented scale."[10] The Unionist Party premier of Punjab, young Khizar Hyat Khan, resigned, leaving Punjab "face to face with the Pakistan issue," as Wavell put it to Pethick-Lawrence.[11] Liaquat now introduced his new budget as finance member of Wavell's council, driving a "wedge deep into the Congress party," Wavell added in that same letter. "He has framed a socialistic budget which appeals to the genuine socialist in the Congress party but horrifies the capitalists." Liaquat's budget called for a 25 percent tax on all profits of over one lakh (100,000) of rupees, the highest tax ever suggested in India to date.

When the House of Commons met on March 5 to discuss India, the leader of the house, Sir Stafford Cripps, rose to move for approval of the transfer of power. "Time is short," Cripps began. "These next few weeks must be decisive of the future of India, and the happiness of its 400 million inhabitants."[12] Former governor of Bengal and member of Churchill's war cabinet Sir John Anderson rose to launch the opposition's attack, warning that His Majesty's Government was making "a cardinal blunder." Anderson feared that the process was being unduly hurried, and he found it impossible to understand how any fixed date could be set for Britain's final withdrawal from India, when it still remained uncertain as to how many parties were to share in the actual transfer of power. He listed many things that would have to be divided, if the transfer were to be made to more than a single party, from British India's army, railway network, judiciary and civil service and taxation systems, to tens of thousands of smaller items of joint ownership, asking, "How is the process to be carried out?" Then Anderson added, from personal experience as Bengal's governor, that the complexity of problems involved in the potential partition of Bengal, Calcutta, and Assam alone would be enough to make any one experienced with Europe's divisions of Danzig and Trieste think those challenges had been simple. He warned that ruin would face entire Indian regions and communities if this hasty process were not reconsidered and its early terminal date pushed back. But his wise warnings fell on deaf ears. Attlee had given Mountbatten his marching orders, and the new viceroy was so eager to get on with the job that he would cut their all too brief allotment of time in half.

In what must be counted one of history's supremely ironic moments, Opposition Leader Winston Churchill, who had always most bitterly opposed India's Congress Party, rose to join the debate on March 6, his voice growling incredulously. Was this merely to be "Operation Scuttle," Churchill asked. "The Government by their 14 months' time limit, have put an end to all prospect of Indian unity. . . . How can one suppose that the thousand year gulf which yawns between Muslim and Hindu will be bridged in 14 months? . . . It is astounding."[13] Churchill called the time limit a "kind of guillotine," designed to cut apart all the long united services and to fragment, not simply partition, all of India. "How can we walk out of India in 14 months and leave behind us a war between 90 million Muslims and 200 million caste Hindus . . . ? Will it not be a terrible disgrace to our name and record if, after our 14 months' time limit, we allow one fifth of the population of the globe . . . to fall into chaos and carnage? Would it not be a world crime . . . that would stain . . . our good name forever?"[14]

"We must face the evils that are coming upon us," Churchill warned, his voice almost breaking as he added, "and that we are powerless to avert. We must do our best in all circumstances. . . . But, at least, let us not add— by shameful flight, by a premature, hurried scuttle—at least, let us not add, to the pangs of sorrow so many of us feel, the taint and smear of shame."[15] His passionately principled eloquence did not, unfortunately, carry the House. Attlee's government's quit-India-quickly policy won the House of Commons vote, by a majority of 337 to 185 votes. The World War was over, India's sterling balance advantage kept growing, and most Englishmen were increasingly sick and tired of squabbling, eternally dissatisfied, forever ungrateful Indians.

The same day that Churchill addressed the Commons, Wavell wrote to ask Governor Jenkins for his "views" of the possible partition of Punjab.

Jenkins replied that he considered Punjab's partition "unthinkable" and "impracticable." Of Punjab's 28 million residents, some 16 million were Muslims, 12 million Hindus and Sikhs. The two western divisions of Rawalpindi and Multan were "Muslim country," and the two eastern divisions of Jullundur and Ambala were non-Muslim. The central Lahore Division was "common ground," with a Muslim majority, but with Sikh "Holy Land," including Guru Nanak's place of birth and death, and mostly non-Muslim "economic interests."[16] Partition would probably "destroy the Punjab economically," he predicted.

> Our minorities problem will not be solved. Both States (particularly the non-Muslim State) will have considerable and probably discontented minorities. . . . Lahore must go to one State or the other. . . . But Lahore has been created by all Punjabis. . . . The non-Muslim State will have the lion's share of our power resources; the Muslim State will inherit the colony districts. . . . We shall have reduced what might be a powerful country to two petty States incapable of real economic development, overloaded with overhead charges, and useful only as 'buffers' between the rest of India and the outer world. Partition solves no problems and does not really make sense,"[17]

Jenkins concluded.

In mid-March, Jenkins replied to a wire from Pethick-Lawrence requesting casualty figures for Punjab, reporting that approximately 500 had been killed in Punjab's cities and towns, and 520 in rural areas, mostly non-Muslims. About 1,000 more people had been "seriously injured" in the recent Punjab riots.[18] The next day, Jenkins visited Attock and Rawalpindi and found some 25,000 terrified non-Muslim refugees and another 35,000 refugee villagers. "Attacks on non-Muslims have been organized with extreme savagery," he reported to Abell. "Deputy Commissioner Rawalpindi believes that in his district alone there may be 5,000 casualties including killed, injured and missing . . . feeling between communities is very bad indeed."[19] A few days after that, Punjab's Muslim League leader, Raja Ghazanfar Ali, came to see Jenkins to urge him to put a League ministry in power in Lahore. "I said I would resign sooner than see one [Muslim League ministry] in office at this juncture," Jenkins replied. "The massacre had been conducted in the name of the Muslim League, and senior Military Officers thought that it had been carefully planned and organised. Non-Muslims with some justice now regarded the Muslims as little better than animals. . . . If a Muslim League Government took office, there would be immediate fighting, and the Government would find it impossible to hold even a single session of the Assembly. . . . I said that the troubles of the Muslim League were due to folly and bad leadership."[20]

Punjab's Commanding General F. W. Messervy reported on those communal riots to Field Marshal Auchinleck:

> The Muslim League, though a political party, has been framing its main propaganda on religious lines. . . . Pakistan and Islam together provide an almost irresistible force on the minds of the mass of comparatively uneducated Muslims. When the intensive Muslim League campaign succeeded in forcing the resignation of the Unionist Punjab Government and was followed by militant anti-Pakistan statements by Master Tara Singh and other Sikh leaders, Muslim feelings were roused to a pitch of fanaticism. It only needed a spark to set alight the raging fires of religious passion. That was provided by anti-Pakistan meetings and processions.

Militant Hindus and Sikhs imprudently joined forces to march down Multan's main road, shouting "Death to Jinnah," raising angry fists, tossing their ragged torches onto communal tinder. "The fires spread rapidly," General Messervy added. "We are dealing with . . . disease and cannot eradicate the disease by military action. The disease comes from the political leaders of all parties. The only complete cure is for them to come to some agreement. . . . An agreement now between the Sikh and Muslim leaders would result in immediate peace. . . . Failing this unlikely contingency the avoidance of provocative statements . . . is the only hope."[21]

On Saturday, March 22, 1947, Lord and Lady Mountbatten and their daughter, Pamela, landed in Delhi. Nehru was waiting at the foot of their plane's ladder with a bouquet of red roses. They drove off together to New Delhi's Rashtrapati Bhavan ("President's House"), where outgoing Wavell waited to receive Mountbatten at the entrance of that palatial domicile of Britain's last few viceroys, soon to become home to independent India's presidents. Mountbatten and Wavell met that night at 10.30 p.m., attended by Ismay, Mieville, and Abell. Wavell, asked by Mountbatten what the next step should be, said, "Everything ultimately depended on securing the co-operation of both the major communities."[22] They discussed how difficult it was to get Indian politicians to "appreciate how little time there was to arrange the transfer of power before June, 1948, and the question was raised whether the partition of Punjab and Bengal could take place inside the Cabinet Mission's plan."[23] Mountbatten thought there was too much "complacency among Indian politicians and that it would be a good thing to have a list of awkward questions which would be put to them." They also discussed the importance of "pressing" the India Office " for quick decisions."

Two days after reaching India, Lord Mountbatten, resplendent in his medal-decked dress whites, the blue sash of the Order of the Garter draped over one broad shoulder, was sworn in as viceroy by British India's chief justice, in the marble domed Durbar Hall of the viceroy's house, filled with

Indian princes and Congress Party politicians, led by bright-eyed Nehru. A crimson canopy was spread over the gilded thrones of the handsome new viceroy and vicerene, whose diamond tiara and emerald jewels were captured by telephoto lenses that preserved each image of that first of many regal spectacles that were to mark Mountbatten's months at the helm of the British Raj.

"His Majesty's Government are resolved to transfer power by June 1948," the new viceroy told his hushed audience, "and since new constitutional arrangements must be made and many complicated questions of administration resolved—all of which will take time . . . a solution must be reached within the next few months. I believe that every political leader in India feels as I do the urgency of the task before us. . . . In the meantime every one of us must do what he can to avoid any word or action which might lead to further bitterness or add to the toll of innocent victims."[24]

Mountbatten met that afternoon with the Muslim Nawab of Bhopal, chancellor of the chamber of princes and an old friend of Jinnah's, who told him that "nothing" would induce Jinnah to join a unified government. The nawab hoped that a number of princely states might join forces to become an independent dominion, and asked about the possibility of buying arms from the UK or the United States. He also wondered if HMG might consider extending the time limit of retaining their powers over India beyond June 1948.[25] That same day, Mountbatten met with Nehru, who "struck me as most sincere." He asked Nehru about Jinnah, whose personality he disliked as much as his politics. Nehru, who himself had never really liked to practice law, even called him a "mediocre lawyer," though Jinnah was the most successful and possibly the most brilliant barrister of British India. He told Mountbatten that Jinnah's "creed" was to "refuse to hold meetings or to answer questions," and "never to make a progressive statement."[26] Nehru's negative assessment of Jinnah would never be erased from Mountbatten's mind and probably did more damage to Pakistan, influencing Mountbatten's decisions on the drawing of Partition's border lines in India's favor, than has been realized. Of course, Jinnah's refusal to accept Mountbatten's repeated offer to serve as Pakistan's governor-general, which Nehru so warmly invited him to do for India, was also important in tilting what should have been Great Britain's even-handed transfer of power balance in favor of India. Mountbatten informed Nehru, "I intended to approach the problem in an atmosphere of stark realism. In connection with the time factor, I pointed out that it took two years to separate Burma. I was less interested that India should be handed over on lines which might ultimately prove correct than that mechanism should be set up to avoid bloodshed after the departure of the British."[27]

Mountbatten's next interview was with Liaquat Ali Khan, "who gave me his version of how the Coalition Government has been formed—a totally different version to that rendered by Nehru—and quite untrue."[28] Mountbatten's deep trust of Nehru and negative feelings about Jinnah affected his view of Liaquat as well as of other leaders of the League. He also stressed "the time factor" to Liaquat and asked if he agreed that the Army was "the final guarantor of law and order," to which he did agree.

Mountbatten met with his staff on the morning of March 25 and reported that Nehru had suggested "a temporary partition" of Punjab into three areas, one Muslim, the other Hindu, the third "mixed." Nehru had noted that Jinnah was "much opposed to partition."[29] Lord Ismay doubted the "possibility of ever re-uniting the Punjab, once a partition, however temporary, was made." Sir Eric Mieville noted that some Sikhs had insisted on Punjab's partition, vowing to "resist" any Muslim ministry there. Mountbatten deferred further discussion and went to interview Sardar Patel, who was waiting. "He told me . . . to dismiss the Muslim League members of the Cabinet because . . . their 'direct action' resolution had the avowed intention of attacking the central organisation."[30]

At his fourth staff meeting on March 28, Mountbatten reported what Field Marshal Auchinleck had told him at dinner the night before, that it would take from five to ten years to divide the Indian Army. Non-Muslim parties would be much stronger if the army were communally divided, Hindus and Sikhs taking over general headquarters, major supply dumps and "a large majority" of officers.[31] Ismay added that there was not a single unit in the Indian Army that was totally Muslim.

That same day in London, the British cabinet listened to Lord Wavell's final assessment of the Indian situation. He claimed, astonishingly, that the situation in Punjab was "now in hand," but saw no alternative to governor's rule under Section 93, since Muslim rule was impossible and a coalition unlikely. Though Nehru advocated partition, Wavell considered it too difficult. Punjab's governor was worried about the safety of British families and might have to call for their evacuation. India's princes were now divided. Some were ready to join with the Congress Party and enter the constituent assembly, while the Nizam of Hyderabad expected the rich lands of Berar to be returned to his state when British power was finally transferred, and also insisted on having a suitable port. Wavell concluded by noting that "all sensible Indians were anxious for a pacific settlement but none were prepared to make concessions."[32]

Mountbatten met with his staff again on the morning of March 29 and stressed to them that the importance "of coming to the right decision very quickly will be very great: but it must be the right decision. . . . if a decision could be made quickly, it might well be possible to establish some form of Dominion status in India . . . he would return to London to see that solution put through. He felt that he had great powers to speed the process of legislation."[33] He was obsessed with the idea of speed, convinced that the best way to achieve his twin goals for India and for his naval career was to move with such swift assurance that every politician he met would be swept along with the plan. He had discussed dominion status with Nehru, who rejected the idea, as he and his Congress Party had done since the passage of their *Purna Swaraj* ("Complete Freedom") resolution in 1930, when Nehru first presided over his party. But Mountbatten knew that India's acceptance of dominion status was vital if he was to keep Churchill and his Tory Party happy with any agreement finally reached. He was also aware that keeping India in the British Commonwealth would ensure military cooperation and long-range defense agreements and contracts with the UK.

On March 31, Mahatma Gandhi arrived at 5 p.m. for his first meeting with Mountbatten. Lady Mountbatten remained with them for the first hour, all facing up to "a barrage of cameras, and then . . . purely social, friendly talks," Mountbatten noted. Gandhi " talked of his life in England, of his life in South Africa, his recent tour of Bihar, his discussions with former Viceroys and Members of the Cabinet."[34] Since Gandhi "promised to give me two hours every day for the rest of the week, I felt there was no hurry," Mountbatten added, "and deemed it advisable to let him talk along any lines that entered his mind." He clearly decided during this first meeting that prolix old Gandhi was too popular an iconic figure to offend by cutting him short, but that nothing he said was very practical or important enough to take seriously. When Gandhi returned for a second meeting the next day, he told Mountbatten that the "solution" to the recent communal conflicts that had shaken north India was to invite Jinnah to form a new central interim government with Muslim League members, replacing the current one led by Nehru. "I need not say that this solution . . . staggered me," Mountbatten reported. "I asked 'What would Mr. Jinnah say to such a proposal'? 'If you tell him I am the author he will reply 'Wily Gandhi.' I then remarked 'And I presume Mr. Jinnah will be right'? To which he replied with great fervour 'No, I am entirely sincere in my suggestion.'"[35]

That afternoon, Mountbatten told Nehru what Gandhi had said. "Nehru was not surprised . . . since this was the same solution that Mr. Gandhi had put up to the [1946] Cabinet Mission . . . [and] turned down then as being quite impracticable."[36] Nehru added that having been away from Delhi for the last four months, Gandhi was "out of touch with events at the Centre." Nehru then strongly opposed any fresh elections in Punjab, insisting they would only lead to more "bloodshed." Nehru favored the immediate partition of Punjab, calling Mountbatten's attention to a resolution passed by the Congress Party Working Committee to that effect on March 8, 1947, which Gandhi had vigorously opposed but failed to stop.[37] Nehru explained that "Gandhi was immensely keen on a unified India, at any immediate cost, for the benefit of the long term."[38] Mountbatten agreed with Nehru, for they were both most "keen" to avoid more bloodshed, and though they "recognised the high purpose which impelled him [Gandhi] to carry out . . . hopes of healing the sore spot in Bihar . . . as Pandit Nehru so aptly pointed out, Mr. Gandhi was going round with ointment trying to heal one sore spot after another on the body of India, instead of diagnosing the cause of this eruption of sores and participating in the treatment of the body as a whole. I entirely agreed," the viceroy added, "and said that it appeared I would have to be the principal doctor in producing the treatment for the body as a whole, and . . . he agreed." So those two brilliant, powerful men agreed on April Fool's Day of 1947 that a swift surgical "cure" dividing Punjab and Bengal would be India's best medicine for the dreadful sores of communal strife that kept erupting. Thus the knife was drawn that in four and a half brief months would "vivisect," as Mahatma Gandhi called it, "Mother India's body" politic.

In the interest of rushing everything to Partition's hasty conclusion, Mountbatten now urged Sardar Patel to persuade Gandhi to stop pressing the Congress ministry in Bihar to waste any time on an official "inquiry" into the massacre of Muslims that had taken place there. "I told him that the Governor of Bihar was against these inquiries; and that I shared the Governor's view. Sardar Patel promised to speak strongly to Mr. Gandhi on this subject."[39] On that same April 1, Mountbatten also sent off a swift wire to Governor Burrows of Bengal.

> I understand Suhrawardy has been pressing for inquiry into Bihar riots but does not wish to accept simultaneous inquiry into the East Bengal riots. . . My own view is that there should either be inquiries into both areas simultaneously or none at all. Personally I think there should be none at all since it is sufficiently established that the Muslims are responsible for the East Bengal riots and the Hindus responsible for the Bihar riots. Not only will inquiries take much time and cost much money, but . . . they are merely likely to arouse further communal feelings, I therefore trust you will do your best to get Suhrawardy to drop request, which in any case could not be granted unilaterally.[40]

He sent the same wire off to Bihar's governor, thus saving a great deal of time and squashing all shameful records of those monstrous murders and violations of human rights.

Gandhi returned again on April 2, and Mountbatten began by trying to explain to him that holding inquiries in Bihar and Bengal would only be "a waste of time and money, as well as a potential source of further communal strife." But Gandhi "flatly disagreed, and said that it was, in his opinion, essential that the Congress Government in Bihar should in all events show good faith by holding an inquiry which would reveal the appalling excesses committed by the Hindus in Bihar."[41] Gandhi was never as easy for Mountbatten to deal with as Nehru, and, after that first pleasant meeting filled with social chit-chat, the viceroy found the Mahatma more and more difficult and disagreeable. He finally agreed, however, that such riots were matters for the provincial governments to investigate, and he would discuss them with Sardar Patel.

"After this Mr. Gandhi came down firmly for his great plan. . . . He wants me to invite Mr. Jinnah to form a new Central Government . . . to which I am to turn over power. He suggests I should leave it to Mr. Jinnah," Mountbatten reported, but when he "twitted" the Mahatma for being insincere, Gandhi denied that "with burning sincerity." To prove how much he meant what he said and believed in his idea, Gandhi "volunteered to place his whole services at my disposal in trying to get the Jinnah Government through first by exercising his influence with Congress to accept it, and secondly by touring the length and breadth of the country getting all the peoples of India to accept the decision. . . . He agreed as to the supreme importance of complete secrecy, particularly as far as the Press were concerned."[42]

By convincing Gandhi of the "importance" of "complete secrecy" Mountbatten contrived to let that one and only plan, which might have saved India from the horrors of Partition and its aftermath, die stillborn. Mountbatten never breathed a word of Gandhi's idea to Jinnah, discussing it only with Azad and with Nehru, who never forgot that the man he had once considered his political guide, if not guru and Mahatma, so mistrusted him as to advise the viceroy to put his worst enemy into the position of premier power. It is, of course, possible that Jinnah would not have accepted the offer had it been made. But Mountbatten was so profoundly ignorant of the complexities he rushed into, and Nehru was so outraged by Gandhi's "treacherous" idea, that neither was willing to give it the chance of still saving India by proposing it to Jinnah.

Maulana Azad was the only other member of the Congress Party to whom Mountbatten spoke of Gandhi's radical plan, on April 2. "He staggered me by saying that in his opinion it was perfectly feasible of being carried out, since Gandhi could unquestionably influence the whole of Congress to accept it and work it loyally," Mountbatten recorded. "He further thought that there was a chance I might get Jinnah to accept it, and he thought that such a plan would be the quickest way to stop bloodshed, and the simplest way of turning over power."[43] Not only was Azad the only living Muslim former president of the Congress Party, but he personally had suffered Jinnah's harshest insults and slights, from the first Simla summit called by Wavell. Jinnah refused ever to shake Azad's hand, condemning him in public as a "Quisling Muslim," a "showcase Muslim." For Azad, nonetheless, to rise above such insults and honestly inform Lord Mountbatten that Jinnah was, indeed, the only Muslim to whom the vast majority of his fellow-Muslims throughout India would listen was a golden tribute to Azad's integrity and selflessness. Azad neither loved nor admired Pandit Nehru any less than he had before, but he was old enough and wise enough to know that Mahatma Gandhi's solution was the one and only chance to save India, and Maulana Azad, like Mahatma Gandhi, loved India and its people far more than he craved political power for himself or his dynastic heirs.

Lord Mountbatten, who knew more about the strengths and weaknesses of every member of his royal family and could recite the names and number of guns of every major ship of the line in the Royal Navy, understood little about Indian politics and nothing of the weaknesses or the strengths of India's major leaders. He considered Jinnah "mediocre" and "negative," as well as passe, for that was what Nehru had told him, and he found Nehru charming and wise, and just as importantly admired and trusted by Krishna Menon and Lady Edwina. As for Gandhi, everyone said he was a saint, of course, but nation-states were only run by strong men like Nehru and himself, not by half-naked old fakirs. Churchill and Wavell were right about Gandhi, a "treacherous" old "fool," Mountbatten now sensed, especially since he kept pushing Jinnah for Nehru's job—proof positive of how "far out of it" he was, as Nehru had rightly noted.

Mountbatten met Jinnah for the first time on April 5, finding him "most frigid, haughty and disdainful," though more convivial the next evening. Jinnah told him that a "surgical operation" on India, creating Pakistan, was the only way to keep India from perishing.[44] At their April 8 meeting, Mountbatten asked Jinnah why he had called for direct action the previous year, and Jinnah "denied that they had ever instigated bloodshed," insisting that the "Congress had started bloodshed."[45] Asked what his solution for India would be, Jinnah replied "Pakistan, together with a splitting of the Defence Forces." Mountbatten argued that if he accepted Jinnah's logic for the need to partition India, it would also be necessary to partition Punjab and Bengal. Jinnah protested most vigorously against being offered a "moth eaten" Pakistan, arguing strongly that Bengalis and Punjabis were united by their common languages and history. Mountbatten agreed that was true, but even more true of India as a whole. "I am afraid I drove the old gentleman quite mad." Gandhi also felt "most disappointed" by now at Mountbatten's disdainful dismissal of his plan, which had been turned over to Ismay for review and staff criticism. "Mr. Gandhi . . . was hoping for a Mountbatten-Gandhi pact!" Mountbatten told the King. "I have written to him making it clear that at the present stage I have no intention of making up my mind on the solution . . . and that it would be premature to prepare any cut and dried plan."[46] He had, in fact, already made up his mind to sink Gandhi's plan, having no more faith in Gandhi than he had in Jinnah. Years enough had been "wasted" on both by Cripps and Wavell. His mission's plan was clear enough to him now: cut and run, full speed ahead.

On the morning of April 10, Mountbatten told his staff of the "solution, which not only would do justice, but would also make it clear in the eyes of the world that justice was being done. . . It was also important that the Indian people should take the onus of making a decision. Thus Britain could not then be blamed after the event."[47] Punjab and Bengal would be "partitioned," and Jinnah would be offered his moth-eaten Pakistan, but "no mention of Pakistan as such should be made in the announcement giving the plan for India's future." Every one in the Congress Party (except Gandhi), after all, was ready to let Jinnah have his fragmented state as the price of getting rid of him. Nehru and Krishna Menon agreed to it; that was good enough for Mountbatten.

Unable to convince either Nehru or Mountbatten of the wisdom of his plan, Gandhi left for Bihar's capital, Patna, on April 11, hoping he would be able to persuade the Congress government there to launch an investigation into the mass murders of Muslims in that province. But he had no more success in Patna than he had had in Delhi, so he moved on to Bengal's Noakhali District, where many rural Hindus were reportedly being murdered or forcibly converted to Islam. For the next few weeks Gandhi walked barefoot from one small village in East Bengal to another, repeating his message of "non-violent love" (*Ahimsa*) as God, appealing to all who saw and heard him to stop killing one another. He blessed Muslims and Hindus alike, briefly dowsing flames of hate with his fearless presence and calm visage, though as soon as he was out of sight, petty fears and old hatreds erupted into conflict. Bengal's total population at this time was some 60 million, most of whom were Muslims, though about 24 million Hindus dominated the western region. Suhrawardy hoped to lead Bengal to independent dominion statehood, urging Governor Burrows and Mountbatten to help him create an undivided *Bangla Desh*, "Land of Bengali-speakers," in 1947. Nehru and his powerful Bengali Hindu cabinet colleague, Dr. Shyama Prasad Mookerji, refused to consider giving up Calcutta or the Hindu-populace of West Bengal, however, insisting instead on partition. Mookerji led the "Great Hindu-Party" (Hindu *Mahasabha)*, political precursor of modern India's *Bharatiya Janata* ("Indian People's") Party and its more militant wing, Vishva Hindu Parishad. He raised an army of ardent Hindu volunteers, who marched around Calcutta demanding a "Hindu homeland" in Bengal. He became the most eloquent advocate in Nehru's cabinet of a religiously "pure" Hindu *Bharat*, India's Sanskrit name. Local Hindu leaders were afraid to pit themselves against Mookerji or Nehru, so although most preferred to keep Bengal united and independent, they "subordinated" their Bangladeshi "nationalism to communalism."[48]

Two weeks later, Mountbatten asked Jinnah what he thought of Suhrawardy's proposal to create a separate sovereign Bengal, expecting him to be shocked at his Muslim League lieutenant's "treachery." Much to Mountbatten's surprise, Jinnah calmly replied, "I should be delighted. What is the use of Bengal without Calcutta; they had much better remain united and independent; I am sure they would be on friendly terms with us."[49] And when Mountbatten added that Suhrawardy said Bengal would wish to remain within the British Commonwealth, Jinnah retorted, "Of course, just as I indicated to you that Pakistan would wish to remain within the Commonwealth." Had Mountbatten followed the advice of Gandhi, Jinnah, or Suhrawardy, instead of listening only to Nehru, Punjab and Bengal might have been spared their deadly horrors, and a richly united Bangladesh, with its capital in Calcutta, would have emerged instead of the fragmented, impoverished Bangladesh born from its eastern half a quarter century later.

In mid-April, Mountbatten invited all of India's governors to meet with him and his staff in Delhi, informing them that "the dominating impression which he had gathered since his arrival was the necessity for a very early decision on how power was to be transferred."[50] No Indian leader, except for Pandit Nehru, Mountbatten told them, realized what a "terrifying problem" it was to figure out how to hand over so much power by June of 1948. He confessed that Prime Minister Attlee had told him "that he was not to attempt to devote himself to looking after British interests during his Viceroyalty. He was, in fact, to regard himself less as the last British Viceroy than as the first head of the new Indian State." That, he said, was why he invited "an ever growing proportion of Indians to the parties in Viceroy's House." Mountbatten stressed to his governors that "it was of the utmost importance that, in the eyes of the world, it should be Indian opinion rather than a British decision which made the choice as to the future."[51] He then added that in his opinion "partition of India would be a most serious potential source of war . . . [and] that a quick decision would also give Pakistan a greater chance to fail on its demerits. The great problem was to reveal the limits of Pakistan so that the Muslim League could revert to an unified India with honour."

John Tyson, who represented Governor Burrows, informed Mountbatten that if Bengal was partitioned, "Eastern Bengal alone was not a going concern and never would be. It could not feed itself. . . . It would become, in Sir Frederick Burrows' words, a 'rural slum' . . . Muslims knew all this as well as the Hindus—so they felt that the object of the cry to partition Bengal was to 'torpedo' Pakistan."[52] Mountbatten replied, "Anything that resulted in 'torpedoing' Pakistan was of advantage in that it led the way back to a more common-sense solution." He then added "he wished to make it quite clear that he was in no way opposed to the Muslim League and pro-Congress."[53]

Britain's high commissioner to India, Sir Terrence Shone, was asked by Mountbatten to meet with Jinnah and found him "unbending" in his demand for Pakistan. He also insisted that Pakistan must have its own army, and viewed the proposed division of Bengal and Punjab as "a red herring."[54] Jinnah argued that with 60 percent of Bengal's population Muslim and only half of the remaining 40 percent "caste Hindus" (the rest being untouchables) the threat of offering him a "moth-eaten" Pakistan was ridiculous. As for Punjab, he insisted that its 3.5 million Sikhs would be "making a great mistake" if they refused his offer to join Pakistan, since if Punjab were divided, the line would be drawn through their rural heartland. He had promised Tara Singh whatever he "wanted," but as Jinnah told Shone, Sikhs were "in many ways admirable people," only "they lacked leadership of a high order."[55]

By mid-April Mountbatten informed Pethick-Lawrence that "partition is probably inevitable."[56] In his third personal weekly report to his cousin the king and Prime Minister Attlee, Mountbatten went into greater detail, stressing the "unsettled state of the whole country," especially the riots in Punjab and the North-West Frontier Province. His "incessant talks" with Indian leaders of all parties had "convinced" him that "we have got to make up our minds."[57] Mountbatten's mind was already made up, and he planned to meet with the major party leaders in Simla on May 15. He would invite Nehru and Jinnah and ask them to bring their working committees as well. "I shall have to fire my last shot in the shape of our announcement of partition," he decided.[58] He saw no point in waiting any longer. He was India's "best surgeon," after all, and believed that the sooner he performed major surgery on its body politic the better it would be for all concerned.

Pethick-Lawrence, frustrated and depressed at Mountbatten's failure to listen to his advice to slow down, resigned the day Mountbatten wrote that report, and Attlee informed the viceroy that the Fifth Earl of Listowel, who had served as parliamentary under secretary of state for India for two years, would now take over the India Office. Young "Billy" Listowel was easy for Mountbatten to work with, posing no challenges to the hastily accelerated timetable or the ill-considered disastrous plan to partition both major multicommunal provinces.

Krishna Menon met with Mountbatten on the evening of April 17 to discuss ways to work out a formula acceptable both to India and Britain for retaining British officers in India's army after independence. Since the term "dominion status" had been rejected by the Congress Party in 1930, the problem was how to change the name, yet keep India's connection to Britain's Crown. They agreed that Commonwealth was much easier for Congress to accept, as would be "Union of India," which the constituent assembly finally drafted into its constitution. Menon also agreed that if Great Britain offered India "dominion status, well ahead of June 1948, we should be so grateful that not a voice would be heard . . . suggesting any change."[59] Krishna Menon was eager to become free India's first high commissioner in London, the job Nehru promised him, and Mountbatten was willing to agree to remain in Delhi for a few months as the first governor general of the Dominion of India, as long as he could be back in the royal navy by June 1948. Mountbatten also used the "threat" that Pakistan was willing to remain in the Commonwealth to help convince Nehru's Congress to agree to "take the plunge."[60]

Mountbatten asked Ismay to fly to London in early May to brief the cabinet on his plan. "He emphasized that the need for speed had arisen from the deplorable deterioration in the situation over the last eight months. It was evident that . . . members of the Cabinet Mission did not realise the situation produced by this deterioration. For all they knew . . . they might as well have got back to London in 1895."[61] Ismay met with the India committee of the cabinet on May 5, informing them that "the Viceroy had found the communal feeling in India was far more bitter than he had expected." His proposals, Ismay explained, were "designed to place the responsibility for dividing India conspicuously on the Indians themselves."[62] The viceroy hoped to meet Indian leaders no later than May 20 and hoped "to make them admit openly that there was no possibility of securing agreement on a unified India."[63]

Gandhi tried once again to stop the juggernaut about to be unleashed. "Whatever may be said to the contrary," the Mahatma wrote to "Dear Friend" Mountbatten on May 8, "it would be a blunder of first magnitude for the British to be a party in any way whatsoever to the division of India."[64] One of the things Mountbatten had urged Ismay to assure the British cabinet was that all of India's leaders either "acquiesced" or "seemed to be reconciled to some form of partition," but clearly that was not the case. Now the Mahatma wrote: "I feel sure that partition of the Punjab and Bengal is wrong in every case and a needless irritant for the League. . . . Whilst the British power is functioning in India, it must be held principally responsible for the preservation of peace. . . . If you are not to leave a legacy of chaos behind, you have to make your choice and leave the government of the whole of India including the States to one party."[65] Mountbatten wrote to "thank" Gandhi for that letter, but ignored it. His mind was firmly made up.

On May 10, Mountbatten invited Nehru, Jinnah, Patel, Liaquat, and Baldev Singh to meet with him in Delhi one week later to "have a final talk" about "certain conclusions, with which I have reason to believe H. M. G.

will agree."[66] Nehru now felt grave misgivings about some of those "conclusions." With characteristic ambivalence, he admitted: "I am anxious . . . that in our hurry a wrong step might not be taken. . . . I find that my mind is not at all clear about the various possible developments. . . . [W]e have to consider carefully what the final outcome might be. I confess that I do not see much light and many things trouble me."[67] He had just learned of Gandhi's strong negative reactions, as well as some misgivings expressed by Sardar Patel. "I read the draft proposals you gave me," Nehru wrote Mountbatten a day later. "I reacted to them very strongly. . . . [T]he Cabinet Mission's scheme and subsequent developments were set aside, and an entirely new picture presented—a picture of fragmentation and conflict and disorder. . . . [T]hese proposals . . . I am convinced, will be resented and bitterly disliked all over the country."[68]

Cripps, too, became very concerned about the new plan Ismay had presented. "I have been and am very worried about the Punjab part of our plan," he wrote to Attlee on May 10. "I think we have gone a long way . . . but we must remember that the Sikhs can bust this arrangement as well as Jinnah! If we were to adopt Dickie's last alternative and hand over the Punjab to the Muslims that would mean immediate civil war. We must in the last resort divide out the Sikhs somehow or we shall never get through."[69] But it was too late. There was no time for that, so one and a half million Sikhs would be trapped in the western Pakistan-half of Punjab in mid-August, only three months away.

Mountbatten and his wife had driven Nehru and Krishna Menon up to Simla in early May for a "quite glorious" week of relaxation and some last minute work on his partition and transfer of power plan, which Ismay had taken to London. Nehru suddenly feared now that "India was being balkanised. . . . [T]he Cabinet Mission's plan . . . completely thrown away . . . gave rise to the idea that there was nothing final in H. M. G.'s announcements . . . no assurances of what was going to happen."[70] It unnerved him, but he "personally hoped that the conception of Partition would recede."[71] Nehru failed as yet to realize that Mountbatten's plan to partition India was steaming full speed ahead. Mountbatten wired Attlee that evening to inform him that he would meet with all the important political leaders on June 2 to confirm his plan, rather than on May 17. "I am sorry about this especially after the splendid way the Cabinet Committee have worked to meet earlier date."[72] Pethick-Lawrence was gone and Cripps remained unhappy, but the rest of the cabinet were almost as eager as Mountbatten to be rid of their Indian albatross and to extricate His Majesty's Government without too much pain or enduring blame.

Mountbatten wired Ismay later that same night, to be sure he had HMG's "general approval to the line which I am taking. You must make them realise that speed is the essence of the contract. Without speed, we will miss the opportunity. . . . I am convinced that, in order to have the best chance of obtaining our long-term object, the grant of Dominion Status must take place during 1947."[73] And what was that "object?" He spelled out all the "advantages" he assumed would accrue to Great Britain from his speedy operation: "(a) the terrific world-wide enhancement of British prestige and . . . of the present Government. (b) the completion of the framework of world strategy from the point of view of Empire defence. (c) the early termination of present responsibilities, especially in the field of law and order. . . . (d) A further strengthening of Indo-British relations which have enormously improved."[74] There were some "complications" perhaps "resulting from the partition of India," but nothing worth slowing down for.

Lord Ismay met with the chiefs of staff next day to brief them on "the political background" which led to Mountbatten's new plan. "Communal feeling dominated and influenced the whole attitude and outlook," he told them. "It was far worse than he had imagined. . . . The outlook of the leading politicians was entirely coloured by race hatred."[75] Unless an announcement was made very soon, he feared, there would be "civil war." Even though most leaders agreed with the new plan, there might be "the risk of disorders" in Punjab and Bengal, as a result of partition. There was no contingency for dealing with that "risk" in Mountbatten's plan, so those "disorders" were soon to leave approximately one million Hindus, Muslims, and Sikhs dead. The chiefs of staff agreed that from a strategic point of view there were many advantages to allowing western Pakistan to remain within the Commonwealth. Those included strategic facilities in "the port of Karachi, air bases and support of Moslem manpower . . . the continued integrity of Afghanistan . . . our prestige . . . throughout the Moslem world."[76] British martial "presence in Pakistan" would also have "a stabilising effect on India as a whole, and . . . the frontier might well become more settled," they thought.

Cripps remained unhappy about the plan, and, after Nehru wrote to complain about several details, he offered to fly out to Delhi to speak to Mountbatten unless the viceroy could fly home, which he immediately agreed to do. Before leaving, Mountbatten tried to persuade Jinnah and Liaquat to sign a copy of his proposed final plan, indicating their agreement to it, but both adamantly refused. Mountbatten told the cabinet on May 19 that "it had become clear that the Muslim League would resort to arms if Pakistan in some form were not conceded. In the face of this threat, the Congress leaders had modified their former attitude; indeed, they were now inclined to feel that it would be to their advantage to be relieved of responsibility for the Provinces that would form Pakistan, while at the same time they were confident that those Provinces would ultimately have to seek re-union with the remainder of India."[77] Mountbatten added that though Jinnah would be happy for Pakistan to remain in the Commonwealth, Congress insisted on becoming an independent republic, and he had since been at great pains to explain to them the advantages of remaining a dominion instead, which he believed they would now agree to do, but only if all British power was transferred this year. The viceroy then proposed that an immediate announcement be made of HMG's intention to grant dominion status to both India and Pakistan.

Prime Minister Attlee would first have to inform the leader of the opposition, Winston Churchill, of these sudden changes and momentous proposals, seeking his cooperation. He would then have to invite the lord chancellor and law officers to enact appropriate legislation, amending the Government of India Act of 1935 to allow two new dominions to be born in 1947.

On May 17, Jinnah made one final attempt to warn Mountbatten and the British cabinet against partitioning Bengal and Punjab.

> The Muslim League cannot agree to the partition of Bengal and the Punjab. . . . It cannot be justified historically, economically, geographically, politically or morally. These provinces have built up their respective lives for nearly a century. . . . The principle underlying the demand for establishment of Pakistan and Hindustan is totally different . . . [I]n the name of justice and fair play, [do] not submit . . . to this clamour. For it will be sowing the seeds of future serious trouble and the results will be disastrous for the life of these two provinces.[78]

But human frailty and the pressures of time, compounded by the growing burden of Britain's sterling debt to India as the economic legacy of World War II, had so swiftly eroded British support for their once glorious empire that few members of Parliament cared enough about India or Pakistan to pay attention to the worthy warnings of Jinnah or of Gandhi, the only two leaders left who could see where the rush to Partition would lead all of South Asia.

Churchill also understood what Jinnah meant, of course, but realized too late just how much damage Mountbatten's frenzied rush to retreat would inflict on moth-eaten Pakistan and the princes he loved and admired. A year later, Mountbatten came home to a hero's welcome in London. Anthony Eden threw a grand Tory party for him, to which Churchill was invited. When Mountbatten saw "Winston," he headed toward him with open arms and a warm smile on his face. "Dickie, stand there!" Churchill shouted, pointing a paralyzing finger at his admiral's jacket, instantly bringing the taller man to a halt. "What you did in India was like whipping your riding crop across my face!"[79] The noisy room had fallen so silent that Churchill's stentorian voice could be clearly heard by every ear in Westminster. The older man turned on his heel and strode out of the room, never speaking again to Mountbatten for seven years.

Sir Eric Mieville met with Jinnah several times in May, and on May 20 he wired Mountbatten in London: "Jinnah . . . told me that he thought we were going too fast. . . . At the end of our talk he took my arm and said 'I am not speaking as a Partisan, but I beg you to tell Lord Mountbatten once again that he will be making a grave mistake if he agrees to the partition of Bengal and the Punjab."[80] To no avail. Mountbatten neither listened nor responded. On the evening of May 20 Mountbatten met with the cabinet's India committee again and told them he had just received word from Governor Burrows of Bengal that Suhrawardy and Bengal's Congress Party leader K. S. Roy had reached agreement that would allow them to unite in governing a "Free State of Bengal," which the governor agreed was "the only chance of averting grave disturbances in Bengal."[81] Instead of warmly supporting that option Mountbatten crushed it, negatively noting that it would "involve the establishment of a third Dominion, with all the further complications," wasting too much time.[82]

Punjab's Governor Jenkins reported that same May 21 from Lahore that "Muslims seem determined to burn Hindus and Sikhs out of greater Lahore and are concentrating on incendiarism. Hindus and Sikhs are retaliating in kind but are concentrating mainly on acquisition of arms with a view to personal vengeance."[83] Old Lahore's narrow streets and lanes made it all but impossible for fire trucks to come close enough to put out the flames, and police were too "tired" and inadequate for the job of maintaining order. Troops were urgently needed, and Jenkins had appealed to the army commander, as Sardar Patel had to Acting Viceroy Colville. Patel reminded Colville that "Lord Mountbatten gave the assurance that in future such disturbances would be put down with an iron hand."[84] But Mountbatten was too busy in London to worry about arson and murder in the streets of Lahore.

Mountbatten told the cabinet on May 22 that after returning to India, he would give the Congress Party and the Muslim League twenty-four hours to consult their working committees about his plan, which he would present to them on June 2. He would invite Nehru and Jinnah to broadcast announcements the next day, appealing to their parties to cooperate in working the plan. He said his "prospects of securing agreement and a quick decision" would be much enhanced if the cabinet would give him "discretion to settle . . . points of minor importance" without reference to London. The cabinet agreed, caught up in the magic web of speed and rush their viceroy wove. Several cabinet members expressed concern about what the governor of Punjab had said, but Mountbatten reassured them that "no solution could now be found which would not result in some disorder."[85]

There were still a few questions about potential "disorders" in Punjab at the next day's cabinet meeting, which Mountbatten allayed, explaining that "the only hope of checking widespread communal warfare was to suppress the first signs of it promptly and ruthlessly, using . . . all the force required, including tanks and aircraft."[86] He never did that, but he sounded so firm in his promise that Attlee ended his cabinet meeting with a "tribute to the remarkable skill and initiative which the Viceroy had shown in his conduct of these difficult negotiations with the Indian leaders."[87]

In Delhi that same day, Nehru wrote Acting Viceroy Colville, urging immediate martial action against the "complete lack of control" in Lahore, some parts of which were "reduced to ashes."[88] Since March 4, some 3,600 Punjabis were officially reported to have died violently, most of them non-Muslims murdered in Lahore and Rawalpindi, though most of the latter's dead had not as yet been counted. On May 26, Liaquat Ali Khan visited Government House in Lahore, to meet with Governor Jenkins's secretary, insisting that the Muslims were "not the aggressors, but the present administration in the Punjab was bitterly hostile to them."[89]

Mieville met with Nehru on May 27 and "I asked him how he viewed . . . an independent Bengal. He reacted strongly and said there was no chance of the Hindus there agreeing to put themselves under permanent Muslim domination, which was what the proposed agreement really amounted to. He did not, however, rule out the possibility of the whole of Bengal joining up with Hindustan."[90] The next morning Mountbatten told the cabinet that since Nehru had been quoted in the press as insisting that the Congress Party would only agree to Bengal remaining united if it joined the Union of India that "gravely prejudiced" any chance of establishing a third dominion of Bengal.[91] Governor Burrows wired Mountbatten that day to brief him on the "prospects" of a coalition in Bengal. Suhrawardy had just gone to Delhi with Bengal's Congress Party leader, Kiran Shankar Roy, to meet with their respective party leaders, and Burrows shared "Suhrawardy's apprehension that, if Nehru and Patel prove adamant, Roy is not the man to move them and Bengal will be sacrificed on the altar of Nehru's All-India outlook."[92] This is precisely what happened. Gandhi had been willing to help Bengal win its peaceful independence, and most of the Hindus in east Bengal would have much preferred that to partition, but Nehru's insistence that West Bengal's Hindu majority districts and Calcutta must remain in India's Union sealed Bengal's fate. Mountbatten agreed with Nehru's judgment that eastern Bengal was "likely to be a great embarrassment to Pakistan" and "bound sooner or later to rejoin India."[93] A quarter century later, thanks to Indo-Soviet arms and support in the 1971 Indo-Pak War, the impoverished independent state of Bangladesh would emerge out of what had hitherto been East Pakistan.

Mountbatten wired his governors on May 31 to report that before flying to London, "It was clear to me that if we waited till constitutions for both Hindustan and Pakistan had been framed and all the negotiations about partition settled we should have to wait a very long time, and things would get more difficult. . . . There would be likely to be chaos in June 1948. . . . British troops will probably be withdrawn directly after the transfer of power. . . . We must go ahead at once with provisional administrative plans for partition." With staggering disingenuousness he told them: "I have left H. M. G. in no doubt about the possible dangers and difficulties. These are now fully appreciated at home. But H. M. G. are confident they can rely on all of us to do our best."[94]

Mountbatten met with his staff on the afternoon of June 1 and reported that he had just seen the Nawab of Bhopal, who still served as chancellor of the chamber of princes, and told him about the plan, pledging him to secrecy. "He had asked whether it was intended that Dominion status should be granted to the States. . . . The Viceroy said that . . . this was not the intention of His Majesty's Government. . . . The Nawab . . . complained that His Majesty's Government had once more let the States down . . . and . . . declared that he would not join either Constituent Assembly in these circumstances."[95] The Maharaja of Bikaner state, however, had already joined the Congress Party constituent assembly with several other Hindu princes, and Mountbatten suspected that no more than a handful of states, including a few others under Muslim rulers, like Hyderabad and Mysore, would follow the Nawab of Bhopal's lead in this regard. He intended to meet with the states negotiating committee on June 4 to speak with them about his plan. Sir Eric Mieville pointed out that any state which failed to join either constituent assembly "would be outside the British Commonwealth and no longer eligible for decorations."[96] Most Indian princes were very proud of their British decorations and enjoyed other princely privileges whenever they went to London to receive such honors.

Suhrawardy and Roy failed to convince the Congress high command to agree to allowing Bengal to become independent, but Suhrawardy still hoped to persuade them to agree that Calcutta be left as "a free city. Otherwise he feared that nothing he could do would prevent riots and great damage in the City before partition."[97] Mountbatten sent his reforms commissioner, V. P. Menon, to appeal to Sardar Patel on his behalf to allow Calcutta to remain under the joint control of India and Pakistan for six months. "Not even for six hours!" Patel replied.[98]

On the morning of June 2, Mountbatten met around a small table in the Viceroy's House with the most important leaders of Congress and the League, assuring them that what they decided that day would have "a profound influence on world history . . . not only India."[99] He told them that before coming to India as viceroy he had been given "no indication in London of the necessity for speed in formulating proposals for the transfer of power. . . . However, from the moment of his arrival [in Delhi] a terrific sense of urgency had been impressed upon him by everybody. . . . He had come to realise that the sooner power was transferred the better it would be."

During his most recent London visit, Mountbatten told them how "very impressed" he was by the "intense feeling of goodwill for India." He was "most distressed," however, about the "position of the Sikhs. . . . He had repeatedly asked the Sikhs whether they desired the partition of the Punjab, as they were so spread over that Province that any partition would necessarily divide their community."[100] Of course, they always told him "they did . . . but it was apparent that there would be frightful difficulties. . . . The Boundary Commission, on which Sikh interests would of course be represented, would have to work out the best . . . solution." Then he turned to Calcutta, where again there were many difficulties, but "[h]e had done his best, while in London, to be [the] advocate of the different party issues on Calcutta, but the definite decision of the Cabinet had been that no exception . . . could be made in this case."[101]

He then stressed "the supreme need for secrecy" until his plan had been approved in Britain's House of Commons. All present promised to keep it secret. He asked Jinnah and Nehru to take copies of the statement that would be made by His Majesty's Government to show to their working committees, but to let him know, no later than midnight, what they thought of it. He then asked them all to "accept" his plan "in a peaceful spirit and to make it work without bloodshed."[102]

Nehru asked for Mountbatten's definition of "the difference between agreement and acceptance. . . . The Viceroy explained that agreement would imply belief that the right principles were being employed. . . . What he asked was for acceptance, in order to denote belief that the plan was a fair and sincere solution for the good of the country. . . . Nehru stated that there could never be complete approval of the plan from Congress, but . . . they accepted it."[103] Jinnah then said that "neither side agreed with certain points in the plan. . . . The decision could not be left to the leaders and the Working Committee . . . alone. . . . [They] would have to bring the people round. Much explanation would be necessary. . . . [H]e would rather say that the plan had been fully examined and that they would do their best to see that the proposals were effected peacefully." To Mountbatten, that was enough. He was "willing to take the risk of accepting the words of the leaders," for he was "completely confident" in their "loyalty and straightforwardness."

Jinnah, however, persisted in saying that "to give a definite answer, it was necessary to make the people understand. The Muslim League was a democratic organisation. He and his Working Committee would have to go before their masters, the people, for a final decision."[104] Lord Mountbatten, always thinking first as a martial, rather than a political, leader, replied that "there were times when leaders had to make vital decisions without consulting their followers." But Jinnah continued to shake his weary head, unable to understand why this Englishman was in such a dreadful rush, when it was so clear to him how dangerously destructive to countless Punjabi and Bengali lives this hastily ill-conceived new plan would be.

Mahatma Gandhi came to see Mountbatten separately that day, as he had not been invited to the meeting convened with the most "important" Congress leaders. Since it was his "silent day" (Monday), Gandhi did not speak, but handed Mountbatten a note written in pencil on the backs of five old envelopes. "I am sorry I can't speak. . . . But I know you do not want me to break my silence. Have I said one word against you during my speeches? . . . There are one or two things I must talk about, but not today. If we meet again, I shall speak."[105] The Mahatma knew too well what the viceroy thought of him, how little he valued his words of wisdom, so he would waste as few as possible now. If neither of his two oldest political disciples, Patel and Nehru, listened to him any more, then why should this foreign admiral? Silence was, indeed, golden.

"Both Nehru and Jinnah gave me their personal assurances. . . .[T]hey were prepared to do their utmost to make it [the plan] work in a practical and peaceful spirit . . . without bloodshed," Mountbatten euphorically wired Secretary of State Listowel that evening. "God must be on our side, since Gandhi, who came to see me after the conference (presumably to implement his declared policy of stopping the present agreement) was afflicted by a day of silence."[106] Jinnah returned to see Mountbatten at 11 p.m. and remained until midnight arguing in vain for more time to give his League members a chance to consider this plan, but the viceroy would not wait. He merely urged Jinnah to "support me personally." But Jinnah refused to invite Mountbatten to become the dominion of Pakistan's first governor-general, as Nehru had invited him to be for India.

On the morning of June 3, Mountbatten convened another meeting of those same leaders and told them that though all their parties "had raised a number of points in the Plan with which they . . . could not be in complete agreement," he considered that all of them had "accepted" it "in principle," which is what he wired to Attlee.[107] Then on the morning of June 3 in London, Attlee's cabinet met, and "the Prime Minister informed the Cabinet that the Viceroy had reported that the plan for the transfer of power in India had been favourably received by the leaders of the . . . political parties."[108] The cabinet then "invited the Prime Minister to convey to the Viceroy on their behalf a message of congratulation on the successful outcome of his negotiations."

The last Chukka was over. Dickie's team had won.

8

Partitioned Transfer of Power, June–August 1947

O N THE NIGHT OF JUNE 3, after Nehru had swallowed the bitter pill of Partition, he broadcast the news over All-India Radio to his friends and comrades. "The sands of time run out and decisions cannot await the normal course of events. . . . We have, therefore, decided to accept these proposals. . . . It is with no joy in my heart that I commend these proposals to you. . . . For generations we have . . . struggled for a free and independent united India. The proposals to allow certain parts to secede, if they so will, is painful for any of us to contemplate. . . . It may be that in this way we shall reach that united India sooner than otherwise."[1] He vainly hoped, as did Sardar Patel, that Pakistan would prove insolvent after it was born and, in the not-too-distant future, Jinnah and Liaquat would beg forgiveness and ask for permission to rejoin India's union. He continued: "There has been violence—shameful, degrading and revolting violence—in various parts of the country. This must end. . . . We must make it clear that political ends are not to be achieved by methods of violence now or in the future."

Jinnah also broadcast nationwide that evening, his eloquent high-pitched voice sounding more English than Nehru's. "I most earnestly appeal to every community and particularly to Moslems in India to maintain peace and order. We must examine the plan . . . and come to our conclusions and take our decisions. . . . It is clear the plan does not meet in some important respects our point of view. . . . It is for us to consider whether the plan as presented to us by His Majesty's Government should be accepted by us. . . . The decision of the Council of the All India Moslem League . . . can only be taken . . . according to our constitution."[2] He ended by "most earnestly" appealing to all "to maintain peace and order. *Pakistan Zindabad* [Victory to Pakistan]." Englishmen, who misunderstood that Urdu phrase, thought he said, "Pakistan's in the bag!" Sardar Patel, distressed over Jinnah's remarks, protested to Mountbatten the "abuse . . . of the hospitality extended to him by the All-India Radio . . . by making a political, partisan and propagandist broadcast."[3]

But the next morning it was Mahatma Gandhi who sounded most disturbed, Krishna Menon reported to Mountbatten in a "Very Urgent" letter. Gandhi asked for a private meeting with Mountbatten, and Krishna urged the viceroy to reassure the Mahatma that all "the perils" over which "he is distressed" were uppermost in Mountbatten's mind. "I think that much can be done to allay his reasonable anxieties. . . . It is a pity that he will speak about them today. . . . Jawaharlal also had talks with me about the 'hereafter' and wants me to talk them over with you. . . . I shall . . . come over whenever required."[4] Nehru promised to appoint Krishna Menon India's first "Ambassador" (high commissioner) to England, and Krishna was eager to report that "vital hereafter" news.

Mountbatten met the press on June 4, telling them: "My own feeling was that a united India was, of course, the right answer but only if communal feeling and goodwill allowed it. So, while I did my best to get the Cabinet Mission scheme accepted . . . the riots and bloodshed throughout the country made the prospects of its acceptance obviously pretty remote."[5] He reported that he had learned from meetings with leaders of the League as well as the Congress Party "that the people of India should take it upon themselves to make up their own minds what they wanted to do for the future of their country." Clearly, the best way to ascertain that would have been by "the adult franchise plebiscite," for that was the "democratic" way, Mountbatten conceded. Only "such a process was utterly impracticable . . . when we wanted a very quick answer and speed was the one thing which everybody desired." Mountbatten clearly equated himself with "everybody."

He was particularly anxious to try to explain how he had agreed to partition the Punjab, knowing full well it would cut the Sikh community in half. " I found that it was mainly at the request of the Sikh community that Congress had put forward the Resolution on the partition of the Punjab. . . . I was not aware of all the details . . . but when I sent for a map and studied the distribution of the Sikh population under this proposal, I must say I was astounded to find that the plan which they had produced divided their community into two almost equal parts. I have spent a great deal of time . . . seeing whether there was any solution which would keep the Sikh community more together. . . . I am not a miracle worker and I have not found that solution."[6] His confession that he had approved a plan affecting the lives of millions of people without knowing "the details" or looking at a map reflecting his monumental ignorance of the dangers and indifference to the consequences of Partition were hallmarks of his tenure in India. But his ego made him add how many "solutions" he had found "in the course of these very high-speed talks," when it "became apparent" to him that "all leaders wanted speed in the actual transfer of power . . . anxious to assume their full responsibility at the earliest possible moment." Perhaps unaware of his own confession, he rhetorically asked, "Why should we wait? Waiting would only mean that I should be responsible ultimately for law and order."[7] Mountbatten understood by then how impossibly ugly and crushingly difficult a job that would become, how far beyond him, and deleterious to his royal reputation and to that of the British Raj.

He concluded by promising that British "power will be transferred as completely this year as it ever would have been by June 1948. . . . This Bill will be rushed through in record time . . . a legislative record . . . because of the measure of extreme goodwill that exists . . . in England today . . . for the good of India."[8] Master of doublespeak that he was, Mountbatten thus turned "abject disinterest" into "extreme goodwill." A new high-speed record would, indeed, be set by completely dividing in ten weeks what had taken all of British India's army, and its total corps of governor-generals, viceroys, and civil servants, well over a century to unite.

Mountbatten needed constant reassurance about his every official act and speech, and his personal press attache, Alan Campbell-Johnson, waxed ecstatic over press reactions to the announcement. "Mellor of the *Daily Herald* describes himself as 'stunned by the performance,'" Campbell-Johnson reported to Dickie's personal secretary, Captain Ronnie Brockman. "Stimson of the B.B.C. said it made a most tremendous impression on Indian and foreign Correspondents, in particular on the Americans. . . . Britter of *The Times* described it as a '*tour de force*.'"[9]

But that evening Gandhi arrived and angrily accused Mountbatten of using "magic tricks" to get the Congress Party and Muslim League "to agree on anything."[10] He clearly saw through Mountbatten's aura of self-confidence and bonhomie to the darkest heart of the insoluble problems he glossed over, leaving them for the infant dominions of India and Pakistan to confront and fight over the day after Great Britain would fly away. "Gandhi was in a very unhappy and emotional mood, and some of the Congress leaders feared he might denounce the plan and its acceptance at his prayer meeting," Mountbatten noted, reflecting Krishna Menon's earlier warnings. Gandhi was "very keen on going to Kashmir." Nehru also wished to travel there, much to the anxiety of its maharaja, who hated Nehru. So Mountbatten immediately "suggested that perhaps the best course might be for me myself to go."[11]

The princely state of Jammu and Kashmir was the largest of South Asia's 562 states and the most problematic, with a Muslim majority ruled by an autocratic Hindu maharaja. Geographically, the state was contiguous to both India and Pakistan, all the great rivers of Punjab springing from its Himalayan ice and snow. Gandhi sensed how distressed the people of Kashmir felt on the eve of the dreadfully hasty Partition that would soon turn their valley into a battleground between newborn Pakistan and his Mother India. Ever alert to the danger of adverse publicity, Mountbatten tried to mollify the Mahatma by telling him that what the press called his "Mountbatten Plan" should really have been christened the "Gandhi Plan, since all the salient ingredients were suggested to me by . . . Mr. Gandhi." Even the Mahatma was not totally immune to the viceroy's flattery and charm, so he silently bowed his head and smiled, but never changed his mind about the vivisection of India or the shameful speed of Lord Mountbatten's exit strategy.

Trying to keep his staff moving at top speed, Mountbatten met with them that evening to review a long paper the India office had prepared titled the "The Administrative Consequences of Partition."[12] It was a uniquely daunting list, reflecting an impossible undertaking never before attempted at so swift a pace in recorded history, the "divorce" in ten weeks of a continent of 400 million people. The first task on that list was "Final demarcation of *boundaries*," which soon had to be turned over to a boundary commission. The second was "Division of . . . the *Indian Armed Forces*," which was giving Commander-in-Chief Auchinleck sleepless nights. The third was "Division of the staff . . . of Central Civil Departments . . . Railways, Posts and Telegraphs, Broadcasting, Civil Aviation . . . Public Works, Income Tax, Customs, Central Excise . . . Central Power Board." Then came "divisions of the assets and liabilities of the Government of India including fixed installations and stores. . . . " Next, the *"Division of Assets and Liabilities of the Reserve Bank including* Currency . . . and foreign exchange." After that came the high courts and federal courts, and diplomatic representation abroad. Similar decisions would have to be made for each of the provinces. Mountbatten relied heavily on his brilliant young reforms commissioner V. P. Menon, who was as close to Sardar Patel as Krishna Menon was to Nehru. Patel was to use V. P. Menon most effectively in convincing all but three of South Asia's princes within India's territory to accept life pensions and sign agreements merging their states into the dominion of India by mid-August.

Arguments erupted daily on the "coalition" interim government's executive council. Krishna Menon said that Nehru wanted Mountbatten to throw out all the Muslim League members, but Sardar Patel was more cool-tempered and practical. V. P. Menon argued that such a move would only waste time and energy during the brief two and half months before power was transferred. The Congress Party members on the viceroy's council would all be "extremely busy on the problems of Partition" and should try to ignore the League's opposition. V. P. Menon then tactfully told Mountbatten's staff that "Sardar Patel and Pandit Nehru were invariably in complete agreement on fundamental issues."[13]

Meanwhile, the real consequence of Partition was that Punjab's major cities had become killing fields for communal arsonists. Governor Jenkins wired the viceroy: "Lahore reports five dead . . . and five fires. Amritsar has had two communal riots and four fires. . . . Gurgaon disorders still widespread. . . . Total number of villages burned now estimated at sixty. Casualties unknown. . . . Known dead over one hundred. . . . Troops not yet reinforced. . . . Reception of partition plan very mixed. . . . Sikhs angry and bellicose. . . . Muslims also angry and critical . . . threatening to destroy Amritsar completely."[14] It was too late for Mountbatten to change his decision to partition the Punjab, so the next day he met with Nehru, Jinnah, and their lieutenants to consider the "administrative consequences of partition."

Nehru insisted he did not understand references to a "division" of the staff and records of the central civil departments. "As he saw it, there was . . . an Entity of India. Certain parts of India were being given the opportunity to secede from this Entity. The functions of the Government of India would continue. The seceding parts would have to build up their own Government."[15] Jinnah angrily disagreed: "It was not a question of secession, but of division." The very words used to describe the events about to explode thus became a subject of bitter conflict between the leaders of the new dominions on the eve of their births.

"The Viceroy explained that it would be necessary for those members of the staff of Central Civil Departments who lived in Pakistan to transfer to the Pakistan Service. Similarly, British officials would have to be divided between the two States. Back files would have to be copied." There was so much to be done, and at such high speed. Boundary commissions had to be selected, one each to divide Punjab and Bengal. Four judges would be chosen, two by the Congress Party and two by the League, for each province, but since every one expected those four always to be equally divided, an impartial chairman must be found, one who would serve as the final arbitrator of all contentious issues and questions.

Barrister Sir Cyril Radcliffe, who had never before set foot on Indian soil, was chosen to chair both commissions. He would fly out to undertake in a month work that should have taken at least a year to do properly. Once his job was done, Radcliffe left India, never to return, fearing both sides would try to kill him. Nehru and Mountbatten agreed that the "terms of reference" for the boundary commissions should be "very simple and brief," leaving them maximum flexibility to change proposed lines of demarcation in Punjab and Bengal at the last moment, should "other factors" than "the contiguous majority areas of Muslims and non-Muslims," require alteration.[16] In Punjab, one major "other factor" was to assure India winter highway access to the Vale of Kashmir.

"There has been no relaxation of the pace here," Mountbatten reported to Secretary of State Listowel. "The pace is so hot that we are still three or four lengths ahead . . . but certainly June in Delhi is not a month in which anyone . . . can be expected to give of his best."[17] That same day he reported to the kng and Attlee that "many of the troops . . . are obviously concerned at the inevitable splitting of the Services."[18] He also told of Patel's "Congress spy!" in the Council of the Muslim League, who had brought him a copy of the League's resolution, which was passed in a secret session and now raised a "howl of indignation" in the Congress in view of its failure to accept the settlement plan he announced. Congress feared Jinnah would "back out at the last moment," as the League accused the Congress of having done earlier in dealing with the cabinet mission's Plan in 1946.[19] The mistrust between Congress and League leaders was so intense that Nehru and Liaquat almost came to blows in the council chamber of the interim government over Nehru's insistence on appointing his sister, Madame Pandit, to serve as India's ambassador to Russia. Liaquat loudly refused to agree. "Nehru announced that he would not tolerate interference by the League. . . . Pandemonium then broke loose and everyone talked at once."

A few days later, Jenkins wrote from Punjab that there was "a complete absence of enthusiasm for the partition plan—nobody seems pleased." Political parties had accepted the plan for "widely differing reasons. Muslim Leaguers think it a master stroke by Jinnah, who has secured the recognition of Pakistan. . . . Congressmen think it a master-stroke by Patel, who, having pushed the Muslims into a corner (or into two corners) will be able to destroy them before very long. . . . [A] Minister in the Coalition Government told me he had heard him [Patel] say that Hindustan could quickly make an end of its Muslim inhabitants if Pakistan did not behave."[20]

With almost as many Muslims remaining inside India as would comprise Pakistan's population, that view of India's Muslim minority as Patel's "hostages" for Pakistan's behavior remained alive as long as he did (until 1950), after which even tolerant pro-Muslim Prime Minister Nehru at times discreetly whispered that should India ever "lose" Kashmir to Pakistani invaders there was no way of predicting the "terrible" dimensions of the "tragedy" that might befall India's Muslim minority.[21] Jenkins also reported the "flight of capital" from Lahore and "falling land values" in central Punjab's hitherto rich Sikh colony wheat districts.[22]

Nehru addressed his All India Congress Committee on June 15, expressing his "horror and disgust" at the riots in Punjab and asking how it was that "British officers who coped with civil disturbance movements in the past were unable to cope with the present disturbances?"[23] Jenkins insisted that Nehru was "wrong" both with respect to his facts as well as his reasoning, reporting to Mountbatten that Punjab was experiencing "what amounts to a revolution." Nehru charged that the flash points of conflict ignited where "callous" British officers, no longer "desirous of shouldering any further responsibility," were in charge.

Liaquat Ali Khan wrote the next day to Mountbatten, bitterly complaining that the Muslims of Gurgaon, in Punjab, were unprotected against a "full-scale war of extermination which is being waged against them by armed hosts of Hindus."[24] Those Hindus were helped in their killing of Muslim villagers by the forces from neighboring Sikh states. Each side blamed the other, or the British, for the escalating violence that now threatened to engulf all of Punjab and much of northern India. Mahatma Gandhi returned to Delhi from east Bengal, where he had walked barefoot from one burning village to the next, trying to teach his message of "Love"–Ahimsa–"God" to Hindus and Muslims alike. He had warned Nehru and Patel against trusting Mountbatten, "an unknown friend," as he called him, more "dangerous to us" than such "known enemies" as the previous viceroys Linlithgow and Wavell.[25] Partition was a "curse," Gandhi warned them, and "like eating wooden loaves" would only poison India's starving children.

Mountbatten's swiftly shifting attention focused now on other matters. He telegraphed to Listowel to request modification of a previous secretary of state's 1925 "Secret Despatch," which had decreed that Indian princely state rulers who were entitled to no more than "a salute of nine guns" could not be called "His Highness." "Many of those States are more important than certain eleven gun States," Mountbatten noted, "and the extension of the courtesy of the style of His Highness to all Rulers of salute States would be widely welcomed by them, and would be of much advantage in the future. . . .[A]void all publicity about this, as far as possible."[26] The latter comment at least reflects Mountbatten's own awareness of how inconsequential this subject would be seen, in light of the urgent life and death problems affecting hundreds of millions of Indians. Listowel did as requested and a month later conveyed the king's "approval" of the royal title "Highness" to all "9 Gun" rulers and their "lawful wives and widows."

A few days later, Nehru sent Mountbatten, who was vacationing in Kashmir, his most deeply troubled personal letter.

> I am distressed . . . about what is happening in Lahore . . . where fires are raging and consuming hundreds of houses. It is reported that 100 houses were burnt down last night and this morning. During the previous two days about 250 houses were set fire to and burnt. At this rate the city of Lahore will be just a heap of ashes. . . . The human aspect of this is appalling to contemplate. Amritsar is already a city of ruins, and Lahore is likely to be in a much worse state very soon. . . . My mother came from Lahore and part of my childhood was spent there. . . . Human beings have an amazing capacity to . . . bear calamity after calamity; but it is very difficult

to have to bear something which can apparently be avoided. . . . I do not know who is to blame and I do not want to blame anybody for it. But the fact remains that horror succeeds horror. . . . [V]ast numbers of human beings, men, women and children, live in the midst of this horror. . . . [P]eople have come from Lahore to see me today and . . . [t]hey tell me that . . . when houses were set fire to, the residents of those houses rushed out into the streets and lanes and these people were fired at by the police for breach of the curfew order. Most of the fires occurred at the time of the curfew. . . . Something effective has to be done to stop this tragedy. . . . As I told you once, the insistent demand is either for the military to take charge, or for the withdrawal of the police and military so that the people can look after themselves. You were surprised at this last demand. . . . But it is passionately repeated. All manner of charges are made against the police of committing arson. . . . [T]he situation continues to deteriorate. Are we to be passive spectators while a great city ceases to exist?[27]

Mountbatten met with Nehru, two days after he wrote his urgent letter about Lahore, which the viceroy's secretary George Abell filed as "a long rigmarole about the Punjab."[28] At their meeting Mountbatten discussed with Nehru not the deaths and desecration in Lahore, but "my painting of a proposed flag for the Dominion of India which I had designed. This consisted of a Congress flag with a small Union Jack in the upper canton," he noted in his "TOP SECRET" record of that interview on June 24.[29] Nehru agreed to take Dickie's flag away with him and report back, but none of Nehru's Congress Party colleagues found it as attractive as their saffron, white, and green tricolor, which would become the flag of independent India.

After Nehru left his office on the 24th, Mountbatten called Jenkins to report that Nehru suggested he should declare martial law in Lahore and Amritsar "forthwith," and that all Punjabi police should be "withdrawn for rest and recuperation." Nehru urged that Punjab's "troops should be empowered to be utterly ruthless and to shoot on sight." Remarkably, Jinnah agreed: "I don't care whether you shoot Moslems or not, it has got to be stopped."[30] But Jenkins, who discussed this matter with his Lahore area military commander and Punjab's inspector general of police, refused to declare martial law. They feared there were not enough British troops left to "succeed immediately" in restoring civil control, and once martial law was declared British troops would "be exposed to same communal attack as Police."[31] They would have played their highest card, and if they "lost," it would leave every non-Indian in Punjab "vulnerable to attack." That was the ultimate terror that kept Jenkins too paralyzed to declare martial law in Lahore and Mountbatten and Auchinleck afraid to order him to do so. In part it was because they felt too impotent to stop the butchery and arson unleashed by the threat of imminent partition. But it was also that they lost their will to fight any more in defense of an "ingrate" India that wanted only to be left alone as soon as British soldiers locked up all the communal killers and arsonists. "Police are physically tired and services generally are disintegrating," Jenkins glumly concluded. Ismay was asked to comment on Jenkins's report, and he agreed that "if the military fail, we will have played our last card."[32] So instead of risking the humiliation of exposure before "Natives," they retained the pretense and illusion of impervious power and failed to act, biding their time until their return to Britain.

Meanwhile, in London, Attlee met with his cabinet almost daily to work out details for the final transfer of power. On June 25 the cabinet discussed the date on which to start the withdrawal of all British armed forces from India. Mountbatten wanted to announce that withdrawal would begin on August 15 and end in February. Minister of Defence A. V. Alexander was "doubtful whether the stage had yet been reached when a firm date for the transfer of power could be announced," and, in any case, he thought the "first announcement" of such plans should be made in the House of Commons.[33] They decided to put off that decision until July. Then they turned to details of the Indian Independence Bill, for which they received many last-minute changes from the viceroy. The phrase "the Indian Dominions" would have to be changed to "the new Dominions," and to adjust to forthcoming provincial partitions, new titles for East and West Punjab and East and West Bengal would have to be given to the governors of each. "Time is getting very short," Secretary of State Listowel wired to remind Mountbatten that afternoon. "We must show Bill in substantially its final form to Opposition on Friday . . . and obtain their views on Monday."[34]

The next morning Mountbatten met with his new small partition committee of the Indian cabinet, Liaquat Ali Khan and the North-West Frontier's Abdur Rab Nishtar representing the League, and Sardar Patel and Bihar's Dr. Rajendra Prasad for the Congress Party. Mountbatten asked if they wanted to follow the Dominion of Canada's practice for appointments of governors, which were made on recommendations of the governor-general-in-council, or if they would prefer the practice of the Dominion of Australia, which made such appointments on recommendations of state governments. Mountbatten thought "the Canadian practice was the more suitable one." Sardar Patel said that Congress agreed. Liaquat said "he wished to consider the matter further."[35] Next they turned to preliminary arrangements for "setting up the Central Pakistan Government in Karachi." After that, Auchinleck briefed them on the "retention of British Officers" by either or both new dominions, if desired, and how best that could be done. Then they focused on the boundary commissions, and Mountbatten explained that the secretary of state had found the most eminent and suitable person to chair both commissions, Cyril Radcliffe, describing his "high integrity," legal reputation, and wide experience in the law. None of them objected to the fact that he had never set foot in Punjab or Bengal.

On June 26 Auchlinleck sent a "TOP SECRET" report to Mountbatten about a request from Jinnah that the withdrawal of British troops should "not be conducted too quickly as he considered that troubles might possibly arise."[36] Auchinleck hoped that "Mr. Jinnah clearly realizes British Troops will not be available in communal disturbances." Except for Gandhi, none of India's leaders, not even Jinnah or Nehru, nor as cool a realist as Patel, realized how quickly the British sword and shield that so long had served—even if just as an "illusion"—as India's ultimate defense against communal killings and terror, was about to disappear, never again to "be available in communal disturbances." Great Britain would no longer "be responsible" for maintaining India's "law and order." It would not even be in place until June of 1948, for Mountbatten had advanced that date to mid-August of 1947.

The last meeting of Mountbatten's partition committee proved

> highly acrimonious. When Liaquat asked that one of the six Government printing presses should be moved from Delhi to Karachi . . . Patel flared up. He said that all six presses were fully occupied with Government of India work and could not be spared. . . . he said 'No one asked Pakistan to secede. We do not mind their taking their property with them but we have no intention of allowing them to injure the work of the Government of the rest of India.' . . . Liaquat remarked that if that spirit persisted there would be no possible hope of the Pakistan Government being ready to take over on the 15th August.[37]

With only seven weeks left before the actual transfer of power, a new states department was established to deal with the future of Princely states, a subject on which Mountbatten considered "Nehru and Gandhi . . . both pathological."[38] He was relieved, therefore, to report that "sensible realist" Patel was assigned to take charge of that department by Nehru, and he invited V. P. Menon to serve as its secretary. On July 5, Patel launched his new department, urging the princely rulers in Delhi to send representatives to India's constituent assembly. "Now that British rule is ending, the demand has been made that the States should regain their independence," Patel told them.

> I do not think it can be their desire to utilise this freedom . . . in a manner which . . . militates against the ultimate paramountcy of popular interest and welfare. . . . The great majority of Indian States have already come into the Constituent Assembly. To those who have not done so, I appeal that they should join now. The States have already accepted the basic principle that for defence, foreign affairs and communications they would come into the Indian Union. We ask no more of them. . . . In other matters, we would scrupulously respect their autonomous existence.[39]

He appealed to the common "proud heritage" that India's princes shared with its people, "all knit together by bonds of blood and feeling. . . . We are at a momentous stage in the history of India. By common endeavour, we can raise this country to new greatness, while a lack of unity will expose us to fresh calamities. I hope the Indian States will bear in mind that the alternative to co-operation in the general interest is anarchy and chaos. . . . Let not future generations curse us for having had the opportunity but failed to turn it to our mutual advantage . . . to leave a legacy of . . . peace and prosperity."

Most princes signed accession agreements that V. P. Menon drafted, promising them annual pensions that sufficed to allow them to retain their princely lifestyles, at least for the first decade of India's independence. Only three states refused to join India's union by mid-August of 1947. Hyderabad was the most populous state, whose Muslim nizam autocratically controlled a predominantly Hindu population. Patel allowed the nizam to sign a standstill agreement with India, and waited until September of 1948 before ordering India's army into Hyderabad, taking control of it in a few days. Junagadh was one of the smallest Muslim-ruled states of India, located on the Arabian Sea, facing Pakistan. Its nawab tried to accede to Pakistan, but Patel ordered the Indian army to crush that rebellion, which it did without any difficulty. The state of Jammu and Kashmir proved a more formidably enduring problem for both India and Pakistan.

Mountbatten tried to convince Jinnah of the value of accepting him, Mountbatten, as Pakistan's first governor-general, but Jinnah refused to be moved from his determination to take that job himself. "Mr. Jinnah came to see me last night," Mountbatten wired Attlee in early July, "and told me that he wanted to be Governor-General of Pakistan." Mountbatten argued with him for four hours, "trying to make him realise the advantages that Pakistan would gain from having the same Governor-General as India . . . until partition is complete. He is so adamant that he openly says that he would prefer to lose the crores' [tens of millions of rupees] worth of assets . . . than share a Governor-General."[40] Jinnah knew that his lungs were failing him, and he wanted to lead the nation he'd sired, if only for the briefest period of time vouchsafed to him. Mountbatten's ego was jolted by Jinnah's "rejection" of what he considered his "generous" offer to help Pakistan gain advantages in its early months of life. "I am now faced with the appalling problem of whether to accept Nehru's offer to stay as Governor-General of India or whether to pull out on August 15th," he confided to Attlee, alerting him to what could be an awkward situation, appearing as it would to the world as a clear sign of Britain's partiality to India in the aftermath of Partition.

Mountbatten was so upset by Jinnah's refusal to allow him to govern the dominion of Pakistan that he had Ismay fly to London the day after he met with Jinnah, carrying his TOP SECRET report to the cabinet and king. "He is suffering from megalomania in its worst form," Mountbatten reported of

Pakistan's first governor-general and "Great Leader." So angered by Jinnah's stubborn refusal to do what he wanted, he finally "got up and left the room," after warning Jinnah "somewhat acidly 'It may cost you the whole of your assets and the future of Pakistan.'"[41] Sheer vanity or prophetic warning? "I have always felt and said that I considered it morally wrong to stay on with only one of the two sides," Mountbatten confessed in the last paragraph of that personal report to Attlee and the king. Yet he decided, after Jinnah's rejection, to do just that, fearing that otherwise Nehru would "never forgive me for allowing Jinnah once more to have his way." So Mountbatten convinced himself that he was doing the right thing by becoming governor-general of India's dominion alone, even though he had "always felt" it was "morally wrong."

"I must say," Bengal's Secretary John Dawson Tyson wrote from Calcutta on July 5,

> Mountbatten is a hustler: ever since he came out he has pursued shock tactics. . . . He made his plan [and] soon after that the blitz began. And since the time when he launched his blitz he has given no one any rest—the Indian leaders least of all. He has kept them so busy—so much on the run—that they have not had time to draw breath and criticise. Before they know where they are we shall be out—and I believe now, we shall withdraw in fairly peaceful conditions—whatever may happen after we have gone. . . . I think there will be very unsettled conditions in India for some time to come . . . but the trouble will be primarily between Hindus and Muslims—not anti-European. . . . [T]he India of "after-August 15th" will not be the kind of country I should want to live in.[42]

Many of Tyson's Indian civil service contemporaries felt much the way he did, eager to leave India's chaos and conflicts behind them and to head home.

Throughout July Punjab sizzled, not only from lack of rain but from growing fears among its Sikhs and Hindus as well as its Muslim majority. Most of Punjab's Sikhs started to wear black armbands of mourning as well as black turbans, and Sikh shops in Lahore and Amritsar remained locked shut on July 8 to protest the province's partition. "There is great soreness in the Punjab . . . among the Sikhs," Jenkins warned Mountbatten.[43] He feared that unless the Sikhs retained their major gurdwaras ("guru's house" temples) east of the Chenab River and "Nankana Sahib," the sacred gurdwara near Lahore where the founder of their faith, Guru Nanak, was born, they would launch a revolt that could start a civil war. He worried about the impact of the release of the boundary commission's report, which he expected to trigger Sikh violence, either just before or shortly after August 15, the date not only of India's independence but also the day Mountbatten had chosen for the start of the final withdrawal of all British troops from Punjab. Instead of urging the viceroy to send more troops to his province immediately to avert that disaster, however, Jenkins advised the opposite: "I think it will be wise to avoid postponing the relief of British troops for too long. It would be awkward if trouble on a large scale started while the relief was in progress. My own advice would therefore be to make the change before the end of July."[44]

As with his handling of the arson that ravaged Lahore, Jenkins feared the engagement of any British troops in Punjab's worst communal conflicts, and Mountbatten was eager to agree with him. He visited Lahore in late July to accelerate the "relief" of British troops, and to meet with Punjab's partition committee, urging Radcliffe to work faster, since "the risk of disorder would be greatly increased if the [boundary] award had to be announced at the very last moment" before August 15. "We should be grateful for every extra day earlier that you could manage to get the award announced."[45] But in August, when Radcliffe delivered his maps early, Mountbatten put them under his strictest embargo until after all the jubilant independence day celebrations had ended, by which time all of Punjab's British troops were fully relieved.

Two weeks before Mountbatten's partition deadline, violence escalated. On July 30, Jenkins reported, "Feeling in Lahore is perhaps worse than it has ever been . . . daily fires, stabbings and bomb explosions."[46] Bombs were thrown in railway workshops and stations and inside crowded cinemas. The death toll rose daily. In Amritsar a bomb wounded fifty people inside a courthouse. Outside Amritsar, rural villages and towns were attacked by Sikhs, leaving many dead. On August 5 the Sikhs planned a Punjab-wide strike, and Jenkins feared "a considerable muddle" by mid-month. "It would be difficult enough to partition within six weeks a country of 30 million people which had been governed as a unit for 93 years, even if all concerned were friendly," he wrote Mountbatten, as if the enormity of what they were about to do had only just dawned on him. Migrations from among the 27 percent non-Muslim minority of West Punjab had begun moving east, even as some of the 33 percent Muslim minority around Amritsar started moving west. Soon those early trickles grew to giant snaking processions of millions, bearing all they owned on their backs or in bullock carts, continuing to move until they dropped dead.

"I am more than ever convinced that if the date of transfer had been 1st October there would have been a serious risk of a complete breakdown," Mountbatten wired the cabinet on the next day. He kept trying to assure Attlee's cabinet, as well as his own council, and his own weak and troubled mind that he was really doing the right thing. "The country as a whole is quiet, with the exception of Punjab, where there have been continued disturbances . . . [because] the Sikhs have 'ratted' on the undertaking they gave me."[47] Attlee had just congratulated him on doing so "remarkable" a job and proposed his name to the king for an earldom, so Mountbatten did not want to alarm London with any depressing details. [48] "I visited Calcutta for 20 hours. . . . I feel that part of their trouble is that Suhrawardy is rather a gas bag, who likes to score debating points. Another weakness is that in Bengal, unlike Delhi, the Separation Council start arguing on general principles and . . . [t]he Council has got bogged down over three main points." Other than "ratting" Sikhs in Punjab and a "gas bag" running Bengal, however, all was going quite well, the viceroy informed his king and cabinet.

That first day of August, intelligence reports from Amritsar told of twenty-three Muslims murdered by Sikhs, and thirty more left wounded. [49] A few days later, Mountbatten met with Punjab's police captain Gerald Savage, who informed him that Master Tara Singh had recently purchased "rifles" and "grenades" for a number of young Sikhs "planning to blow up the Pakistan Special with remote control firing apparatus and after wrecking the Special, set it on fire, and shoot the occupants." [50] Savage also reported that Tara Singh planned to have Jinnah "killed" during the ceremonies in Karachi celebrating Pakistan's birth. Mountbatten informed Jinnah and Liaquat, the latter taking precautions to secure all Pakistan Special trains. The viceroy told Governor Jenkins about Tara Singh, leaving it to him to decide whether or not to arrest the Sikh leader before mid-August. Jenkins characteristically decided to do nothing rather than risk rocking the boat. Jinnah, who had faced down several previous assassination attempts, was unperturbed by learning of this latest "threat" to his life, which never occurred.

Gandhi left for Calcutta a week before mid-August, moving into an abandoned old mansion in the heart of Bengal's capital which he shared with Suhrawardy, so that both could help keep that City of Dreadful Night calm in the aftermath of the independence day partition of Bengal. "Gandhi's absence from the celebrations in Delhi is, of course, intentional," Mountbatten explained in his TOP SECRET personal report to Attlee and the king on August 8. "He has never given the 3rd June plan his unqualified blessing. . . . [I]t would not be possible to fit him into the programme in the way to which he would feel himself entitled. . . . Gandhi has announced his decision to spend the rest of his life in Pakistan looking after the minorities. This will infuriate Jinnah, but will be a great relief to Congress . . . [H]is influence is largely negative and even destructive." [51]

Radcliffe was more eager than Mountbatten to finish his job and escape from India before mid-August, surprising the viceroy by reporting he was ready to "announce" his Punjab Boundary Commission's "award" on August 9. Mountbatten immediately met with his staff to ask them "whether it would in fact be desirable to publish it straight away," since "without question, the earlier it was published, the more the British would have to bear the responsibility for the disturbances which would undoubtedly result." [52]

He cared nothing for the fact that a week's advance notice of the actual location of the new boundary would have given all those people most frightened and eager to move enough time to do so before they found themselves trapped in the wrong country. Mountbatten's chief concern was to avoid British responsibility for the hurricane they could all see looming on Punjab's horizon. Hoping to escape blame for what he had so ominously accelerated by his passion for speed, "the Viceroy emphasised the necessity for maintaining secrecy, not only on the terms of the award, but also on the fact that it would be ready that day."[53] Campbell-Johnson reported that "on administrative grounds it was argued that earliest possible announcement would be of help to Jenkins and would enable last-minute troop movements to be made into the affected areas in advance of the transfer of power. . . . Mountbatten said that if he could exercise some discretion in the matter he would much prefer to postpone its appearance until after the Independence Day celebrations, feeling that . . . the controversy and grief that it was bound to arouse on both sides should not be allowed to mar Independence Day itself."

Radcliffe tried his best to be fair in tackling what became an impossible job. He could not understand why Nehru's and Mountbatten's greatest concern over the new Punjab border line was to make sure that neither of the Muslim-majority "sub-districts" (*tehsils*) of Ferozepur and Zira nor the Muslim-majority district of Gurdaspur should go to Pakistan, since that would have deprived India of direct road access to Kashmir. The Punjab Boundary Commission Radcliffe chaired, after all, was simply asked to divide the province along lines of "Muslim versus non-Muslim majority Districts." Since the numbers clearly favored Muslims, Radcliffe awarded the Ferozepur subdistricts and Gurdaspur to Pakistan in his initial maps. He was quite sensibly ready to recommend, moreover, joint Indo-Pak "control of the canal system and electricity" generated in the Rajput princely state of Bikaner, whose Hindu maharaja controlled the state dam, canal headwaters, and hydroelectric generators that fed power to Ferozepur, Montgomery, and Lahore districts. Bikaner's power distribution system had proved the key to central Punjab's rich economic growth and development. Nehru sent an urgent message to Mountbatten as soon as he learned of Radcliffe's initial "award" in early August, that "both from the strategic and irrigation point of view it will be most dangerous to let Ferozepur go to Pakistan. Whatever may be the decision about area west of [River] Sutlej, no area east of the Sutlej must on any account go to Pakistan. The joint control of irrigation canals must on no account be accepted, even as a recommendation of the Boundary Commission. . . . Similarly no joint control of electricity must be accepted."[54]

The Maharaja of Bikaner wired Mountbatten the next day to express his "every confidence that Your Excellency in finally arriving at decision on award of Boundary Commission will be good enough to safeguard interests of Bikaner State."[55] The maharaja sent that message with his prime minister, K. M. Panikkar, Nehru's close friend, who warned Mountbatten that "Bikaner would have no option but to join Pakistan," unless the Ferozepur Headworks were protected by India. That strategic risk was judged by Mountbatten to be too high a price to pay , and though he never admitted he told Radcliffe to change his initial Punjab award, the maps were altered accordingly and the award itself kept under Mountbatten's personal embargo until after his August 15 celebrations ended. On August 10, Maharaja Sadul Singh of Bikaner sent a confidential private letter to Mountbatten to "convey my most grateful thanks" for "the action which you so kindly and promptly took after your talk with Mr. Panikkar in regard to the protection of the interests . . . of my State."[56] Pakistan was thus, strategically, obliged to "pay" a very high price, as Mountbatten warned Jinnah it would, for refusing to grant him the pleasure of becoming governor-general of Pakistan as well as India.

Then, on August 11, when Liaquat learned that much of Punjab's Muslim-majority Gurdaspur District, with its highway access to Kashmir, was awarded to India, he angrily informed Ismay that Pakistan considered that a "political decision" as well as a British "breach of faith." Lord Ismay claimed to be "dumbfounded" by that "private message."[57] As chief of staff to Mountbatten, however, he must have known of the alterations, but disingenuously assured Liaquat that "the Viceroy has always been, and is determined to keep clear of the whole business. . . . I am at a loss to know what action you wish me to take. . . . In the first place, I am told that the final report of Sir Cyril Radcliffe is not ready yet, and therefore I do not know what grounds you have for saying that Gurdaspur *has been* allotted to the East Punjab. . . . [Y]ou surely do not . . . imply that the Viceroy has influenced this award. . . . I never for one moment thought that you, who are completely in the know, should ever imagine that he could do such a thing."[58]

On August 11, Jinnah flew from Delhi to Karachi, the city of his youth, first capital of Sind Province, now to become the capital of Pakistan. As president of Pakistan's Constituent Assembly, Quaid-i-Azam Jinnah addressed his elected followers that evening. "A division had to take place," Jinnah told them. "Any idea of a United India could never have worked and in my judgement it would have led us to terrific disaster. . . . Now what shall we do? . . . [I]f we want to make this great State of Pakistan happy and prosperous we should wholly and solely concentrate on the well-being of the people, and especially of the masses and the poor." It was Jinnah's noblest speech, a statement of his personal vision of Pakistan as a liberal, egalitarian state, where everyone would "work together in a spirit that everyone of you, no matter to what community he belongs . . . no matter what is his colour, caste or creed, is first, second and last a citizen of this State with equal rights, privileges and obligations." The Pakistan Jinnah envisioned was neither a narrow-minded theocracy nor a feudal tyranny or martial dictatorship, but a democratic polity governed by law and equal opportunities for all. "You are free; you are free to go to your temples, you are free to go to your mosques or to any other place of worship in this State of Pakistan. . . . You may belong to any religion or caste or creed. . . . We are starting with this fundamental principle that we are all citizens of one State. . . . My guiding principle will be justice and complete impartiality, and I am sure that with your support and co-operation I can look forward to Pakistan becoming one of the greatest Nations of the world."[59] Jinnah meant every word of it, but tragically, he was mortally ill and could barely continue to work. He could do little more than to articulate his secular and liberal ideals to his Muslim followers, many of whom found them impossible to comprehend. For most of his last pain-filled year, Governor-General Jinnah lacked the strength to help Pakistan create and securely establish the vital democratic institutions it so desperately needed. He was so frail during his last months that he remained bed-ridden in Baluchistan's hill station of Ziarat.

Admiral Lord Mountbatten flew to Karachi in his best dress whites on August 13 to attend the ceremonial flag-raising birth of the Dominion of Pakistan with Governor-General Jinnah on August 14, flying back to Delhi that evening to prepare for Dominion India's midnight birth. Midnight of the 14/15 was chosen after several Hindu astrologers warned that August 15 was a most "inauspicious" day. Nehru hoped that by inaugurating India's dominion with his eloquent "Tryst with Destiny" speech in New Delhi's Constituent Assembly Hall of Parliament shortly before midnight, India might elude astral rage and fury for ignoring the warnings of heavenly map-readers.

Jenkins's final letter as governor of Punjab was his most grim. "Raids and murders are now so frequent that it is difficult to keep track. . . . Amritsar district has become generally unsafe. There have been several attacks on trains. . . . Most of rural casualties—and they have been very heavy—have been caused by Sikhs . . . raiding Muslim villages. . . . Parties of unescorted Muslim refugees have been attacked and butchered."[60] As the news of Sikh brutality spread to Lahore, Muslim vengeance against Sikhs and Hindus grew so violent that "neither the railways nor the main roads are safe," Jenkins reported. He now felt that Amritsar district alone would have needed two more "full-strength" British brigades, since the Lahore attacks would lead to Sikh retaliation raids against Muslim villages, with communal hatreds escalating by the hour. But the British brigades had all been relieved. "Hindus are thoroughly terrified, and the Muslim movement from the East is balanced by a similar movement of Hindus from the West." Human chains of tragedy would grow from fifty to one hundred miles in length over the next few months, the refugees moving in opposite directions toward accelerated death.

Field Marshal Auchinleck's assessment of Punjab's "situation" on that inauspicious mid-August day was this: "The area is large and the troops are few. There is no remedy for this, unless the troops are permanently posted in villages as armed police and this is neither practicable or desirable. . . . Several houses were burning in Amritsar City as I flew over it and four or five villages within ten miles of the City were apparently completely destroyed by fire and still burning."[61] As for Lahore itself, most of its police had "defected" and joined the looters and arsonist-killers roaming through the old city. "But for the presence of the Army there would by now be a complete holocaust in the City. . . . "A large number of houses were still burning and a thick pall of smoke hung over the City. "Delay in announcing the award of the Boundary Commission is having a most disturbing and harmful effect. . . . It is realised of course that the announcement may add fresh fuel to the fire, but lacking an announcement, the wildest rumours are being spread by mischief makers. . . . The position is thoroughly bad and is getting worse."[62]

"The last week of British rule in India has been the most hectic," Mountbatten wrote in his final TOP SECRET "Personal Report" to King George and Attlee on August 16. "We got back from Karachi on the afternoon of the 14. At twenty minutes past midnight on that night the President of the Constituent Assembly, Rajendra Prasad, and the new Prime Minister, Nehru, arrived to tell me that at the midnight session of the Constituent Assembly they had taken over power, and endorsed the request of the leaders that I should become their first Governor General. . . . Nehru said in ceremonious tones 'May I submit to you the portfolios of the new Cabinet.' He then handed me a carefully addressed envelope (on opening it after his departure I found it to be empty!)"[63]

> The 15th August has certainly turned out to be the most remarkable and inspiring day of my life. We started at 8.30 with the Swearing-in ceremony in the Durbar Hall in front of an official audience of some 500 . . . Ambassadors, Princes and the Cabinet then drove in procession from Government House to the Council Chamber. Never have such crowds been seen within the memory of anyone. . . . [I]t had fortunately been arranged that there should be two Guards of Honour of 100 men each. . . . The ceremony in the Council Chamber was extremely dignified. . . . Fortunately two more Guards of Honour of the Indian Army were due for the departure. . . . As we were about to depart they said that it was doubtful whether the 400 men could keep the way clear to the coach, so Nehru went on to the roof and waved the crowd to go back; the door was then opened and surrounded by our staff we fought our way through to the coach. . . . A parade had been arranged of the units of the three Services. . . . [R]ehearsals had been going on for days, and seats on raised platforms had been provided. The crowds however were far beyond the control of the police. . . . [O]fficials estimate that there were 600,000 people. . . . Nehru and I . . .

decided that the only thing to do was to hoist the flag and fire the salute.
. . . This was done amid scenes of the most fantastic rejoicing, and as the
flag broke a brilliant rainbow appeared in the sky. . . . Close to 3,000
people came to our evening party at Government House and stayed till
after two o'clock in the morning.[64]

When asked why he did not remain in New Delhi to "celebrate" the
birth of India's dominion, Gandhi replied that he would "fast" in Calcutta
instead. "We do not have food grains, clothes, ghee or oil," he sadly explained. "So where is the need for celebrations? On that day we have to fast
. . . and pray to God."[65] He was sleeping when Nehru spoke of him and how

> long years ago, we made a tryst with destiny, and now the time comes
> when we shall redeem our pledge. . . . [N]ot wholly or in full measure, but
> very substantially. At the stroke of the midnight hour, when the world
> sleeps, India will awake to life and freedom. . . . The future is not one of
> ease or resting but of incessant striving so that we might fulfill the pledge
> we have so often taken. . . . The service of India means the service of the
> millions who suffer. It means the ending of poverty and ignorance and
> disease and inequality of opportunity. The ambition of the greatest man of
> our generation has been to wipe every tear from every eye.[66]

King George sent a personal message to be read aloud to the Dominion of
India's Constituent Assembly on August 15, and Governor General
Mountbatten did so as all the cameras rolled and flashed. "Freedom loving
people everywhere will wish to share in your celebrations, for with this
transfer of power by consent comes the fulfilment of a great democratic
ideal to which the British and Indian peoples alike are firmly dedicated. It is
inspiring to think that all this has been achieved by means of peaceful
change."[67]

9

Freedom's Wooden Loaf,
September–December 1947

AHORE'S RAILWAY STATION became a veritable death trap by August 12, Justice Gopal Das Khosla reported. "On the evening of August 11, the railway station was packed with passengers . . . when news came that the Sind Express, on its way to Lahore, had been attacked by Muslims, panic spread. . . . They found that men, women and children had been brutally murdered and were lying in pools of blood. . . . The dead bodies were carried across several platforms . . . while all that was visible in the city of Lahore was a huge tower of smoke."[1] Passengers on the Frontier Mail were murdered near Wagah. Next day no Hindu or Sikh reached Lahore station alive; Muslim gangs were prowling the environs of the city in armed packs. In June 1947 some 300,000 Hindus and Sikhs lived in Lahore. By August 19 fewer than 10,000 remained; and by August 30, fewer than one thousand. Endless caravans of Hindu-Sikh refugees moved out of that smoking pyre of death, trekking west to try and reach the new Punjab border at Wagah, twenty miles away, hoping to stay alive for another twenty miles to Amritsar.

"Nearly the whole of India celebrated the coming of independence, but not so the unhappy . . . Punjab," Prime Minister Nehru broadcast to his nation on August 19. "Both in the East and the West, there was disaster and sorrow. . . . There was murder and arson and looting in many places and streams of refugees poured out from one place to another."[2] Three days later he wrote to Gandhi in despair, "All this killing business has reached a stage of complete madness, and vast populations are deserting their habitations and trekking to the west or to the east."[3] But Gandhi was not surprised. When the Congress Party first passed its resolution favoring Partition, he had warned that the "only peace" Partition would bring to India was "the peace of the grave."⁴ He stayed for a week in Calcutta with Suhrawardy, trying to pacify raucous crowds of Bengalis, who were at first moved by the symbolism of Hindu-Muslim friendship and unity presented by this "odd couple" of old leaders living together in a burned-out building. Having "drunk the poison of mutual hatred," as Gandhi explained it, "this nectar of fraternization tastes all the sweeter."⁵ But it did not last very long. "What was regarded as a miracle has proved a short-lived nine-day wonder," Gandhi confessed to Vallabhbhai Patel, after he was almost killed by brick-throwing students who rudely awakened him, compelling him to launch a fast in response.⁶ "Today we have lost all our senses, we have become stupid," Gandhi cried aloud at his prayer meeting in Delhi the next month. "It is not only the Sikhs have gone mad, or only the Hindus or the Muslims. . . . India is today in the plight of the [sinking] elephant king [a Hindu fable]. . . . What should I do?"⁷ He wanted to fly to Lahore in Pakistan, but, fearing he might be murdered there, Nehru and Patel dissuaded him from going.

With the death toll in Punjab constantly rising, the new governor of East Punjab, C. M. Trivedi, urgently appealed to Prime Minister Nehru, requesting that two brigades of troops be sent at once to Amritsar. Nehru passed that message to Governor-General Mountbatten, who sent it on to Field Marshal Auchinleck, who had no more troops to send anywhere but home to England. "It is the duty of the Hindus and Sikhs of East Punjab to protect the minorities," Nehru told a large audience of anxious Punjabis who came to hear him speak in Jullundur on August 24. "Peaceful conditions must be restored and every citizen must share this responsibility." The desperate prime minister promised that "all possible assistance will be provided in evacuating people rendered homeless. . . . I appeal once again to the people to create a peaceful atmosphere . . . and help the administration in restoring law and order."⁸ But precious little assistance was available to restore any modicum of law and order.

In West Punjab's Sheikhupura District, Guru Nanak was born and his birthplace Gurdwara, or temple, named Nankana Sahib, was erected; this temple was the place of worship for many Sikhs. It later became the region's center for the massacre of Sikhs by Muslims, and that once worshipful district's name became a synonym for terror in the minds of Sikhs. "The minorities were taken at a disadvantage, arrangements for evacuation could not be made immediately," Justice Khosla noted, "and, while men, women and children, uprooted from their homes, ran hither and thither like hunted animals and crowded into refugee camps, a most ruthless campaign of murder, rape, arson and loot was launched upon them. . . . Sheikhupura became a by-word. . . . In West Punjab hooligans used it to intimidate the minorities into handing over their property, accepting Islam or quitting their homes. 'If you do not do as you are told,' they said, 'we shall enact another Sheikhupura here.'"⁹ Nehru wrote to tell Mountbatten that he was "sick with horror," after he visited Sheikhupura at the end of August. "There is still an odour of death, a smell of blood and burning human flesh. . . . This Punjab business becomes bigger and bigger. . . . I imagine that quite a million have been uprooted. Another million are in refugee camps either in West or East Punjab, or are wandering about."¹⁰

By August 25 more than 100,000 Hindus and Sikhs sought permanent refuge in Delhi. Refugee camps were quickly built to the north of the old city and soon filled with Punjabi families, most of whom remained. The camps grew into the new cities of Kurukshetra and Panipat, urban centers of salvation for millions of refugee Punjabi Hindus and Sikhs. Convoys of Hindus and Sikhs rushing to escape from Lahore stretched over forty miles before the end of August, those of Muslims escaping Amritsar almost as long. Children too young to walk were carried by their elder sisters or mothers, and those too old were wheeled in barrows until the axles broke. Punjab's unrelenting heat proved too much even for able-bodied men who collapsed, many dying before they reached their promised land on the far side of Radcliffe's line. Sir Cyril had sailed home by then, as W. H. Auden put it: "In seven weeks it was done. . . . A continent for better or worse divided/ The next day he sailed for England. . . . Return he would not/ Afraid, as he told his Clerk, that he might be shot."¹¹

Nehru, who couldn't escape to England, wrote remorsefully to his Congress comrade, Rajendra Prasad, president of the constituent assembly, who would soon become president of the Republic of India: "I must confess to you that recent happenings in the Punjab and Delhi have shaken me greatly. . . . I could not conceive of the gross brutality and sadistic cruelty that people have indulged in. . . . Little children are butchered in the streets. The houses in many parts of Delhi are still full of corpses. . . . I am fairly thick-skinned but I find this kind of thing more than I can bear . . . 50,000 or 100,000 people have been murdered."¹² That was the situation in Old Delhi, where Muslims were murdered inside mansions owned for generations by their families, dating back to the heyday of Mughal power.

"Has the city of Delhi which always appeared gay turned into a city of the dead?" asked Mahatma Gandhi when he returned there from Calcutta in September.¹³ Thousands of terrified Muslims squatted along roads and in dark alleys of the old city, afraid to be caught inside their abandoned homes. The venerable vice-chancellor of Delhi's Muslim University (Jamia Millia), Dr. Zakir Husain, told Gandhi how he had been attacked in East Punjab by a Sikh mob and his life saved by a Sikh captain, who chased the bullies away by drawing his revolver and shouting. The most painful stories Nehru and Gandhi heard were of Hindu and Sikh women, abducted by Muslims who tried either to rape or first to convert and "marry" them, and if they were lucky enough to escape that torture, were then driven away by their own husbands and fathers who treated them as "damaged goods" or "polluted" untouchables. "Dishonoured" wives and daughters were encouraged to take their own lives, in some cases shot dead by their husbands or fathers, who self-righteously insisted they were "protecting" their women from "a fate worse than death!"[14]

Justice Khosla estimates that half a million Punjabi Hindus and Sikhs were murdered or died of exhaustion before reaching safe havens in Delhi that September; Penderel Moon set the total number of Punjabi deaths lower, at about 180,00.[15] In both Punjab and Bengal, however, after August 16, between 500,000 and one million people died as refugees of Partition. More extreme "estimates of deaths vary between 200,000 and three million," Mushirul Hasan noted in his introduction to *The Partition Omnibus*, but neither of those seems credible.[16]

On August 27, Nehru received a phone call from India's high commissioner in Pakistan, Sri Prakasha, reporting that so many "persons" were "being done to death daily." When he conveyed Prakasha's news to Mountbatten, he added "I do not mention the figure he gave because it is incredible. . . . Still he is not a man to be easily led away."[17] Nehru's self-confidence was severely shaken by these dark reports, and though he could not bring himself directly to accuse Mountbatten of having made a most horrible mistake by rushing headlong into the tragedy erupting now all over Punjab, he alluded to his deepest feelings and fears, confessing distractedly, "I do not quite know why I am writing to you. . . . I suppose I am not directly responsible for what is taking place in the Punjab. I do not quite know who is responsible." He did know, but how could he openly say it to the man he had chosen to serve as free India's first head of state. Having ignored the advice and warnings of Mahatma Gandhi, lured instead by the rose-colored promises of Lord and Lady Mountbatten, and half blinded by the glitter of posh parties they hosted in Government House, Nehru rightly recognized now that he was as much to blame for what was happening in Punjab as was Mountbatten, perhaps because he understood so much more than the fast-moving viceroy. Mountbatten rushed over to see him the same day he received that troubled letter, but he came not to commiserate with Nehru about the daily deaths in Punjab or to suggest emergency steps they should take to alleviate the suffering and restore order, but to invite Nehru to Princess Elizabeth's wedding in London to his favorite nephew, Philip. Nehru, incredulous, refused, "doubtful of the psychological effect" his absence from India for so frivolous a reason might have.

On September 9, in a broadcast to his nation—the "Crisis in the Spirit of India"—Nehru said: "I am ashamed of the acts that my people have done and I fear that the disgrace and the consequences of evil deeds will remain with us for a long time. . . . We must rescue our people from West Punjab. We must cooperate in the process of exchange of populations wherever that is possible."[18] He had previously refused to agree to the massive population transfers proposed by Punjab's Sikhs, but he now realized it was perhaps the only way to save countless lives. Three days later, on September 12, Nehru informed his cabinet that more than 1.25 million Hindus and Sikhs had come into India as refugees in the past month, and almost as many Muslims had left India for Pakistan. "Are we to aim at . . . elimination of the Muslim population from India, or are we to consolidate, make secure and absorb as full citizens the Muslims who remain in India?"[19] Nehru had long been in the vanguard of those Congress Party leaders to insist that India must become a truly secular multicultural society, neither Hindu-only nor Hindu-first, refusing to imitate Pakistan's Islamic state. He loved Persian and Urdu poetry and the fine arts and architecture of the great Mughals, who had so enriched Delhi and Agra. The savagery he saw all around him now in Delhi and Punjab left Nehru shaken to the core of his faith in civilized human behavior and the possibilities of a harmonious progressive Socialist society emerging in India now that the martial restraints of foreign imperial rule were so suddenly removed

Dr. Zakir Husain, soon to become India's first Muslim president, warned Nehru's cabinet on September 16 that Delhi's "Old Fort—Purana Quila— and Mughal emperor Humayun's tomb had become "human dumps," occupied by thousands of Punjabi refugees without adequate water or sanitation facilities. The dangers of potential cholera and typhoid epidemics loomed larger every day in hot and overcrowded Delhi. Mahatma Gandhi also spoke out every evening against the mistreatment of Muslims, appealing to those who came to his prayer meetings to take care of Muslims forced out of their homes and to treat them with loving kindness. Hindu fanatics called him "Jinnah's stooge!" and "Mohammad Gandhi!" Vallabhbhai Patel was in charge of Delhi's police, and Nehru urged him to work harder to activate them to apprehend Hindu Rashtriya Svayamsevak Sangh (RSS, "National Volunteer Association") thugs, who terrorized Muslims. Patel himself sympathized with and strongly supported the RSS. When Nehru wrote to tell him that RSS gangs, working together with armed Sikhs, committed "most of the murders" in Delhi, as part of their "wave of fascism which is gripping India now," Patel exploded and threatened to resign from the cabinet.[20] But Gandhi urged them both to stop squabbling and to carry on, insisting there was no escape, short of death, for any of them. India was forced to suffer the poison diet of Partition's wooden loaf, since they had agreed to it for her starving children.

By mid-September, Lieutenant General Tuker described Amritsar railway station, through which he passed on his last tour of Punjab: "Hindu and Sikh evacuees are everywhere, and the . . . whole station stinks of hu-man excreta and urine. Masses of flies are carrying infection from the filth all round to the food the evacuees are eating, as they sit in this scene of 'Disgrace Abounding.'"[21] All rail travel in Punjab had by now been offi-cially declared "unsafe." Even those Refugee Specials, trains that were sent out with armed guards aboard, proved virtual mass coffins on wheels. In-spector General Gilbert Waddell of the Punjab Railway Police reported "with horror . . . the slaughter of Muslims between stations all through the Sikh-dominated area [of Patiala State and Mahendargarh]."[22] Another train ar-rived in Jullundur with 145 dead, one hundred of whom had been murdered and the rest of whom had died of thirst.

Punjabi Sikhs and Muslims had long served in both British Indian and princely state armies of that province, which during World War II had sup-plied 715,000 soldiers for the British Indian Army and another 633,000 for the princely states. That martial experience gave sword-wielding Sikh horse-men, who attacked Muslim-filled trains in the countryside, fearless furor and deadly aim in their killings. Muslim "guards" were equally brutal in exacting vengeance on carriages filled with Hindus and Sikhs moving the other way, and in East Punjab's cities, as well as Delhi, the RSS paramilitary forces proved almost as effective at committing murders in the service of "God"—whether named Waheguru, Allah, or Ram.

Bengalis, on the other hand, had long been labeled "non-martial" Indi-ans by post-1857 Sepoy "Mutiny" British administrators, who effectively closed all British martial recruiting offices to "Bengali traitors." Bengal, long the most prosperous and intellectual center of British India, with its capital at Calcutta, turned in the aftermath of Partition into two sadly di-minished fragments: West Bengal, which retained Calcutta, joined the In-dian Union; and East Bengal became a rural slum as East Pakistan, whose less populous but martially and administratively dominant West Pakistan was divided from it by almost a thousand miles of North India.[23] Muslim ex-Chief Minister of Bengal H. S. Suhrawardy tried his best to keep Bengal united as an independent dominion, but Nehru and Patel so strongly op-posed this that they convinced Mountbatten of the futility of considering it.

Many of Bengal's Hindus supported Suhrawardy's attempt to bring a much larger, more powerful "Land of Bengali-speakers" (Bangladesh) to life fully a quarter century before its impoverished East Pakistani fragment was finally born in the wake of the Indo-Pak War of 1971. Sarat Bose, elder brother of Netaji Subhas, so strongly supported Suhrawardy's valiant ef-fort, that in June of 1947 he discussed the prospect with Jinnah, who readily agreed to "Bengal remaining united and becoming independent."[24] Bengali Congress Party leader Kiran Shankar Roy also agreed with Suhrawardy, until he was called to Delhi by Nehru and Patel and told in no uncertain terms that Congress's "High Command" had definitely rejected any prospect of letting go of Calcutta or the Hindu-majority districts of West Bengal.[25] Nehru may well have imagined that Jinnah would never accept what he called a "moth-eaten" Pakistan, without Calcutta or East Punjab. Or perhaps he agreed with Patel that, even if Jinnah did accept the fragments Mountbatten offered him, they would prove so unviable that "Pakistan" would before long be forced to beg Congress to permit it to rejoin the Indian Union. Neither happened, however.

The partition of Bengal, so long and deeply united by its Bengali language and poetic literature, proved as tragic as that of Punjab, displacing even more people. Far from the glare of Delhi's publicity Calcutta and Dacca were neglected by journalists and later by scholars. Nehru and Patel were so angry at Radcliffe when they learned of his "disastrous" award of the predominantly "tribal" [neither Hindu nor Muslim] Chittagong Hill Tracts to East Pakistan that they threatened to "boycott" Mountbatten's Independence Day party unless that award was "rectified."[26] Nehru went so far as to insist that those Hill Tracts "people would be justified in resisting this award by force and that the Central Government would be bound to support them! So much for his undertaking . . . to accept and implement the awards whatever they might be," Mountbatten wrote Attlee and the king.[27] Mountbatten, therefore, found yet another reason for keeping the new boundaries top secret, sealing up the Bengal award as well as Punjab's until after independence, by which time Nehru had cooled off. But when the Bengal boundary award was finally revealed, it became clear that some 42 percent of undivided Bengal's Hindu population, about 11.4 million people, were left in East Pakistan. Of those, only 344,000 Hindu refugees initially fled to West Bengal, most Bengali minorities clearly hoping to live "peacefully" in East Pakistan.[28] Just as Mahatma Gandhi's best effort to keep the peace in Calcutta by living under one roof with Suhrawardy proved but a "nine-day wonder," so too did the peaceful dreams of most Bengali Hindus.

Millions of Bengali Hindu refugees kept moving west as their persecution by East Pakistani officials and police grew harsher. Punjabi and Pathan martial bullies, who had been flown to Dacca from Karachi, Lahore, and Rawalpindi, could not even speak or understand Bengali. In 1948, 786,000 terrified East Bengali refugees fled to West Bengal, and another 213,000 came in 1949, the tide continuing to build over the next two decades. Generations of impoverished Bengali refugees lived out their lives on the crowded railway platforms of Calcutta's Central Station.

"I have seen great crowds many times in various parts of India and I wondered," Nehru broadcast from Calcutta two months after Partition, "whether I was right, whether it was with the approval of our people I was sitting in Delhi as the Prime Minister of India." He tried now to stem the tide of Bengali Hindus eager to escape from Pakistan and seek work in overcrowded Calcutta, ending up as beggars at the station. "We must behave like men," Nehru told them. "I would beg you not to behave in a manner which shows lack of discipline."[29] He appealed to Prime Minister Liaquat Ali Khan in Karachi as well, but Liaquat could do no more to stop the mounting tide of Bengalis leaving East Pakistan than Nehru could. By March 1948, the situation, Nehru warned his new chief minister of West Bengal, Dr. B. C. Roy, was so "rapidly deteriorating" that "we might well have to face a crisis of unprecedented dimensions which might overwhelm us."[30]

Jinnah had as much reason to worry about Pakistan's Bengali majority, which grew more restive every day, demanding that its rich language be recognized, together with Urdu, as the national language of Pakistan. For all Bengalis, Muslims as well as Hindus, love of their language, the most powerful magnet for its people, was a unifying force much greater for them than either Islam or Hinduism alone. On Pakistan Day, March 21, 1948, Jinnah flew to Dacca, his only visit as governor-general to East Pakistan's capital. He made his worst political blunder by insisting that Urdu must remain the only national language of Pakistan, addressing a third of a million Bengalis, who had waited all day in the sun to hear him speak bitter words in a foreign language. Six months later Jinnah would die, and twenty-three years after that East Pakistan was reborn as "The Land of Bengali-speakers," *Bangla-Desh*.

Freedom brought no economic boom to Calcutta, no increase in the bare subsistence economy of most of its millions of residents, many of whom remained refugee beggars. The labor unions of Bengal, the most effective of which were run by communists, threatened strikes in several major industries. Nehru, himself a socialist, if not a Marxist, was embarrassed by strike threats and tried his best to negotiate settlements. But Bengal's communist leaders refused to be talked out of what they all believed to be labor's major weapon in the class war against indigenous industrial capital and imperialist financiers. "We have no desire whatever to come in the way of legitimate industrial activity including strikes," Nehru told West Bengal's union leaders, "but it seems clear to us that there is a fear of sabotage. . . . [T]herefore . . . any Government employees joining the strike in Calcutta will be liable to be dismissed."[31] Many of Nehru's socialist comrades lost faith in him now that he had become prime minister, and the Communist Party members of Bengal were angry to find their party banned, not by officials of the British Raj, but by their own comrades in power. "There was no intention of banning the Communist Party or indeed of large-scale arrests," Nehru insisted, only of "dangerous" troublemakers, especially "in the security services." The Calcutta strike lasted more than a week. Those "guilty of violence" and all Bengali communist "ring leaders" were arrested.[32]

Governor-General and Lady Mountbatten embarked on their "grand tour" of eastern India in March 1948, the entire party, including servants, comprising "over fifty persons." Their nine-day itinerary schedule started and ended in Calcutta, and was beautifully printed up in tastefully colored "booklets."[33] Alan Campbell-Johnson accompanied them in their Rolls as they drove around Calcutta's slums, "always with the same sense of foreboding, bordering on despair, at the sprawling squalor of the life it reveals— life lived below the margin of human rights and hopes. . . . Emancipation is far away—from hunger and poverty, from industrial exploitation, from communal terror; and lying in wait to solve it all, the great Communist cheat. We hurried past."[34] Amidst the celebrations, the mayor sharply criticized Partition, which he termed a "violation of an axiom of history" in this ancient land "undivided and indivisible."

In Calcutta, Lord and Lady Mountbatten visited Fort William, its two square miles of somber gray stone walls and six sturdy gates epitomizing the solid powers of the Raj. That fort was begun two centuries earlier by Bengal's thirty-two-year-old governor, Bob Clive, soon after his small force of British soldiers blasted a brash young nawab's subverted Mughal army to bits in Plassey's "Mango Grove."[35] Fort William took twenty-two years to complete, costing Bengal's treasury two million pounds sterling to mount its six hundred twenty-nine cannon, while famine wiped out a third of Bengal's starving population during the heyday of "Nabob" Clive's plunder. The officers of the Armed Forces of Calcutta hosted a splendid reception for the Mountbattens at Fort William's officers' club. "We left afterwards for dinner at the Royal Tolley Gunge," the oldest golf club in India, Campbell-Johnson reported. "The British colony were here in full force. . . . [T]he Mountbattens were at their phenomenal best during all the small talk, setting the conversational ball rolling . . . breaking down reserve and shyness without apparent effort."[36]

Nehru had by then acquired some of Lord Mountbatten's most passionate interests. He devoted most of a long letter to Bengal's chief minister to discussion of India's anthem, "Jana Gana Mana," telling him that it had been played "at the Waldorf Astoria Hotel . . . before an international gathering . . . at the time of the United Nations meeting. It produced a sensation. . . . There was a tremendous demand for it among Americans. . . . [W]e suggested that Army bands should practice it . . . and it is now regularly played by the Army, the Navy and the Air Force. . . . [W]e considered it in Cabinet here."[37] Nehru also gave Dr. Roy detailed instructions about where and when to display India's flag and exactly which officials were obliged to fly it over their residences and on their cars.

Was the rising refugee death toll in the aftermath of Partition simply too painful for Prime Minister Nehru to focus on every hour of each day?

Or was it the ineptitude of his colleagues in the cabinet and their subordinates in the field? Or the impotence of all of them to stop the slaughter and heal wounds opening wider in Bengal as well as Punjab? Now the awful responsibility was on Nehru's shoulders, not Mountbatten's. No longer could the British Raj be blamed, for they had pulled out overnight. It was in his hands alone now—his and Patel's. Why not focus on the national anthem, then, and the flag? What better ways to escape at least some of the pain of great power?

10

Indo-Pak War over Kashmir, October 1947–July 1948

THE MOST TRAGIC, still unresolved legacy of Partition was the Indo-Pak Wars over Kashmir, the first of which erupted in October 1947. The state of Jammu and Kashmir had a population of some four million people, three-fourths of whom were Muslim. Its autocratic maharaja, Hari Singh, was a Hindu, and he alone was given the option by Mountbatten of deciding to which dominion, India or Pakistan, his state should accede by August 15. Kashmir's Maharaja, who preferred to keep his state independent, hoping it might become a Switzerland of Asia, signed standstill agreements with both dominions late in August. In October, however, Maharaja Hari Singh's time to choose between India and Pakistan ran out.

The battle for Kashmir started among poor Muslim peasants in the district of Poonch, who rebelled against their Hindu Rajput landlords early in October 1947. On October 10 the London *Times* reported that Muslims were "systematically exterminated" in Poonch by forces of the Hindu maharaja of Kashmir.[1] Many of Poonch's Muslim peasants fled to Pakistan, where they were armed and supported by Pakistanis, who listened sympathetically to their tales of Hindu terror. Before month's end they were joined by Frontier Pathan tribals, eager to climb into British army trucks with their rifles loaded, heading toward Kashmir.

Though Prime Minister Nehru's Kashmiri Pandit ancestors had abandoned Kashmir's Vale almost two centuries before Jawaharlal was born in 1889, "Pandit" Nehru always spoke of Kashmir as his "family home." He was, in fact, born in his father Motilal Nehru's princely mansion in Allahabad, and, after returning from years of study at Harrow and Cambridge in England, he was married there, and then took his bride to Kashmir for their honeymoon. In Kashmir, Nehru shot and killed a bear in the mountains, and then almost fell to his death in a glacial crevasse beyond Zoji-la Pass. Nehru wrote of Kashmir as a "beautiful woman," retaining his romantic fascination for and devotion to her the rest of his life.[2] Unfortunately, Nehru's personal passion for Kashmir affected his political and diplomatic judgment. He lavished India's martial and material resources on the "defense" of Kashmir's Muslim-majority Vale throughout his nearly two decades of premier power, without first asking the people of Kashmir if they wanted him to do so.

"What happens in Kashmir will affect the rest of India," Nehru wrote to the popular "Lion of Kashmir" Sheikh Mohammad Abdullah, whose release from prison Patel secured from Hari Singh in October. "For me Kashmir's future is of the most intimate personal significance. On no account do I want Kashmir to become a kind of colony of foreign interests. I fear Pakistan is likely to become that if it survives at all."[3] Nehru and Patel hoped that as chief minister of Kashmir, Sheikh Abdullah would be able to convince his fellow Muslim majority in the Vale to remain happy within India's union, rather than so anxious to join their Muslim brothers in Pakistan as to be willing to fight and die for their freedom. On October 22, several thousand armed Pathan tribesmen invaded Kashmir in British army trucks, capturing Muzaffarabad, which was to become the capital of Pakistan's Azad ("Free") Kashmir. Maharaja Hari Singh soon fled with his family and treasured jewels from his endangered winter capital of Srinagar, south to Jammu. There he subsequently refused to sign the instrument of accession to India's union that V. P. Menon had brought for him.

Nehru and Patel ordered all of north India's more than 100 civil and military transport planes fueled up and kept ready to fly India's First Sikh Battalion to Srinagar from Delhi's airport on October 26. They reached Srinagar before the invading tribals could and forced all of them back up the Baramulla Road to the outskirts of Muzaffarabad. A few days later Hari Singh agreed to sign the instrument of accession, "requesting" help from India "against raiders" who invaded his state. Nehru also convinced the maharaja and his chosen prime minister Mahajan to accept Sheikh Abdullah as Kashmir's new chief minister. "No looseness or weakness should be tolerated," Nehru cautioned Abdullah. "We have taken on a tough job. But I am dead sure that we shall pull through . . . and we shall swim across to the other shore."[4]

To allay international opposition to his precipitous martial action, Nehru wired Attlee to assure him that "aiding Kashmir in this emergency is not designed in any way to influence the State to accede to India. Our view . . . is that the question of accession in any disputed territory of State must be decided in accordance with wishes of the people and we adhere to this view."[5]

That had always been Gandhi's view, of course, which he stressed at his daily prayer meetings in Delhi, saying, "The people of Kashmir should be asked whether they want to join Pakistan or India. Let them do as they want. The ruler is nothing. The people are everything."[6] Nehru said he "agreed" that a plebiscite should be held in the state, but first he insisted that "law and order" must be restored there and all the "invading forces" completely withdrawn.

Gandhi was asked each evening by people who attended his prayer meetings what he thought of the conflict in Kashmir. "If the people of Kashmir are in favour of opting for Pakistan, no power on earth can stop them from doing so," the Mahatma replied. "But they should be left free to decide for themselves. . . . If the people of Kashmir, in spite of its Muslim majority, wish to accede to India no one can stop them. . . . If the people of the Indian Union are going there to force the Kashmiris, they should be stopped . . . they should stop by themselves. About this I have no doubt."[7]

Nehru sent Kashmiri Pandit general Hiralal Atal to Srinagar to launch secret operations throughout Kashmir, including trying to bomb several bridges over the Jhelum River. "It is a very risky job, but worth doing."[8] Nehru was more enthusiastic about and attentive to the war in Kashmir than to any of the more urgent and painful refugee problems awaiting his attention in Delhi. "The trouble in Kashmir . . . may well be the saving of us in many ways," Nehru confessed to General Atal. "It may go a long way in settling our problem with Pakistan . . . and I hope it will change the entire communal atmosphere in India. The fact that Hindus, Muslims and Sikhs are cooperating for the defence of Kashmir will tone up our whole system."[9]

Attlee did not like the reports he received of heavy fighting between the newborn dominions of His Majesty's Commonwealth and asked Nehru for details. "Some 2,000 or more fully-armed and well-equipped men came in motor transport, crossed over to Kashmir," Nehru wired the prime minister on October 28.

> The Maharaja appealed urgently to us for help. He further suggested accession to Indian Union. . . . We decided at first not to send any troops. . . . But later developments made it clear that, unless we send troops immediately, complete disaster would overtake Kashmir. . . . We therefore elected to send troops. . . . Early this morning one battalion . . . was flown to Srinagar. . . . Our attitude and policy have been, as I have stated to you, that in case of any disputed State territory, the problem of accession should be decided amicably and in accordance with the wishes of the people. . . . Our military intervention is purely defensive in aim and scope.[10]

That day Nehru also reassured Pakistan's Prime Minister Liaquat, who was even more anxious than Attlee about the swiftness and extent of India's martial airlift and operation. The "action Government of India has taken has been forced upon them by circumstances and imminent and grave danger to Srinagar. They have no desire to intervene in the affairs of Kashmir State after raiders have been driven away," Nehru insisted. "Government of India have no desire to impose any decision and will abide by people's wishes."[11] Over the next decade, whenever the United Nations Security Council's Commission on India and Pakistan (UNCIP) sent its three most distinguished chairmen to India to ask Nehru to agree to a plebiscite in Kashmir, supervised and monitored by the UN, he always adamantly refused. Nehru finally withdrew any pretense of supporting a UN-supervised plebiscite, arguing that India's "elections" in Kashmir were as "valid" as such a plebiscite. By then Nehru had ordered the imprisonment of his "friend" Sheikh Abdullah for denouncing India's growing martial presence in Kashmir and favoring a "free and fair" plebiscite throughout the state.

Jinnah tried in late October to send "two brigades" of Pakistan's regular army into Kashmir to fight India's army there, but Field Marshal Auchinleck stopped him. The "Auk" flew immediately to Lahore to explain to Pakistan's governor-general that unless he withdrew his order every British officer in Pakistan's army would be ordered immediately to "stand down." That stand-down order would begin with General Douglas Gracey, Pakistan's commander-in-chief, who still served under Field Marshal Auchinleck, Supreme Commander of all British Forces in South Asia. Pakistan's army would thus be left leaderless. So Jinnah backed down, more fully aware of just how high a price he had to pay for thwarting Mountbatten's desire to become Pakistan's governor-general as well as India's.

Jinnah still hoped, however, that Mountbatten would agree to fly with Nehru to Lahore on October 29 to discuss with him and Liaquat how best to resolve their conflict over Kashmir. Mountbatten accepted Jinnah's invitation, but Nehru claimed he was "ill" and refused to go. Mountbatten phoned Jinnah the next morning to explain how "sick" Nehru was and to request a postponement of their meeting, inviting Jinnah and Liaquat to fly to Delhi instead. Jinnah was dying, however, and Liaquat was bedridden with a bleeding ulcer. So Mountbatten promised to bring Nehru to Lahore with him on November 1. But then, Nehru's temper flared up and he refused to "discuss anything" with Jinnah, leaving Mountbatten to fly with Ismay to Lahore for their last meeting with Jinnah. Pakistan's Quaid-i-Azam was barely more than a skeleton by then, his voice faint as he told those robust British lords that he had "lost interest in what the world thought of him since the British Commonwealth had let him down when he asked them to come to the rescue of Pakistan."[12]

Soon after that meeting Jinnah's health deteriorated, a mood of fatalism shrouding his spirit. "We have been the victims of a deeply-laid and well-planned conspiracy executed with utter disregard of the elementary principles of honesty, chivalry and honour," Jinnah told his compatriots at month's end in Lahore's University stadium. "We thank Providence for giving us courage and faith to fight these forces of evil. . . . Do not be afraid of death. . . . We should face it bravely to save the honour of Pakistan and Islam."[13] It was "the first time" his sister Fatima heard her brother speak of death, but he spoke and thought of little else from then until his death in Karachi on September 11, 1948.

Despite what Nehru had told Attlee a few days earlier, he wrote to Kashmir's Prime Minister Mahajan, who had proposed going to meet Jinnah to discuss a cease-fire in Kashmir:

> You will appreciate, we have made a tremendous effort to pour in troops and equipment into the valley of Kashmir. A brigade has also gone to Jammu. . . . I hope that soon our troops will take the offensive. This has been done at tremendous cost to us and holding up most of our other activities in India. All our air services have stopped and every available plane is going to Kashmir. . . . I see no reason why any of you should go to Lahore to confer with Mr. Jinnah. . . . Our position is perfectly clear and there is very little to discuss. . . . It is obvious that a plebiscite cannot take place till complete law and order have been established. I see no chance of this happening for some months.[14]

Nehru also warned Sheikh Abdullah not to think of going to Pakistan to meet with Jinnah. "Any direct contacts should be avoided."[15]

Gandhi was asked if he had abandoned his faith in nonviolence and approved what India's Army was doing in Kashmir. He replied sadly:

> I am a nobody and no one listens to me. . . . I have never abandoned my non-violence. . . . [I]t was acceptable till we attained independence. Now they [Nehru and Patel] wonder how they can rule with non-violence. . . . If I could have my way of nonviolence and everybody listened to me, we would not send our army as we are doing now. And if we did send, it would be a non-violent army. . . . It would be a non-violent war. . . . But to whom can I say this? Today poison has spread on all sides and people kill each other in barbarous manner.[16]

Gandhi offered to go to Pakistan at the head of a nonviolent Indian "shanti-sena" (army of peace), but Nehru refused to agree.

Nehru sent his toughest Sikh general, Kalwant Singh, to Kashmir to take "overall" command of India's troops there. "He is able and strong," Nehru told Sheikh Abdullah, "just the man for taking the offensive. . . . Our orders to him are to take Baramula at any cost and very soon. . . . Having cleared up the Valley completely we shall proceed along Jhelum Valley Road to Kohala and clear that up. It is possible that a number of raiders might take refuge in the mountains. . . . Every army has to face this kind of thing."[17] Half a century later, with the size of India's army in Kashmir having grown to over half a million men, that "kind of thing" continued to harass them.

On November 11, Nehru flew up to Srinagar to rally his troops there, assuring them that "during the past two weeks, the eyes of India have been fixed on Kashmir, where a battle is in progress between freedom and slavery. . . . I am proud of you. I congratulate you all, officers and men belonging to all branches. . . . You have not only saved Kashmir, you have also restored the prestige of India, your mother country."[18] While he was in Kashmir, however, Nehru was "horrified to learn" that on November 5 and 6 some 5,000 Muslims had been driven from their homes in Jammu and sent off in convoys under the "protection" of Kashmir state Dogra Hindu troops, who drove them outside the city limits and left them to be gunned down by RSS terrorists from Punjab.[19] That news sobered the compassionate Pandit Nehru, but did not make him change his mind about agreeing to hold a plebiscite in Kashmir, or even allowing Sheikh Abdullah, or Mahajan, or Hari Singh, who was by now also eager to fly to Pakistan himself, to speak with Jinnah. Revered as he was by all Pakistanis, Jinnah could have put an end overnight to the dreadful conflict that continued to drain the wealth and energies of India and Pakistan, and so much of the blood of Kashmir's poor people. Then a plebiscite could have been held, supervised by the UN, to ascertain the true wishes of all Kashmiris.

Prime Minister Attlee was wise enough to realize what a dreadful mistake he had made in relying on Mountbatten's inept judgment to accelerate his cabinet's timetable for withdrawing Britain's martial shield from South Asia. Mountbatten's hyperactive passion for speed and his focus on secrecy had only added international war to refugee chaos and slaughter in Partition's hasty wake, turning India's internal communal conflict into an ever-escalating war over Kashmir. So Attlee cabled Nehru again in November to "suggest" that perhaps the "speediest and most satisfactory way" to arrange for an impartial test of the preference of Kashmir's people, as to which dominion they wished to join, was to appeal to the International Court of Justice as an impartial arbiter. "I am grateful to you for your message regarding Kashmir," Nehru replied defensively. "We do not, however, consider the International Court of Justice to be the appropriate organ for providing requisite machinery."[20] Nehru dared not contemplate the possibility of "losing" his beloved Kashmir.

"Kashmir has gone through fire," Nehru emoted to India's constituent assembly in Delhi two days after rejecting Attlee's sensible advice. "This fair land which nature has made so lovely has been desecrated by the people who have indulged in murder, arson, loot and foul attacks on women and children. . . . Whatever the future may hold, this chapter in the history of Kashmir will be worth reading."[21]

Yet even as Nehru spoke of the battle raging in Kashmir, his own high commissioner [ambassador] to Pakistan, Sri Prakasa, admitted to Mountbatten that "for the sake of peace all round," the "best thing" India could do was to hand over Kashmir to Pakistan. "I was amazed," Nehru wrote Sri Prakasa as soon as Mountbatten reported what he had said,

> that you hinted at Kashmir being handed over to Pakistan. . . . If we did anything of the kind our Government would not last many days and there would be no peace. . . . It would lead to war with Pakistan because of public opinion here and of war-like elements coming in control of our policy. We cannot and we will not leave Kashmir to its fate. . . . The fact is that Kashmir is of the most vital significance to India. . . . [H]ere lies the rub. . . . We have to see this through to the end. . . . Kashmir is going to be a drain on our resources, but it is going to be a greater drain on Pakistan.[22]

Nehru was not only obsessed with protecting and at all costs defending Kashmir, but believed, as did Patel, that the war over Kashmir would swiftly bankrupt Pakistan, even as it had put an end to all urban welfare and rural development projects throughout India.

Mahatma Gandhi was repeatedly asked in Delhi by Rural Uplift and Constructive Program workers to whom he spoke why "so little headway" was made in rural reconstruction work, to which India's Congress Party [now in power] had always been committed. "It may be that we have no heart. Because if we were endowed with a heart we would have been sensitive to the pain of others," Gandhi replied. "The freedom that came was not true freedom. . . . My eyes have now been opened. . . . Today, everybody in the Congress is running after power. That presages grave danger."[23] He tried to end that political power game by earlier advising the Congress to "disband" its party entirely, but neither Nehru nor Patel, and certainly no other members of Congress's Working Committee, liked that idea. Gandhi then tried to convince them to stop the fighting in Kashmir, but that too evoked no positive response. He understood that Nehru and Patel hoped to bankrupt Pakistan by escalating the Kashmir war and by continuing to withhold overdue payments of a substantial sum of money India owed to Karachi's treasury, Pakistan's share of British India's cash assets, all kept in Delhi's Central Bank. He urged his friends as earnestly as he could to remit those funds, since it was not "honorable" to withhold promised payments. Gandhi had always been as scrupulous about paying his debts as he was about keeping vows.

By mid-December Gandhi was convinced that by airlifting "everything to support the war" in Kashmir, India was recklessly throwing away its fortune while ignoring the needs of its "starving millions." "It is a tragedy and a shame. For so long we fought through the charkha [spinning wheel] and the moment we have power in our hands we forget it. Today we look up to the army. . . . [W]e throw away money so recklessly."[24] He believed now that only "a handful of persons" were "behind" this "communal conflict" in Kashmir. He tried his best to urge Nehru to give up premier power and become the "secretary" to a "peasant" prime minister. "Our peasant ministers would stay not in a palace but in a mud-house, and would toil on the land. . . . Then alone can there be a true peasant rule."[25] Nehru, like Mountbatten, however, thought that Gandhi had "lost" his wisdom, if not his sanity, and that such "strange" ideas were too bizarre for serious consideration. Nehru came to Gandhi to complain about Patel never doing what he should to stop the persecution of Delhi's Muslims. Patel came to complain about Nehru, threatening to resign from the cabinet because the prime minister never listened to him, or any one. Each blamed the other for not releasing the millions that India owed Pakistan.

Moved by the spirit of Christmas, Gandhi offered a simple solution to end the Kashmir War on December 25: "Can we not settle the issue between ourselves? . . . One should always admit one's mistakes. . . . I shall advise Pakistan and India to sit together and decide the matter. . . . The Maharaja can step aside. . . . If they want an arbitrator they can appoint one."[26] It was Mahatma Gandhi's last offer to serve India in the way he knew best: as an impartial arbitrator for peace. Instead of thanks from his former disciples and an immediate invitation to serve as he so generously offered, "I have been severely reprimanded for what I said concerning Kashmir," Gandhi reported a few days later. "Occasionally it becomes one's duty to offer such advice. . . . The raiders . . . say that the Muslims of Kashmir are being ground down under the tyranny of a Hindu raj and that they have come for their succour. . . . It seems obvious to me, as it should seem obvious to others . . . that if Sheikh Abdullah cannot carry with him the minority as well as the majority . . . Kashmir cannot be saved by military might alone."[27] The minority Hindu Pandits had lost faith in Sheikh Abdullah, urging their fellow Pandit Nehru to remove him from high office and to return one of their own community to the premier power that Pandits long held over Kashmir's state. If Nehru had only listened to Gandhi, inviting him to arbitrate the Kashmir conflict with Jinnah, India and Pakistan might have been spared three wars and the tragic loss of countless lives, at least 50,000 of whom were Kashmiri.

On December 30, 1947, Gandhi wrote, "I hold that self-government is . . . only a means to good government. . . . And true democracy is what promotes the welfare of the people. The test of good government lies in the largest good of the people with the minimum of control. . . . [A] system that admits of poverty and unemployment is not fit to survive even for a day."[28] Gandhi was called "Mohammad" Gandhi by angry Hindus, too blind from the pain of lost loved ones to understand that India's saintly father was only trying to save all its children from the dreadful traumas and deprivations of war.

On January 12, 1948, Mahatma Gandhi launched his last fast, the "fiery" ultimate weapon of his passionate nature, which he used to deliver his message of love to ears deaf to any verbal appeal. "I yearn for heart friendship between Hindus, Sikhs and Muslims," Gandhi told his friends. "Today it is non-existent. . . . Fasting is a satyagrahi's last resort. . . . This time my fast is not only against Hindus and Muslims but also against the Judases who put on false appearances and betray themselves, myself and society."[29] He was thus fasting for much more than the simple payment to Pakistan of the 550 million rupees of British India's cash balance debt, long since promised by Nehru and Patel. Many Hindus believed, however, that his desire to pay Pakistan was Gandhi's sole reason for launching this final "blackmail" fast, and cried aloud that he should "fast unto death," not simply to "capacity," as he initially announced he would. Three days after he stopped taking food, India's cabinet announced its agreement to transfer the funds to Pakistan, and on the fourth day Gandhi thanked the cabinet, hoping this would lead to "an honourable settlement not only of the Kashmir question, but of all the differences between the two Dominions. Friendship should replace the present enmity."[30] He was too weak to stand but soon recovered enough strength to walk to his evening prayer meetings.

Then on Friday, January 30, 1948, hate-crazed Hindu Brahman Nathuram Godse fired three bullets at close range into Mahatma Gandhi's chest. Calling out to God—"Heh, Ram"—the Mahatma collapsed, dying in the garden of Birla House as the sun set over Delhi. "The light has gone out of our lives and there is darkness everywhere," Nehru declaimed over Radio India. "A madman has put an end to his life, for I can only call him mad who did it, and yet there has been enough of poison spread in this country during the past years and months, and this poison has had an effect on people's minds."[31] All extremist Hindu parties were banned. Riots targeting Hindu leaders of the RSS in Delhi, Bombay, Pune, and Nasik left many dead, their houses burned to the ground, before relative calm was restored to those terror-torn cities. Mahatma Gandhi and his philosophy of peace and love thus became the most tragic victims of the violent Partition he had struggled to avert. That his wise warnings were totally misunderstood by Lord Mountbatten was much less surprising than that they had also been ignored by his disciples, Pandit Nehru and Sardar Patel, prime minister and deputy prime minister of free India's first Congress government.

The war over Kashmir continued daily to take an exorbitant toll, which worried many wise Indians, as it had Mahatma Gandhi. One of those most concerned was Chakravarti Rajagopalachari (C. R.), West Bengal's first governor, who abhorred Nehru's profligate "squandering" on Kashmir of India's precious "resources . . . like trying to mend a broken tea-cup" during a state banquet "and forgetting all about the guests."[32] A few months later, when Nehru invited C. R. to succeed Mountbatten as India's governor-general, he initially demurred, suggesting that Nehru himself should become India's next head of state, letting Patel be prime minister. Nehru rejected that advice as "completely impracticable."[33] Though always introspective and subject to sudden shifts of mood, Nehru more often questioned the wisdom of his own decisions now, feeling more deeply depressed and weary, as he told Mountbatten on the eve of his departure: "May be, we have made many mistakes, you and we . . . but I do believe that we did try to do right . . . the right thing by India."[34]

Nehru was even more forthright in expressing his fears of foolish failure to his sad Muslim friend, the Nawab of Bhopal, to whom he wrote a few weeks later:

> It has been our misfortune . . . the misfortune of India and Pakistan, that evil impulses triumphed. . . . I have spent the greater part of my adult life in pursuing and trying to realise certain ideals. . . . Can you imagine the sorrow that confronts me when I see after more than thirty years of incessant effort the failure of much that I longed for passionately? . . . I know that we have been to blame in many matters. . . . Partition came and we accepted it because we thought that perhaps that way, however painful it was, we might have some peace. . . . Perhaps we acted wrongly. It is difficult to judge now. And yet, the consequences of that partition have been so terrible that one is inclined to think that anything else would have been preferable. . . . [A]ll my sense of history rebels against this unnatural state of affairs that has been created in India and Pakistan. . . . There is no settling down to it and conflicts continue. Perhaps these conflicts are due to the folly or littleness of those in authority in India and Pakistan. . . . Ultimately I have no doubt that India and Pakistan will come close together . . . some kind of federal link. . . . There is no other way to peace. The alternative is . . . war.[35]

Nehru finally had awakened. The historian he so long had been gained dominance, at least temporarily, over the powerful politician he had of late become, seduced by all the charming allures of high office. Mountbatten's frenzied plans had blinded him to the wretched realities of Partition's monstrous problems, the cause of so many deaths, and sixty more years at least of fighting and hatred. The sheer waste of it all now shocked and truly staggered Nehru as he looked back and realized how much better off India would have been had he warmly embraced Cripps's 1942 offer or that of the later cabinet mission. Any plan, indeed, would have been "preferable" to Partition. He saw that quite clearly now. But for India, as for all of South

Asia, the rainbow of federated peace would remain more than half a century away, on a distant horizon obscured by wars and a potential atomic cloud hovering darkly over Kashmir's Himalayan Valley—bitter legacies of Great Britain's hasty, shameful flight.

NOTES

INTRODUCTION

1. See *Pangs of Partition*, II, *The Human Dimension*, ed. S. Settar and Indira B. Gupta (New Delhi: Manohar, 2002); G. D. Khosla, *Stern Reckoning: A Survey of the Events Leading up to and Following the Partition of India* (Delhi: Oxford University Press, 1989); *India's Partition: Process, Strategy and Mobilization,* ed. Mushirul Hasan (Delhi: Oxford University Press, 1993); *The Aftermath of Partition in South Asia,* ed. Tai Yong Tan and Gyanesh Kudaisya (London: Routledge, 2000).
2. John Osman's e-mail of "the Viceroy's verdict," published in London's *The Spectator*, 4 September 2004.
3. Alan Campbell-Johnson, *Mission with Mountbatten* (New York: Dutton, 1953); V. P. Menon, *The Transfer of Power in India* (Princeton: Princeton University Press, 1957); E. W. R. Lumby, *The Transfer of Power* (London: Her Majesty's Stationery Office, 1954); H. V. Hodson, *The Great Divide: Britain—India—Pakistan* (Oxford: Oxford University Press, 1969); Larry Collins and Dominique La Pierre, *Freedom at Midnight* (New York: Simon and Schuster, 1975); Philip Ziegler, *Mountbatten: The Official Biography* (London: Collins, 1971); *End of the British-Indian Empire: Politics of Divide and Quit, Select Documents, March–August 1947,* ed. M. N. Das (Cuttack: Vidyapuri, 1983).
4. Stanley Wolpert, *Tilak and Gokhale: Revolution and Reform in the Making of Modern India* (Berkeley: University of California Press, 1953).
5. Stanley Wolpert, *Gandhi's Passion: The Life and Legacy of Mahatma Gandhi* (New York: Oxford University Press, 2001).
6. Jinnah to Chelmsford, 28 March 1919, reprinted in Stanley Wolpert, *Jinnah of Pakistan* (New York: Oxford University Press, 1989), p. 62.
7. Stanley Wolpert, *Massacre at Jallianwala Bagh* (New Delhi: Penguin, 1989).
8. Wolpert, *Gandhi's Passion*, p. 148.
9. Gandhi's speech to Federal Structure Committee, 15 September 1931, *Collected Works of Mahatma Gandhi*, 47 (New Delhi: Publications Division of Government of India, 1976–1984), pp. 13–14.

10. "Bapu" (Gandhi) to J. Nehru, 16 October 1931, *Collected Works*, p. 173.

11. Stanley Wolpert, *Nehru: A Tryst with Destiny* (New York: Oxford University Press, 1993).

12. Wolpert, *Gandhi's Passion*, p. 165.

13. Stanley Wolpert, *A New History of India,* 6th ed. (New York: Oxford University Press, 2000), p. 329.

14. Ibid., pp. 234–42.

15. N. Mansergh and E. W. R. Lumby, eds., *The Transfer of Power*, 12 vols. (London: Her Majesty's Stationery Office, 1970–83).

CHAPTER 1

1. Churchill to Wavell, 10 February 1942, in Donald and Joanna Moore, *The First 150 Years of Singapore* (Singapore: Donald Moore Press, 1969), p. 616.

2. Churchill to Roosevelt, in Martin Gilbert, *Winston Spencer Churchill* (London: Heinemann, 1986), VII, p. 71.

3. Warren F. Kimball, ed., *Churchill and Roosevelt: The Complete Correspondence,* I, London, 2 March 1942, "Former Naval Person to President" (Princeton: Princeton University Press, 1984), p. 374.

4. Harriman, W. Averell, and Elie Abel, *Special Envoy to Churchill and Stalin, 1941–1946* (New York: Random House, 1975), p. 9.

5. Kimball, *Churchill and Roosevelt*, "Alliance Emerging," p. 3.

6. Simon Burgess, *Stafford Cripps: A Political Life* (London: Victor Gollancz, 1999), p. 43.

7. L. S. Amery, *The Empire at Bay: The Leo Amery Diaries, 1929–1945,* ed. Jon Barnes and David Nicholson (London: Hutchinson, 1988).

8. Stanley Wolpert, *A New History of India*, 6th ed. (New York: Oxford University Press, 2000), pp. 330–31.

9. N. Mansergh and E. W. R. Lumby, eds., *The Transfer of Power: Constitutional Relations between Britain and India,* I, *The Cripps Mission*, ed. (London: Her Majesty's Stationery Office, 1970), no. 290.

10. In his "A Disease of the Will" speech made in Liverpool on 5 March 1931, Churchill spoke of Mahatma Gandhi as "nauseating . . . a seditious Middle Temple lawyer," and "malignant subversive fanatic." Reproduced in *India: Speeches and an Introduction by Winston Spencer Churchill* (London: Thornton Butterworth, 1931), p. 94.

11. Harriman, *Special Envoy*, pp. 126–27.

12. Ibid., p. 128.

13. Ibid., p. 130.

14. Kimball, *Churchill and Roosevelt*, I, "Former Naval Person to President, Personal and Secret, London, March 2,1942," pp. 373–34.
15. Sir H. Dow to Lord Linlithgow, Karachi, 22 March 1942, *Transfer of Power*, I, p. 459.
16. Press Statement by Sir S. Cripps, New Delhi, 23 March 1942, MSS.EUR.F 125/141, in *Transfer of Power*, I, p. 462.
17. Lord Linlithgow to Mr. Amery, New Delhi, 24 March 1942, MSS.EUR.F. 125/11, ibid., I, p. 465.
18. Mr. Amery to the Marquess of Linlithgow, India Office, 10 March 1942, ibid., I, p. 402.
19. Sir H. Twynam to the Marquess of Linlithgow, CAMP, 24 March 1942, *Transfer of Power*, I, pp. 471–73.
20. Notes on Executive Council Meeting at 6 p.m. on Tuesday, 24 March 1942, ibid., I, p. 474.
21. Ibid., p. 475.
22. Linlithgow to Amery, New Delhi, 6 March 1942, *Transfer of Power*, I, pp. 328–89.
23. Note by Cripps L/P&J/10/4: f 13 "My Interview with the Commander-in-Chief," 24 March 1942, ibid., I, p. 464.
24. Note by Cripps, "My Interview with the Governor of the Punjab," 24 March 1942, ibid., I, pp. 464–45.
25. Note by Cripps of his interview with Maulana Azad and Asaf Ali, 25 March 1942, ibid., I, p. 479.
26. Ibid.
27. Note by Cripps of his interview with Mr. Jinnah, 25 March 1942, *Transfer of Power*, I, p. 480.
28. Ibid., p. 481.
29. War Cabinet, Committee on India. I (42) 9th Meeting, in Mr. Attlee's Room, 11 Downing Street, 26 March 1942 at 6 p.m., ibid., p. 493.
30. Note by Cripps, "My Interview with Mahatma Gandhi," 27 March 1942, *Transfer of Power*, I, pp. 498–49.
31. Ibid., p. 499.
32. Ibid.
33. Ibid., p. 500.
34. Note by Cripps, "Interview with a Number of Sikhs (Baldev Singh; Ujjal Singh; Master Tara Singh; Sir Jogendra Singh)," 27 March 1942, *Transfer of Power*, I, p. 496.
35. Ibid., p. 497.
36. Note by Cripps, "My Interview with the Delegation of the Chamber of Princes," 28 March 1942, ibid., pp. 510–11.
37. Note by Cripps, "My Interview with the Hyderabad Delegation," led by the Nawab of Chhatari, who brought with him Nawab Mahdi Yar

Jung Bahadur; Nawab Ali Yavar Jung Bahadur; and Syed Abdul Aziz, ibid., p. 513,

38. Note by Cripps, "My Interview with the Hindu Mahasabha" (V. D. Savarkar; Dr. B. S. Moonje; Dr. S. P. Mookherjee; Sir J. P. Srivastava; Mr. Ganpat Rai), 28 March 1942, *Transfer of Power*, I, p. 513.

39. Note by Cripps, "My Interview with the Congress President" (Maulana Azad), 28 March 1942, ibid., pp. 514–15.

40. Note by Cripps, "My Interview with Congress Members," 29 March 1942, ibid., pp. 527–28.

41. Ibid., p. 528.

42. Note by Cripps, "My Interview with Jawaharlal Nehru and Maulana Azad," 29 March 1942, *Transfer of Power*, I, p. 530.

43. Proceedings of Cripps's Press Conference on 29 March 1942, ibid., pp. 537–58.

44. Ibid., p. 539.

45. Ibid.

46. Ibid.

47. Ibid., p. 541.

48. Note by Cripps, "My Interview with Nehru," 30 March 1942, *Transfer of Power*, I, p. 557.

49. Note by Mr. L. G. Pinnell, MSS.EUR.F 125/141, Diary. 30 March 1942, ibid., pp. 561–62.

50. Broadcast by Cripps, 30 March 1942, ibid., pp. 566–67.

51. Ibid., p. 568.

52. Ibid., p. 569.

53. Ibid., p. 571.

54. Note by Mr. Pinnell, "Interview between Cripps and H.E. this morning," Diary, 31 March 1942, *Transfer of Power*, I, p. 572.

55. Cripps to Churchill, New Delhi, 1 April 1942, ibid., p. 600.

56. Ibid., p. 602.

57. Churchill to Cripps, 10 Downing Street, 2 April 1942, *Transfer of Power*, I, p. 607.

58. Congress Working Committee resolution, quoted in Cripps to Churchill, 2 April 1942, ibid., p. 618.

59. Draft telegram from Prime Minister to Cripps, PERSONAL AND SECRET, 2 April 1942, ibid., pp. 613–14.

60. War Cabinet. W. M. L/PO/6/106c:f60, 2 April 1942, *Transfer of Power*, I, p. 616.

61. Bajpai to Linlithgow, Telegram, MOST SECRET, Washington, 2 April 1942, ibid., p. 619.

62. Gilbert, *Churchill*, VII, p. 84.

63. Wavell to Churchill, MOST SECRET, 6 April 1942, *Transfer of Power*, I, p. 655.

64. Cripps to Churchill, VERY SECRET, 4 April 1942, ibid., p. 636.
65. Ibid., p. 637.
66. Ibid., p. 638.
67. Amery to Linlithgow, PRIVATE, 3 April 1942, *Transfer of Power*, I, pp. 632–33.
68. Ibid., p. 633. Italics in original.
69. Linlithgow to Amery and Churchill, 6 April 1942, ibid., pp. 653–34.
70. Amery to Cripps, PERSONAL, MOST SECRET, 6 April 1942, ibid., p. 663.
71. Enclosure to No. 540, L. G. Pinnell, P.S. to Viceroy, to F. F. Turnbull, P.S. to S. of S. for India, 6 April 1942, *Transfer of Power*, I, p. 665.
72. Linlithgow to Amery, Telegram containing No. 943-G. "Summary of speech by Nehru, reported in Hindustan Times," 8 April 1942, ibid., p. 692.
73. Cripps to Churchill, PERSONAL AND SECRET, 9 April 1942, ibid., p. 697.
74. Note by Linlithgow, "Conversation with Cripps on night of 8 April 1942," ibid., p. 694.
75. Linlithgow to Amery, 9 April 1942, 2.15 a.m., *Transfer of Power,* I, p. 702.
76. War Cabinet to Cripps, 9 April 1942, 4 p.m., ibid., p. 707.
77. Note by Pinnell, "Conversation between Viceroy and Cripps on evening of 9 April 1942," ibid., p. 710.
78. Cripps to War Cabinet, MOST SECRET AND PERSONAL, 10 April 1942, *Transfer of Power*, I, p. 717.
79. Churchill to Cripps, 10 April 1942, ibid., p. 721.
80. Azad to Cripps, 10 April 1942, ibid., p. 727.
81. Cripps to Churchill (via Viceroy and India Office), 10 April 1942, ibid., pp. 730–31.
82. Churchill to Cripps, 11 April 1942, *Transfer of Power*, I, p. 739.

CHAPTER 2

1. Cripps to Churchill, 11 April 1942, *Transfer of Power,* I, pp. 740–41.
2. Azad to Cripps, 11 April 1942, ibid., p. 744.
3. Broadcast by Cripps, 11 April 1942, ibid., pp. 752–53.
4. Amery to Linlithgow, 11 April 1942, *Transfer of Power*, I, p. 756.
5. Ibid., p. 757.
6. Ibid., p. 758.
7. Roosevelt to Hopkins, R/30/1/1:ff 5–8 12 April 1942, ibid., p. 759.
8. Churchill to Roosevelt, 12 April 1942, *Transfer of Power*, I, p. 764.
9. Cripps Mission Debate, in Hansard, *Parliamentary Debates,* 5th series, House of Commons, 379, 28 April 1942, cols. 905–17.

10. Amery to Linlithgow, 6 May 1942, in *Transfer of Power*, II, pp. 42–43.

11. Sir A. Hope to Linlithgow, Guindy, 18 April 1942, *Transfer of Power*, I, pp. 800–801.

12. Ibid., p. 802.

13. That summary of Gandhi's article was sent by Linlithgow to Amery, 20 April 1942, ibid., p. 806.

14. Ibid., p. 807.

15. Summary of the Madras Congress Resolutions of 23 April 1942 is given in Linlithgow's telegram to Amery of 24 April 1942, *Transfer of Power*, I, p. 842.

16. Summary of Nehru's press conference in Calcutta in Linlithgow's telegram to Amery of 26 April 1942, ibid., p. 858.

17. Summary of A-I CC opening meeting in Allahabad, in Linlithgow to Amery, 30 April 1942, ibid., pp. 875–76.

18. Government of India, Home Department, to Secretary of State, 1 May 1942, *Transfer of Power*, II, *"Quit India"* (London, 1971), pp. 3–4.

19. "A.-I.C.C. War Resolution," 1 May 1942," Enclosure to No. 43, ibid., pp. 66–67.

20. Home Department to Secretary of State, telegram, 1 May 1942, *Transfer of Power*, II, p. 6.

21. Amery to Linlithgow, 6 May 1942, ibid., p. 42.

22. Hallett to Linlithgow, 4 May 1942, ibid., p. 24.

23. Summary of Gandhi's article of 3 May 1942, Linlithgow to Amery, 6 May 1942, ibid., p. 37.

24. Hallett to Linlithgow, SECRET, 10 May 1942, ibid., p. 64.

25. Prasad's letter to Acharya Kripalani was dated 5 May 1942, *Transfer of Power*, II, p. 64. Italics in original.

26. Summary of Gandhi's *Harijan* article of 10 May, in Linlithgow to Amery, 11 May 1942, ibid., p. 71.

27. Lumley to Linlithgow, 13 May 1942, ibid., p. 83.

28. Summary enclosed in Linlithgow to Amery, telegram, 19 May 1942, ibid., p. 104.

29. Ibid., p. 105.

30. Harijan of May 24, in Linlithgow to Amery, 25 May 1942, *Transfer of Power*, II, p. 115.

31. SECRET Note by Pilditch, 26 May 1942 L/P7J/8/596:ff 138–43, ibid., pp. 127–28.

32. Amery to Linlithgow, 27 May 1942, ibid., p. 141.

33. Sir G. S. Bajpai to Linlithgow, 29 May 1942, *Transfer of Power*, II, p. 145. Next quotation, ibid.

34. Twynam to Linlithgow, 9 June 1942, ibid., p. 195.
35. Amery to Linlithgow, 16 June 1942, ibid., p. 216.
36. Rajagopalachari's speech reported in Linlithgow to Amery, 18 June 1942, ibid., p. 228.
37. Lumley to Linlithgow, 19 June 1942, *Transfer of Power*, II, p. 240.
38. Jinnah's statement summary in Linlithgow to Amery, 23 June 1942, ibid., p. 251.
39. Ibid., p. 252.
40. Resolution of the Congress Working Committee, Wardha, 14 July 1942, ibid., pp. 385–57.
41. Government of India, Home Department to Secretary of State. Telegram, New Delhi, 24 July 1942, *Transfer of Power*, II, pp. 447–50.
42. Wolpert, *Gandhi's Passion*, p. 205.
43. Text of the Resolution, 8 August 1942, in *Transfer of Power*, II, ibid., pp. 621–24.
44. Anthony Eden to Sir H. Seymour, 7 August 1942, ibid., p. 612.
45. Arun Chandra Bhuyan, *The Quit India Movement* (New Delhi: Manas, 1975), p. 67.
46. Linlithgow to Churchill, 31 August 1942, *Transfer of Power*, II, pp. 853–54.
47. Gandhi to Linlithgow, 14 August 1942, ibid., pp. 702–5.
48. Amery to Linlithgow, 1 September 1942, ibid., pp. 874–76.
49. Jinnah's Press Conference, 13 September 1942, ibid., p. 956.
50. Ibid., p. 958.
51. Linlithgow to Amery, 14 September 1942, ibid., p. 961.
52. Halifax to Eden, 16 September 1942, p. 970.
53. War Cabinet W. M. (42) 125th Conclusions, 16 September 1942, ibid., pp. 971–72.
54. Churchill's Draft Telegram to the Viceroy, 19 September 1942, ibid., pp. 992–93.
55. Linlithgow to Amery, 21 September 1942, ibid., p. 1004.
56. Memo by S. of S. for India to the War Cabinet on "Indian Sterling Balances," 22 Sept 1942, *Transfer of Power*, III, *Reassertion of Authority, Ghandi's Fast and the Succession to the Viceroyalty* (London, 1971), p. 23.
57. Churchill to Amery in "Enclosure to No. 2," ibid., p. 3.
58. Linlithgow to Halifax, 22 September 1942, ibid., p. 16.
59. Churchill's Minute 3 on "Debate on India," 24 September 1942, ibid., p. 35.
60. Churchill to Linlithgow, 24 September 1942, *Transfer of Power*, III, pp. 36–37.
61. Amery to Linlithgow, 26 September 1942, ibid., p. 49. Next quotation, ibid., p. 50.
62. Ibid., p. 51.

63. Linlithgow to Amery, 27 September 1942, ibid., pp. 52–53.
64. Home Department to Secretary of State, 2 October 1942, ibid., pp. 67–68.
65. Lumley to Linlithgow, 22 October 1942, *Transfer of Power*, III, p. 144.

CHAPTER 3

1. Gandhi to Linlithgow, New Year's Eve 1942, *Transfer of Power*, III, p. 440.
2. Linthgow to Amery, the viceroy's draft reply to Gandhi, 6 January 1943, ibid., p. 463.
3. Gandhi to Linlithgow, 19 January 1943, ibid., p. 518.
4. Gandhi to Linlithgow, 29 January 1942, *Transfer of Power*, III, pp. 558–59.
5. Linlithgow to Amery, 2 February 1943, ibid., p. 570.
6. Amery to Linlithgow, 8 February 1943, ibid., p. 617.
7. Amery to Linlithgow, 8 February 1943, *Transfer of Power*, III, pp. 631–32.
8. Lumley to Linlithgow, 2 February 1943, ibid., p. 571.
9. Amery to Linlithgow, 8 February 1943, ibid., p. 636. Next quotation, ibid.
10. Ibid.
11. Linlithgow to Amery, 16 February 1943, *Transfer of Power*, III, p. 675.
12. Linlithgow to Amery, 17 February 1943, ibid., p. 683.
13. Linlithgow to Amery, 19 February 1943, ibid., pp. 687–88.
14. Linlithgow to Amery, 19 February 1943, ibid., p. 690.
15. Amery to Linlithgow, 19 February 1943, *Transfer of Power*, III, p. 699.
16. Ibid., p. 698.
17. Amery to Linlithgow, 21 February 1943, ibid., p. 709.
18. Linlithgow to Churchill, 26 February 1943, ibid., p. 737.
19. Churchill to Linlithgow, 25 February 1943, *Transfer of Power*, III, p. 730.
20. Churchill to Smuts, 26 February 1943, ibid., p. 738.
21. Churchill to Linlithgow, 28 February 1943, ibid., p. 744.
22. Linlithgow to Amery, 2 March 1943, *Transfer of Power*, III, p. 750.
23. Major-General R. H. Candy, 5 March 1943, ibid., pp. 769–71.
24. Hallett to Linlithgow, 9 March 1943, ibid., p. 777.
25. Amery to Linlithgow, 30 October 1942, ibid., p. 172.

26. Amery to Linlithgow, 10 March 1943, *Transfer of Power*, III, p. 782.
27. Amery to Linlithgow, 23 March 1943, ibid., p. 844.
28. Amery to Linlithgow, 26 March 1943, ibid., p. 851.
29. Amery to Linlithgow, 31 March 1943, ibid., p. 870.
30. Amery to Churchill, 16 April 1943, *Transfer of Power*, III, p. 895.
31. Note on proceedings of the All-India Muslim League at Delhi, 24–26 April 1943, ibid., p. 918.
32. Ibid., p. 921.
33. Reuter's report of Mr. Jinnah's speech of 24 April 1943, ibid., p. 982.
34. Gandhi to Jinnah, reported by Linlithgow to Amery, 8 May 1943, *Transfer of Power*, III, pp. 953–54.
35. Gilbert, *Winston S. Churchill*, VII, p. 396.
36. Amery to Linlithgow, 12 May 1943, *Transfer of Power*, III, p. 964.
37. Ibid., p. 969.
38. Gilbert, *Winston S. Churchill*, VII, p. 396.
39. Amery to Churchill, 8 June 1943, *Transfer of Power*, III, p. 1046.
40. Churchill to Linlithgow, 9 June 1943, ibid., p. 1051.
41. *Wavell: The Viceroy's Journal*, ed. Penderel Moon, 27 July 1943 (London: Oxford University Press, 1973), p. 12.
42. Enclose 2 to No. 4 of Amery to Bracken, 16 June 1943, *Transfer of Power*, IV, *The Bengal Famine and the New Viceroyalty* (London, 1973), p. 8.
43. Linlithgow to Wavell, 2 July 1942, ibid., pp. 38–39.
44. Linlithgow to Amery, 2 July 1943, ibid., pp. 39–40.
45. Sir J. Herbert to Linlithgow, 2 July 1943, *Transfer of Power*, IV, p. 43.
46. Government of India, Food Department to Secretary of State, 15 July 1943, ibid., p. 77.
47. Hope to Linlithgow, 15 July 1943, SECRET, ibid., p. 82.
48. Herbert to Linlithgow, 21 July 1943, ibid., p. 112.
49. War Cabinet Paper W.P. (43) 345, 30 July 1943, *Transfer of Power*, IV, pp. 133–38.
50. Auchinleck to Brooke, 8 September 1943, ibid., p. 217.
51. War Cabinet Paper No. 119, 17 September 1943, Annex to "Internal Intelligence," ibid., pp. 272–73.
52. War Cabinet W.M., in P.M.'s Room in House of Commons, 24 September 1943, ibid., p. 319.
53. Wavell to Amery, 1 November 1943, *Transfer of Power*, IV, pp. 431–32.
54. Governor-General to Secretary of State, 3 November 1943, ibid., p. 445.
55. Wavell to Amery, 23 November 1943, ibid., p. 495.

56. Secretary of State to Government of India, Food Department, 1 January 1944, *Transfer of Power,* IV, p. 588.
57. Food Department to Secretary of State, 6 January 1944, ibid., p. 599.
58. Ibid., p. 600.
59. Wavell to Amery, 9 February 1944, ibid., pp. 706–7.
60. Churchill to Wavell, 15 February 1944, ibid., p. 729.
61. Amery to Wavell, 17 February 1944, ibid., p. 741.
62. Gandhi to Wavell, 17 February 1944, *Transfer of Power,* IV, p. 738.
63. Gandhi to "Dear Friend" Wavell, 9 March 1944, ibid., pp. 792–93.
64. Colville to Wavell, 13 March 1944, ibid., pp. 807–8.
65. Wavell to Gandhi, 28 March 1944, ibid., p. 842.
66. Gandhi to "Dear Friend" Wavell, 9 April 1944, ibid., pp. 871–72.
67. Wavell to Amery, 18 April 1944, *Transfer of Power,* IV, p. 895.
68. Wavell to Amery, SECRET, 19 April 1944, ibid., p. 900.
69. Wavell to Amery, SECRET, 26 April 1944, ibid., pp. 925–26.
70. Wavell to Amery, 4 May 1944, ibid., p. 948.
71. Churchill to Amery, 4 May 1944, *Transfer of Power,* IV, p. 951.
72. *Wavell: The Viceroy's Journal,* 5 July 1944, ibid., p. 78.
73. Colville to Wavell, 19 May 1944, *Transfer of Power,* IV, p. 977.
74. Wavell to Amery, SECRET, 23 May 1944, ibid., pp. 983–84.
75. Amery to Wavell, 25 May 1944, ibid., p. 989.
76. Wavell to Amery, 20 June 1944, ibid., p. 1033.
77. Wavell to Amery, 11 July 1944, secret, *Transfer of Power,* IV, pp. 1077–78.
78. Ibid., pp. 1078–79.

CHAPTER 4

1. Sir Ronald Campbell, Head of British Embassy in Washington to Eden, 26 July 1944, *Transfer of Power,* IV, p. 1121.
2. Phillips's entire letter is quoted in Campbell's IMPORTANT report to Eden, ibid., pp. 1121–22.
3. Minute 3 of the War Cabinet's meeting of 3 August 1944, ibid., p. 1155. Next quotation, ibid.
4. Churchill to Wavell, 4 August 1944, *Transfer of Power,* IV, p. 1158.
5. Wavell to Churchill, 4 August 1944, SECRET, ibid., pp. 1159–60.
6. Amery to Wavell, 4 August 1944, ibid., pp. 1165–66.
7. Wavell to Amery, 10 August 1944, SECRET, ibid., p. 1178.
8. Wavell to Amery, 10 August 1944, PRIVATE AND SECRET, *Transfer of Power,* IV, p. 1180.
9. Sir H. Twynam to Wavell, 10 August 1944, ibid., p. 1182.

10. Wavell to Amery, 12 August 1944, ibid., p. 1189.
11. Amery to Wavell, 12 August 1944, ibid.
12. Churchill to Sir. E. Bridges, EMERGENCY, 13 August 1944, ibid., p. 1191.
13. Amery to Wavell, 14 August 1944, *Transfer of Power,* IV, p. 1195.
14. Sir G. Laithwaite to Amery reported Attlee's decision, 16 August 1944, ibid., p. 1204.
15. Amery to Attlee, 16 August 1944, ibid., p. 1205.
16. Amery to Wavell, 16 August 1944, ibid., pp. 1205–6. Next quotation, ibid.
17. Ibid.
18. *Transfer of Power,* IV, p. 1207.
19. Colville to Wavell, 18 August 1944, ibid., p. 1209.
20. Wavell to Amery, 23 August 1944, ibid., p. 1214.
21. Ibid., p. 1215.
22. Glancy to Wavell, 23 August 1944, ibid., p. 1223–34.
23. Amery to Wavell, TOP SECRET, 31 August 1944, ibid., p. 1234.
24. Sir Evan Jenkins's note on Viceroy Wavell's remarks to his Governors Conference on its last day, 31 August 1944, *Transfer of Power,* V, *The Simla Conference* (London, 1974), p. 2.
25. Wolpert, *Gandhi's Passion,* p. 210.
26. Wolpert, *Nehru: A Tryst with Destiny,* p. 337.
27. Gandhi's Talk with Jinnah, September 9, 1944, *Collected Works of Mahatma Gandhi,* 78, pp. 88–89. (Hereafter CWMG.)
28. Wolpert, *Gandhi's Passion,* p. 211.
29. Jinnah to Gandhi, 21 September 1944, Appendix 7, CWMG, 78, pp. 410–11.
30. Gandhi to Dear Quaid-e-Azam [Jinnah], 22 September 1944, ibid., p. 122.
31. Gandhi's interview to the *News Chronicle,* 29 September 1944, ibid., pp. 142–43.
32. Wavell to Amery, 2 October 1944, *Transfer of Power,* V, p. 63.
33. Amery to Wavell, TOP SECRET, 10 October 1944, ibid., p. 96.
34. Wavell to "My dear Prime Minister," Enclosure 64 in Wavell to Amery, 24 October 1944, ibid., pp. 126–27.
35. Ibid., pp. 130–33.
36. Ibid., pp. 130–31.
37. Churchill to Wavell, 26 November 1944, *Transfer of Power,* V, p. 235.
38. W.S.C. to Secretary of State for India, MOST SECRET Minute, 1 January 1945, ibid., p. 344.
39. Wavell's note on his 6 December 1944 conversation with Jinnah, ibid., pp. 279–81.

40. Ibid., p. 280.
41. Wavell to Amery, 7 December 1944, *Transfer of Power*, V, p. 282.
42. Casey to Wavell, 17 December 1944, ibid., pp. 308–9.
43. Wavell to Casey, secret, 1 January 1945, ibid., pp. 345–46.
44. Amery to Wavell, 21 December 1944, ibid., p. 325.
45. "Clem" [Attlee] to "My dear Leo" [Amery], 28 December 1944, *Transfer of Power*, V, pp. 341–42.
46. Memorandum on "The Indian Problem" to War Cabinet by S. of S. Amery, 5 January 1945, ibid., pp. 365–67.
47. Italics in original, ibid., p. 367. The following quotes all are ibid., pp. 368–75.
48. War Cabinet. India Committee, 26 March 1945, ibid., pp. 733–46.
49. *Wavell: The Viceroy's Journal*, March 29, 1945, p. 120.
50. Ibid., May 8, 1945 (VE Day), p. 129.
51. Churchill to Wavell, 28 May 1945, *Transfer of Power*, V, p. 1063.
52. Churchill to Amery, 30 May 1945, ibid., p. 1065.
53. Amery to the Cabinet meeting on the evening of 30 May 1945, ibid., p. 1070.
54. Churchill to Cabinet, morning of 31 May 1945, ibid., p. 1073. Next quotation, ibid., p. 1074.
55. Ambedkar to Wavell, 7 June 1945, *Transfer of Power*, V, p. 1095
56. Wavell to Amery, 7 June 1945, ibid., p. 1093.
57. Wavell to Amery, secret, 12 June 1945, ibid., p. 1116.
58. Broadcast speech by Lord Wavell, 14 June 1945, ibid., p. 1122.
59. Wolpert, *Nehru: A Tryst with Destiny*, p. 346.
60. Wavell to Amery, 18 June 1945, *Transfer of Power*, V, p. 1141.
61. Wavell to Amery, Simla, 25 June 1945, ibid., p. 1152.
62. Ibid.
63. Ibid., pp. 1153–54.
64. Wavell to Amery, 28 June 1945, ibid., p. 1170.
65. Wavell to Amery, 29 June 1945, *Transfer of Power*, V, p. 1173.
66. Note by Wavell of 2 July 1945 interview with Nehru, ibid., p. 1192.
67. Sir B. Glancy to Wavell, 3 July 1945, ibid., p. 1196.
68. Casey to Wavell, 3 July 1945, *Transfer of Power*, V, p. 1196.
69. Jinnah to Wavell, Cecil Hotel, Simla, 7 July 1945, ibid., pp. 1205–6.
70. Wavell to Amery, 9 July 1945, SECRET, ibid., p. 1210.
71. Amery to Wavell, 11 July 1945, SECRET, ibid., p. 1230.
72. Minutes of the Final Conference at Simla, 14 July 1945, *Transfer of Power*, V, pp. 1243–46. The Statement Wavell first read out is No. 600, ibid., pp. 1239–41.
73. Ibid., pp. 1243–44. Next quotation, ibid., pp. 1244–45.
74. Ibid., pp. 1244–45.

75. Wavell's Note of Interview with Nehru, 14 July 1945, ibid., p. 1249.
76. Wavell to King George VI, 19 July 1945, *Transfer of Power,* V, pp. 1275–80.
77. Amery to Wavell, 28 July 1945, ibid., p. 1298.
78. Wavell to Amery, 8 August 1945, ibid., pp. 1299–1300.

CHAPTER 5

1. Martin Gilbert, *Winston S. Churchill*, VIII (London: Heinemann, 1988), p. 81.
2. Ibid., p. 100.
3. Pethick-Lawrence to Indian Press Representatives, London, 8 August 1945, *Transfer of Power*, VI, *The Post-War Phase: New Moves by the Labour Government* (London, 1976), p. 41.
4. Wavell to Pethick-Lawrence, 11 August 1945, ibid., p. 45.
5. Wavell to Pethick-Lawrence, secret, 12 August 1945, ibid., p. 60.
6. Wavell to Pethick-Lawrence, 19 August 1945, ibid., p. 93.
7. Wavell to Pethick-Lawrence, 21 August 1945, *Transfer of Power*, VI, p. 113.
8. Azad to Wavell, 22 August 1945, ibid., p. 119.
9. Wavell to India and Burman Committee of Cabinet, 29 August 1945, ibid., pp. 173–74. Next quotation, ibid.
10. Colville to Wavell, 2 September 1945, ibid., pp. 200–20l.
11. Cripps to Cabinet's India and Burma Committee, 4 September 1945, *Transfer of Power,* VI, pp. 211–13.
12. Enclosure 1 to No. 115, Statesman, New Delhi report of 15 September 1945 A-I W. C. resolutions, in Wavell to Pethick-Lawrence, 18 September 1945, ibid., pp. 273–76. Next quotation, ibid., pp. 273–74.
13. Broadcast from New Delhi by Lord Wavell, 19 September 1945, ibid., pp. 282–83.
14. *Dawn*, 21 September 1945, Enclosure to No. 121, Wavell to P-L, 23 September 1945, ibid., pp. 291–97; extract from *Dawn* on p. 297. Next quotation, ibid., p. 292.
15. Wavell to P-L, 29 October 1945, *Transfer of Power,* VI, p. 420.
16. Wavell to P-L, 2 November 1945, ibid., p. 433.
17. Wavell's Note on his Interview with Nehru, 3 November 1945, SECRET to P-L, 4 November 1945, ibid., pp. 439–40.
18. Ibid., pp. 440–41.
19. Memo Enclosure to No. 194, Wavell to P-L, 6 November 1945, *Transfer of Power*, VI, p. 451. Next quotation, ibid., pp. 451–54
20. Ibid., p. 453. Next quotation, ibid.

21. Pethick-Lawrence to Wavell, 8 November 1945, ibid., p. 463.
22. Ibid.
23. Wavell to P-L, 20 November 1945, *Transfer of Power*, VI, p. 509.
24. India and Burma Committee, 19 November 1945, ibid., pp. 501–3.
25. Pethick-Lawrence to Wavell, 21 November 1945, ibid., pp. 516–17.
26. Cabinet: India and Burma Committee, 28 November 1945, ibid., p. 560. Next quotation ibid.
27. Wavell's TOP SECRET Memo to P.S.V. Abell, 29–30 November 1945, *Transfer of Power*, VI, p. 567.
28. Abell to Y. E. [Wavell] 30.11.45, ibid., 568. Next quotation, ibid., pp. 568–69.
29. Ibid., p. 569.
30. Pethick-Lawrence to Wavell, SECRET, 30 November 1945, ibid., p. 574.
31. Wavell to P-L, 11 December 1945, *Transfer of Power*, VI, p. 633.
32. Enclosure to No. 316, 27 December 1945,Wavell to P-L, ibid., p. 700.
33. Minute MSS.EUR.D 714/72, attached to Pethick-Lawrence to Attlee, 28 December 1945, ibid., pp. 702–3.
34. Cabinet. India and Burma Committee 14 January 1946, ibid., pp. 783–89; quotes p. 788–89.
35. Carl Heath's Memorandum is Enclosure to No. 356, attached to Heath to P-L, 14 January 1945, ibid., pp. 789–94. Quotes from pp. 789–90. Next quotation, ibid.
36. *Transfer of Power*, VI, p. 794.
37. Nehru to Cripps, 27 January 1946, ibid., pp. 851–54. Next quotation, ibid., pp. 855–57.
38. Wavell to P-L, 29 January 1946, ibid., p. 862. Next quotation, ibid.
39. Ibid.
40. Alanbrooke to Auchinleck, 4 February 1946, ibid., p. 879.
41. Mudie to Wavell, 27 February 1946, ibid., p. 1072.
42. Pethick to Wavell, Telegram, 27 February 1946, ibid., pp. 1069–70.
43. Pethick-Lawrence's Statement on arrival in India, 23 March 1946, *Transfer of Power*, VII, *The Cabinet Mission* (London, 1977), p. 1.
44. Cripps, ibid., p. 2.
45. Minutes of Meeting of Executive Council with Cabinet Delegation, 26 March 1946, ibid., p. 9.
46. Ibid., p. 12.
47. Note of Cripps's Conversation with Jinnah, 30 March 1946, *Transfer of Power*, VII, pp. 59–60.
48. Note of Gandhi's interview with Delegation, 3 April 1946, ibid., pp. 116–17.

49. Ibid., p. 118.
50. Record of Jinnah's interview with the Delegation, 4 April 1946, ibid., pp. 119–20. Next quotation, ibid.
51. Ibid., p. 122.
52. Ibid., p. 124.
53. Record of Delegation's meeting with Sikh leaders, 5 April 1946, *Transfer of Power,* VII, p. 138.
54. Cabinet Delegation and Wavell to Attlee, 11 April 1946, ibid., p. 221.
55. Record of interview between Delegation and Jinnah, 16 April 1946, ibid., pp. 281–14.
56. Record of Meeting, 17 April 1946, ibid., p. 288.
57. Record of Meeting between Delegation and Wavell, 18 April 1946, ibid., p. 312.
58. P-L to Attlee, 5 May 1946, *Transfer of Power,* VII, p. 431.
59. Azad to P-L, 6 May 1946, ibid., pp. 433–34.
60. Record of Third Meeting of Second Simla Conference, 6 May 1946, ibid., pp. 436–37.
61. Ibid., pp. 437–38.
62. Record of Fourth Meeting, 6 May 1946, ibid., pp. 441–42.
63. Gandhi to Cripps, 8 May 1946, *Transfer of Power*, VII, pp. 465–66.
64. Abell's Note to the Cabinet Mission, 16 May 1946, ibid., pp. 568–70. Quote, p. 569.
65. Text of Pethick-Lawrence's Broadcast, 16 May 1946, ibid., pp. 592–94.
66. Ibid., p. 593.
67. Ibid., p. 594.
68. Text of Lord Wavell's Broadcast, 17 May 1946, ibid., pp. 611–13. Quotes p. 611 and 613.
69. Gandhi's article in Harijan, Delhi, 17 May 1946, ibid., pp. 614–15.
70. Note by Abell, 18 May 1946, *Transfer of Power,* VII, p. 619.
71. Azad to Pethick-Lawrence, 20 May 1946, ibid., p. 639.
72. *Wavell: The Viceroy's Journal,* 31 May 1946, p. 282
73. Ibid., 2 June 1946, p. 285.

CHAPTER 6

1. Cabinet Conclusions, 6 June 1946, *Transfer of Power*, VII, p. 832.
2. Note by Wavell of his Interview with Jinnah, 7 June, ibid., p. 839.
3. Meeting of Delegation and Viceroy with Azad and Nehru, 10 June 1946, ibid., pp. 853–54.

4. Ibid., p. 855.
5. Ibid., both quotes, pp. 855–56.
6. Abul Kalam Azad, *India Wins Freedom* (New York: Longmans, Green, 1960), p. 189.
7. Secret Note by Wavell of Interview with Patel, 12 June 1946, *Transfer of Power*, VII, p. 884.
8. Gandhi to Wavell, 13 June 1946, ibid., p. 910. Next quotation, ibid.
9. Cabinet Delegation to Attlee, 14 June 1946, ibid., p. 924.
10. Cabinet Defense Committee, 14 June 1946, ibid., p. 926. Next quotation, ibid., pp. 927–28.
11. Statement by Cabinet Delegation and Viceroy, 16 June 1946, ibid., p. 954.
12. Note by Wavell of interview with Jinnah, 18 June 1946, *Transfer of Power*, VII, pp. 971–72.
13. Note by Cripps on meetings with Azad and Gandhi, 19 June 1946, ibid., pp. 985–86.
14. Delegation and Viceroy meeting, Saturday, 22 June 1946, ibid., pp. 1002–5.
15. Ibid., p. 1017.
16. Ibid., pp. 1023–24.
17. Resolution of Congress W. C., 25 June 1946, ibid., p. 1037.
18. Meeting of Delegation and Wavell with Jinnah, 25 June 1946, *Transfer of Power*, VII, p. 1045.
19. Ibid., p. 1046.
20. Ibid., p. 1047.
21. Wavell's Report to King George VI was written in Simla, 8 July 1946, sent to Sir A. Lascalles, from whose cover letter the first quote comes, after which this "Appendix" contains the letter to "Your Majesty" from Wavell, ibid., pp. 1090–95. Second and third quotes from p. 1093.
22. Ibid., p. 1095.
23. Nehru's Press Conference on 10 July 1946, *Transfer of Power*, VIII, *The Interim Government* (London, 1979), pp. 25–26. Next quotation, ibid., pp. 27–30.
24. Jinnah to Attlee in Pethick-Lawrence to Wavell, 23 July 1946, ibid., pp. 106–7.
25. Attlee to Jinnah, 23 July 1946, ibid., p. 111.
26. Nehru to Wavell, 23 July 1946, ibid., pp. 112–13.
27. Wavell to Pethick-Lawrence, TOP SECRET, 24 July 1946, ibid., p. 115.
28. Pethick-Lawrence to Wavell, TOP SECRET, 26 July 1946, ibid., p. 124.
29. *Transfer of Power*, VIII, p. 125.
30. Attlee to Wavell, 22 July 1946, ibid., p. 100. Next quotation, ibid.

31. Wavell to P-L, 28 July 1946, ibid., p. 127.
32. Brief by Abell, 28 July 1946, ibid., pp. 128–29. Next quotation, ibid., p. 130.
33. Texts of M-L Council Resolutions, 29 July 1946, ibid., pp. 135–39. Quote, pp. 137–38. Next quotation, ibid., pp. 138–39.
34. Wavell's interview with Nehru, 30 July 1946, *Transfer of Power*, VIII, p. 144.
35. Ibid., p. 145.
36. Wavell to P-L, 1 August 1946, ibid., p. 168.
37. P-L to Wavell, 2 August 1946, ibid., p. 178.
38. Wylie to Wavell, SECRET, 7 August 1946, ibid., p. 202.
39. Wavell to Pethick-Lawrence, 4 August 1946, but Wavell's letter to Nehru was sent on 6 August 1946, ibid., p. 188, n. 5.
40. Conference of Governors and Wavell, 8 August 1946, *Transfer of Power*, VIII, pp. 204–5.
41. Chiefs of Staff Committee of Cabinet, 13 August 1946, ibid., p. 225. Next quotation, ibid., p. 226.
42. Nehru to Jinnah, Wardha, 13 August 1946, ibid., p. 238. Next quotation, ibid.
43. Ibid. Next quotation, ibid., pp. 238–39.
44. General Francis I. S. Tuker, *While Memory Serves* (London: Cassell, 1950), pp. 160–61.
45. Nehru to Wavell, 22 August 1946, *Transfer of Power*, VIII, pp. 285–86.
46. Wavell's Broadcast, 24 August 1946, ibid., p. 307.
47. Note by Wavell of interview with Nehru and Gandhi, 27 August 1946, ibid., pp. 312–13.
48. Ibid., p. 313.
49. Gandhi to Wavell, 28 August 1946, ibid., p. 322.
50. Jenkins to Wavell, 31 August 1946, *Transfer of Power*, VIII, pp. 371–72.
51. Note by Wavell of interview with Suhrawardy, 8 September 1946, ibid., p. 453.
52. Wavell to Pethick-Lawrence, 8 September 1946, ibid., pp. 454–57.
53. Ibid., p. 455.
54. Ibid., p. 459. Next quotation, ibid.
55. Note by Wavell on discussion with Jinnah, 16 September 1946, ibid., p. 525.
56. Clow to Wavell, 3 October 1946, ibid., p. 648.
57. Ibid., p. 649.
58. Nehru to Wavell, 15 October 1946, *Transfer of Power*, VIII, p. 732.
59. Wavell to Pethick-Lawrence, 15 October 1946, ibid., pp. 737–38.

60. Pethick-Lawrence to Wavell, 18 October 1946, ibid., p. 746.
61. Patel to Wavell, 20 October 1946, ibid., p. 755.
62. Wavell to King George's Secretary, Sir A. Lascelles, 22 October 1946, ibid., pp. 768–69.
63. Wavell to King George VI, ibid., p. 770.
64. Ibid., p. 776.
65. Dow to Wavell, 9 November 1946, *Transfer of Power*, IX, *The Fixing of a Time Limit* (London, 1980), pp. 38–39.
66. Jinnah's statement in *Dawn*, 15 November 1946, in ibid., pp. 73–74.
67. Ibid., p. 75.
68. Nehru to Abell, 15 November 1946, ibid., p. 77.
69. Wavell to Pethick-Lawrence, 17 November 1946, *Transfer of Power*, IX, p. 91.
70. Wavell's Note of his interview with Jinnah, 19 November 1946, ibid., p. 108.
71. Ibid., p. 109.
72. Wavell to P-L, 22 November 1946, ibid., pp. 139–40.
73. TOP SECRET Note by Wavell, 2 December 1946, ibid., pp. 240–42.
74. Ibid., p. 243.
75. Note by P-L of his meeting with Jinnah and Liaquat, 3 December 1946, *Transfer of Power*, IX, pp. 247–48.
76. Note by P-L of his interview with Nehru, 3 December 1946, ibid., p. 249.
77. Secret Record of Cabinet Meeting, 4 December 1946, ibid., p. 256.
78. Ibid., p. 259.
79. Record of Indian Conference, 6 December 1946, ibid., p. 297.
80. Ibid.
81. Confidential Annex to Report of Cabinet meeting on 10 December 1946, *Transfer of Power*, IX, p. 319.
82. Ibid.
83. Ibid., p. 320.

CHAPTER 7

1. Richard Hough, *Mountbatten: A Biography* (New York: Random House, 1981), p. 215.
2. "Dickie" to "My dear Bertie" [Mountbatten to King George VI], 4 January 1947, *Transfer of Power*, IX (London: HMSO, 1980), p. 453.
3. King George VI to Mountbatten, 5 January 1947, ibid., p. 454, n. 6.
4. Mountbatten to Attlee, 3 January 1947, ibid., p. 452.
5. *Wavell: The Viceroy's Journal*, February 13, 1947, p. 419.

6. Wolpert, *Nehru: A Tryst with Destiny*, p. 382; next quotation, ibid., p. 379.
7. Indian Policy, Statement by HMG, 20 February 1947, *Transfer of Power*, IX, pp. 774–75.
8. Article text enclosed in telegram from Abell to Harris, 21 February 1947, ibid., p. 776.
9. Wavell to Pethick-Lawrence, 22 February 1947, ibid., p. 786.
10. Jenkins to Wavell, 5 March 1947, ibid., p. 868.
11. Wavell to P-L, 5 March 1947, *Transfer of Power*, IX, p. 870.
12. Cripps to the Commons, 5 March 1947, Hansard, *Parliamentary Debates*, Fifth Series, 434 (London: HMSO, 1947), col. 510. Next quotations, ibid., cols. 512–14.
13. Winston Churchill, 6 March 1947, ibid., col. 671–72. Next quotations, cols. 673–74.
14. Ibid., cols. 676–67.
15. Ibid., col. 678.
16. Jenkins to Wavell, 7 March 1947, *Transfer of Power*, IX, p. 880. Next quotation, ibid., pp. 880–81.
17. Ibid.
18. Jenkins to P-L, 16 March 1947, ibid., p. 961.
19. Jenkins to Abell, 17 March 1947, ibid., pp. 961–62.
20. Note by Jenkins, 20 March 1947, ibid., pp. 996–97.
21. Lt.-Gen. Messervy to Field Marshal Auchinleck, note enclosed in Auchinleck to Abell, 22 March 1947, *Transfer of Power*, IX, pp. 1005–8.
22. Minutes of Meeting at Viceroy's House, 22 March 1947, 10:30 p.m., ibid., pp. 1011–12.
23. Ibid., p. 1011. Next quote, ibid., p. 1012.
24. Text of Mountbatten's brief address, 24 March 1947, *Transfer of Power*, X, *The Mountbatten Viceroyalty, 22 March–30 May 1947* (London, 1981), p. 9.
25. Interview with Nawab of Bhopal, 24 March 1947, ibid., p. 10.
26. Interview with Nehru, 24 March, ibid., pp. 11–12.
27. Ibid., p. 13.
28. Record of interview with Liaquat, 24 March, ibid., pp. 13–14.
29. M's First Staff Meeting, 25 March, 10:30 a.m., *Transfer of Power*, X, pp. 15–16.
30. Record of Patel interview, 25 March, ibid., p. 17.
31. Viceroy's Fourth Staff meeting, 28 March, ibid., p. 35. Next quote, ibid., pp. 35–36.
32. Cabinet's India Committee Meeting, 28 March, ibid., pp. 39–40.
33. Record of Fifth Staff Meeting, 29 March, *Transfer of Power*, X, p. 47.

34. Record of first interview with Gandhi, 31 March, ibid., p. 55.
35. Record of interview with Gandhi, 1 April, ibid., p. 69.
36. Interview with Nehru, 1 April, ibid., p. 70. Next quotation, ibid., pp. 70–71.
37. That Congress Resolution is in *Transfer of Power*, IX, Enclosure to No. 511, item 3, p. 901.
38. Record of Nehru's interview, 1 April, *Transfer of Power*, X, p. 70. Next quotation, ibid., p. 71.
39. Record of interview with Sardar Patel, 1 April, ibid., p. 73.
40. Mountbatten to Burrows, 1 April, ibid., p. 75
41. Record of Interview with Gandhi, 2 April, ibid., p. 83.
42. Ibid., p. 84.
43. Record of interview with Azad, ibid., p. 86.
44. Record of interviews with Jinnah, 5 and 6 April, *Transfer of Power*, X, p. 138.
45. Record of interview with Jinnah, 8 April, ibid., p. 158 Next quotation, ibid.
46. M's Personal Report, 9 April, ibid., p. 168.
47. Viceroy's Staff Meeting, 10 April, ibid., pp. 176–77.
48. Governor Burrows to Mountbatten, 11 April, ibid., p. 203.
49. Record of M's interview with Jinnah, 26 April, *Transfer of Power*, X, p. 452.
50. Minutes of Governors' Conference, 15 April, ibid., p. 242. Next quotation, ibid., pp. 243–44.
51. Ibid., p. 250; next quotation, ibid., p. 251.
52. Ibid., p. 254; next quotation, ibid.
53. Ibid., p. 255.
54. Note by Sir T. Shone, 16 April, *Transfer of Power*, X, p. 280.
55. Ibid.
56. M to P-L, TOP SECRET, 17 April, ibid., p. 294.
57. M's Personal Report, No. 3., pp. 296–303, quotation from p. 301.
58. Ibid., pp. 301–2.
59. Record of interview of M with Krishna Menon, 17 April, ibid., pp. 310–13; quotation from p. 312.
60. Minutes of M's meeting with staff, 1 May, ibid., p. 523.
61. *Transfer of Power*, X, Item 5, p. 525,
62. India Committee of Cabinet, 5 May, ibid., p. 625.
63. Ibid., p. 626.
64. Gandhi to Mountbatten, 8 May, ibid., p. 667. Next quotation, ibid., pp. 668–69.
65. Ibid., p. 668.
66. M. to Nehru et al., 10 May, ibid., p. 738.
67. Nehru to M., 10 May, *Transfer of Power*, X, p. 740.

68. Nehru to M., 11 May, ibid., pp. 756–57.
69. Cripps to Attlee, 10 May, ibid., p. 741.
70. TOP SECRET Minutes of Viceroy's Simla Meeting, 11 May, ibid., pp. 763–64.
71. Ibid., p. 764.
72. M to Attlee, Simla, 11 May, ibid., p. 772.
73. M. to Ismay, 11 May, *Transfer of Power,* X, p. 774.
74. Ibid. Next quotation, ibid., p. 775.
75. Chiefs of Staff Committee and Ismay, 12 May, ibid., p. 786. Next quotation, ibid., p. 787.
76. Ibid., pp. 791–92.
77. India Committee of Cabinet, 19 May, ibid., p. 896. Next quotation, ibid., p. 897.
78. Jinnah's Muslim League Note against Partitioning Bengal and Punjab, 17 May, *Transfer of Power,* X, p. 852.
79. Mountbatten told this to the author in his London flat, facing the Turk's Head Pub, in the summer of 1975.
80. Mieville to Mountbatten, 20 May, ibid., p. 916.
81. Burrows to Earl of Listowel and Mountbatten, 21 May, ibid., p. 926.
82. India Committee of Cabinet meeting with Mountbatten, 20 May, *Transfer of Power,* X, p. 918.
83. Jenkins to Sir J. Colville, Acting Viceroy, 21 May, ibid., p. 927.
84. Patel to Colville, 21 May, ibid., pp. 928–29.
85. India Committee of Cabinet, 22 May, ibid., pp. 953–54.
86. Cabinet Conclusions, 23 May, ibid., p. 967.
87. *Transfer of Power,* X, pp. 967–68.
88. Nehru to Colville, 23 May, ibid., pp. 968–69.
89. Enclosure 1 to No. 537, attached to Abbott to Brockman, 26 May, ibid., p. 986.
90. Mieville to Abell, 28 May, ibid., p. 1013.
91. India Committee of Cabinet, 28 May, ibid., p. 1014.
92. Burrows to Mountbatten, 28 May, ibid., p. 1025.
93. Mountbatten's Staff Meeting, 31 May, *Transfer of Power*, XI, *The Mountbatten Viceroyalty, 31 May–7 July 1947* (London, 1982), p. 3.
94. Mountbatten to all provincial governors, 31 May, ibid., pp. 29–31.
95. M's Minutes of Staff Meeting, 1 June, ibid., p. 32.
96. Ibid., p. 33.
97. Viceroy's Personal Report, No. 8, 5 June, ibid., p. 158.
98. Ibid.
99. Minutes of Meeting, 2 June, ibid., p. 39. Next quotation, ibid.
100. Ibid., p. 41. Next quotation ibid.
101. Ibid., pp. 41–42.
102. Ibid., p. 45.

103. Ibid. Next quotation, ibid.
104. Ibid., p. 146.
105. Gandhi's Note on Enclosure to No. 24, Record of Mountbatten's meeting with Gandhi, 2 June, ibid., p. 48.
106. Moutbatten to Listowel, 2 June, ibid., pp. 52–53.
107. Minutes of Viceroy's Meeting with Leaders, 3 June, ibid., pp. 72–73.
108. Cabinet Meeting, 3 June, ibid., p. 80. Next quotation, ibid.

CHAPTER 8

1. Nehru's Broadcast, 3 June, *Transfer of Power,* XI, pp. 95–96.
2. Text of Jinnah's Broadcast, 3 June, ibid., pp. 97–98.
3. Patel to Mountbatten, 3 June, ibid., p. 102.
4. Krishna Menon to Mountbatten, 4 June, ibid., p. 109.
5. Press Conference, 10 a.m., 4 June, ibid., p. 110. Next quotation, ibid., pp. 110–11.
6. *Transfer of Power*, XI, p. 112.
7. Ibid., p. 113.
8. Ibid., pp. 114–15.
9. Campbell-Johnson to Captain Brockman, 4 June, ibid., p. 128.
10. Record of interview with Gandhi, 4 June, 6 p.m., ibid., pp. 131–32.
11. Ibid.
12. Annex II to No. 28, *Transfer of Power,* XI, pp. 54–58.
13. Minutes of Viceroy's Staff Meeting, 4 June, 7:30 p.m., ibid., p. 134.
14. Jenkins to Mountbatten, 4 June, 11:50 p.m., ibid., p. 136.
15. Minutes of Viceroy's Meeting, 5 June, 10 a.m., ibid., p. 137. Next quotation, ibid.
16. Nehru to Mountbatten, 12 June, ibid., pp. 292–93.
17. Mountbatten to Listowel, 12 June, *Transfer of Power,* XI, p. 299.
18. Viceroy's TOP SECRET AND PERSONAL Report, 12 June, ibid., pp. 301–2.
19. Ibid., p. 302. Next quotation, ibid., p. 303.
20. Jenkins to Mountbatten, Lahore, 15 June, ibid., pp. 402–3.
21. To Josef Korbel, *Danger in Kashmir*, and to W. Norman Brown, who reported it to me at University of Pennsylvania's South Asia Regional Studies Department.
22. Jenkins to M, 15 June, *Transfer of Power,* XI, pp. 403–4.
23. Extract of Nehru's speech from the *Tribune* of 16 June enclosed in Jenkins to Mountbatten, 16 June, *Transfer of Power,* XI, p. 429. Letter from pp. 427–29.
24. Liaquat Ali Khan to Mountbatten, 17 June, ibid., p. 451. Next quotation, ibid.

25. Wolpert, *Gandhi's Passion*, p. 237. Next quotation, ibid.
26. Mountbatten to Listowel, 17 June, *Transfer of Power*, XI, p. 472.
27. Nehru to Mountbatten, 22 June, ibid., pp. 561–62.
28. Ibid., footnote 2 on p. 563.
29. M's TOP SECRET record of interview with Nehru, 24 June, ibid., p. 591. Next quotation, ibid., pp. 592–93.
30. Moutbatten to Jenkins, by Secraphone, 24 June, ibid., p. 594.
31. Jenkins to Mountbatten, 24 June, *Transfer of Power,* XI, pp. 605–6.
32. Ismay to H. E., 24 June, ibid., pp. 606–7.
33. Cabinet meeting, 25 June, ibid., pp. 638–39. Next quotation, ibid., pp. 639–40.
34. Listowel to Mountbatten, 25 June, ibid., p. 643.
35. Secret meeting of Partition Committee of Indian Cabinet, 26 June, ibid., p. 650.
36. Auchinleck to Mountbatten, 26 June, *Transfer of Power,* XI, p. 660. Next quotation, ibid., p. 661.
37. Viceroy's Personal Report, 27 June, ibid., p. 682.
38. Ibid., p. 687.
39. Patel's speech on "The Future of the States," 5 July, ibid., p. 929. Next quote, ibid., p. 930.
40. Mountbatten to Attlee, TOP SECRET Telegram, 3 July, ibid., p. 863.
41. Viceroy's Personal Report, 4 July, *Transfer of Power,* XI, pp. 898–900.
42. Mr. Tyson's letter home, 5 July, ibid., pp. 939–40.
43. Jenkins to Mountbatten, 10 July 1947, *Transfer of Power,* XII, *The Mountbatten Viceroyalty, 8 July–15 August 1947* (London, 1983), p. 58.
44. Ibid., p. 59.
45. Mountbatten to Radcliffe, 22 July, ibid., pp. 290–91.
46. Jenkins to Mountbatten, 30 July, ibid., p. 426. Next quotations, ibid.
47. TOP SECRET Viceroy's Personal Report, 1 August 1947, ibid., pp. 444–46.
48. Atttlee via Listowel to Mountbatten, 31 July, ibid., p. 440. Next quotations, *Transfer of Power,* XII, pp. 444–46.
49. Telephone message from Mr. Abbott, 1 August, ibid., p. 459.
50. TOP SECRET record of interview with Captain Savage, 5 August, ibid., pp. 537–38.
51. Viceroy's TOP SECRET report, 8 August, ibid., p. 594,
52. Minutes of Viceroy's Staff Meeting, 9 August, ibid., p. 611. Next quotes, ibid.
53. Ibid. Next quote, ibid., n.3.
54. A. N. Kosla's SECRET enclosure of 8.8.47 appended by Nehru to his SECRET letter to Mountbatten of 9 August, ibid., pp. 619–20. See also

V. N. Datta's "Lord Mountbatten and the Punjab Boundary Commission Award," in *Pangs of Partition*, I, *The Parting of Ways*, ed. S. Settar and I. B. Gupta (New Delhi: Manohard, 2002), pp. 13–39.

55. Maharaja Bikaner to Mountbatten, 10 August, *Transfer of Power*, XII, p. 638.
56. Maharaja Bikaner to Mountbatten, 10 August, ibid., p. 645.
57. Ismay to Liaquat Ali Khan, 11 August, ibid., p. 662.
58. Ibid., p. 663. Italics in original.
59. Wolpert, *Jinnah of Pakistan*, pp. 338–40.
60. Jenkins to Mountbatten, 13 August, *Transfer of Power*, XII, p. 700. Next quotation, ibid., pp. 701–4.
61. "Note on Situation in Punjab," by Auchinleck, 15 August, ibid., pp. 734–35. Next quotation, ibid.; following quotation, ibid., p. 736.
62. Ibid., p. 736.
63. Viceroy's Report, 16 August, ibid., p. 771. Next quotation, ibid.
64. *Transfer of Power*, XII, pp. 773–74.
65. Wolpert, *Gandhi's Passion*, p. 240.
66. Wolpert, *Nehru: A Tryst with Destiny*, p. 3.
67. King George VI's Address, delivered by Lord Mountbatten to India's Constituent Assembly, 15 August 1947, Appendix I to no. 489, *Transfer of Power*, XII, p. 776.

CHAPTER 9

1. Gopal Das Khosla, *Stern Reckoning* (New Delhi: Bhawnani & Sons, 1949), p. 122.
2. "Unhappy Land of the Five Rivers," 19 August 1947, in *Selected Works of Jawaharlal Nehru* [hereafter SWJN; second series will be indicated as (2), followed by the volume number as a roman numeral], ed. S. Gopal, Second Series, IV (New Delhi: Nehru Memorial Fund, 1986), p 7.
3. Nehru to Gandhi, 22 August 1947, ibid., p. 14.
4. Mahatma Gandhi's speech at his prayer meeting, 23 March 1947, *Collected Works of Mahatma Gandhi* (hereafter CWMG), (Ahmedabad: Navajivan Trust, 1967–84), 87, p. 146.
5. Gandhi's "Miracle or Accident?" in CWMG, 89, p. 49.
6. Bapu [Gandhi] to Dear Vallabhbhai, 2 September 1947, CWMG, 89, pp. 133–34.
7. Gandhi's speech at his prayer meeting, 17 September 1947, CWMG, 89, p. 195, n.2.
8. Nehru's "No Retaliation," 24 August 1947, SWJN, IV, pp. 17–18.
9. Khosla, *Stern Reckoning*, p. 126.

10. Nehru to Mountbatten, 31 August 1947, SWJN (2), IV, pp. 44–45.
11. W. H. Auden, "The Partition of India," quoted in Edmund Heward, *The Great and the Good*.
12. Nehru to Prasad, 17 September 1947, SWJN (2), IV, pp. 83–84.
13. Gandhi's speech at prayer meeting, 10 September 1947, CWMG, 89, p. 167.
14. Ritu Menon and Kamla Bhasin, *Borders & Boundaries: Women in India's Partition* (New Delhi: Kali for Women, 1998), pp. 49ff.
15. Khosla, *Stern Reckoning*, pp. 298–99; Penderel Moon, *Divide and Quit* (Berkeley: University of California Press, 1962), p. 293.
16. Mushirul Hasan's "Partition Narratives," Introduction to *The Partition Omnibus* (New Delhi: Oxford University Press, 2002), p. xxiv.
17. Nehru to Mountbatten, 27 August 1947, SWJN (2), IV, pp. 25–26. Next quotation, ibid.
18. Nehru's broadcast, 9 September 1947, ibid., pp. 54–55.
19. Nehru's "A Uniform Refugee Policy," 12 September 1947, ibid., p. 62.
20. Nehru to Patel, 30 September 1947, SWJN (2), IV, pp. 113–18.
21. Sir Francis Tuker, *While Memory Serves* (London: Cassell, 1950), p. 482, quoted by Swarna Aiyar, "'August Anarchy': The Partition Massacres in Punjab, 1947," in *Freedom, Trauma, Continuities: Northern India and Independence*, ed. D. A. Low and Howard Brasted (Walnut Creek, CA: Alta Mira Press, 1998).
22. Aiyar, *Freedom, Trauma, Continuities*, p. 20.
23. West Bengal became India's smallest province with only 34,000 square miles and 24.3 million people; East Pakistan had 54,501 square miles and 41.8 million people. Gyanesh Kudaisya, "Divided Landscapes, Fragmented Identities: East Bengal Refugees and Their Rehabilitation in India, 1947–79," in Aiyar, *Freedom, Trauma, Continuities*, pp. 105–31.
24. Leonard A. Gordon, *Brothers Against the Raj: A Biography of Indian Nationalists Sarat and Subhas Chandra Bose* (New York: Columbia University Press, 1990), p. 593.
25. Sabyasachi Bhattacharya, "The Division of Hearts: Mahatma Gandhi and the Partition of Bengal, 1947," in *The Partition in Retrospect*, ed. Amrik Singh, pp. 199–211. Also in the same book, see Parthasarathi Gupta, "Who Divided the Bengalees?" pp. 212–21; and Sucheta Mahajan, "Congress and Partition of Provinces," pp. 222–45.
26. Viceroy's TOP SECRET Personal Report, 16 August, *Transfer of Power*, XII, p. 760.
27. Ibid., p. 761.
28. Kudaisya's "Divided Landscapes," pp. 108–9; next quotation, ibid., pp. 109–113.

29. Nehru's broadcast from Calcutta, 15 December, SWJN (2), IV, p. 211.
30. Nehru to B. C. Roy, 22 March 1948, SWJN (2), V, p. 162.
31. Nehru to State Premiers, 1 April 1948, ibid., pp. 339–40.
32. Nehru to Premiers, 15 April 1948, ibid., VI, p. 255.
33. Campbell-Johnson, *Mission with Mountbatten,* 8 March 1948, pp. 296–97. Next quotation, ibid.
34. Ibid., p. 296. Next quotation, ibid., pp. 297–98.
35. Wolpert, *A New History of India,* pp. 180–88.
36. Alan Campbell-Johnson, *Mission with Mountbatten,* 9 March 1948, pp. 298–99.
37. Nehru to Roy, 15 June 1948, SWJN (2), VI, p. 282. Next quotation, ibid., p. 283.

CHAPTER 10

1. Chaudhuri Muhammad Ali, *The Emergence of Pakistan* (New York: Columbia University Press, 1967), p. 289.
2. Wolpert, *Nehru: A Tryst with Destiny,* pp. 34ff.
3. Nehru to Sheikh Abdullah, 10 October 1947, SWJN (2), IV, pp. 270–71.
4. Nehru to Abdullah, 27 October 1947, ibid., pp. 279–82.
5. Nehru to Attlee, 25 October 1947, ibid., p. 275.
6. Gandhi's prayer meeting, 29 July 1947, CWMG, 88, p. 461.
7. Gandhi's prayer meeting, 26 October 1947, CWMG, 89, pp. 413–14.
8. Nehru to Atal, 27 October 1947, SWJN (2), 4, pp. 283–84.
9. Ibid., pp. 285–86.
10. Nehru to Attlee, 28 October 1947, SWJN (2), 4, pp. 286–88a.
11. Nehru to Liaquat Ali Khan, 28 October 1947, ibid., p. 289.
12. Wolpert, *Jinnah of Pakistan*, p. 352.
13. Ibid., p. 353.
14. Nehru to Mahajan, 30 October 1947, SWJN (2), 4, pp. 292–93.
15. Nehru to Sheikh Abdullah, 1 November 1947, ibid., p. 300.
16. Gandhi to prayer meeting, 5 November 1947, CWMG , 89, pp. 480–81.
17. Nehru to Abdullah, 4 November 1947, SWJN (2), 4, pp. 318–19.
18. Nehru's speech in Srinagar, 11 November 1947, ibid., pp. 321–22.
19. Nehru to Pandit Kachru, 21 November 1947, ibid., p. 329.
20. Nehru to Attlee, 23 November 1947, ibid., pp. 338–39.
21. Nehru to Delhi's Constituent Assembly, 25 November 1947, ibid., p. 345.
22. Nehru to Sri Prakasha, 25 November 1947, ibid., pp. 346–47.

23. Gandhi to Constructive Workers, 11–12 December 1947, CWMG, 90 (1984), pp. 215–17, 223–34.
24. Gandhi's prayer meeting speeches, 13 and 16 December 1946, ibid., pp. 233, 244–45.
25. Gandhi's prayer meeting, 26 November 1947, ibid., pp. 112–13.
26. Gandhi's prayer meeting speech, 25 December 1947, ibid., p. 298.
27. Gandhi's prayer speech on 29 December 1947, ibid., pp. 318–19.
28. Gandhi's "Fragment of a letter," 30 December 1947, ibid., p. 325.
29. Gandhi's prayer meeting speech, 12 January 1948, ibid., p. 409.
30. Gandhi's prayer meeting speech, 16 January 1948, ibid., pp. 435–36.
31. Nehru's speech on 30 January 1948, in Dorothy Norman, *Nehru*, II, 364–65.
32. "C.R.'s statement, Calcutta, 8 March 1948," in Campbell-Johnson, *Mission with Mountbatten*, p. 297.
33. Nehru to C. R., 21 May 1948, SWJN, VI, p. 356.
34. Nehru's speech to Mountbatten, 20 June 1948, ibid., pp. 358–60.
35. Nehru to Nawab of Bhopal, 9 July 1948, SWJN, VII (1988), pp. 5–6.

BIBLIOGRAPHY

The most important primary source documents for this period are the twelve volumes on constitutional relations between Britain and India, entitled *The Transfer of Power, 1942–7*, edited by Nicholas Mansergh; he was assisted for the first three volumes by E. W. R. Lumby, after whose death in 1972 Penderel Moon took up that job, with the help of D. M. Blake and L. J. Carter. Each of these volumes covered primary sources in British Archives from the India Office, the cabinet's India Committee and the cabinet's London records, as well as documents from records kept by successive viceroys of the period and their advisers in New Delhi. The subtitles and publication dates of each volume are as follows:

Volume I, The Cripps Mission, January–April 1942. London: Her Majesty's Stationery Office, 1970.

Volume II, "Quit India," 30 April–21 September 1942. London: Her Majesty's Stationery Office, 1971.

Volume III, Reassertion of Authority, Gandhi's Fast and the Succession to the Viceroyalty, 21 September 1942–12 June 1943. London: Her Majesty's Stationery Office, 1971.

Volume IV, The Bengal Famine and the New Viceroyalty, 15 June 1943–31 August 1944. London: Her Majesty's Stationery Office, 1973.

Volume V, The Simla Conference: Background and Proceedings. London: Her Majesty's Stationery Office, 1975.

Volume VI, The Post-War Phase: New Moves by the Labour Government, 1 August 1945–22 March 1946. London: Her Majesty's Stationery Office, 1976.

Volume VII, The Cabinet Mission, 23 March–29 June 1946. London: Her Majesty's Stationery Office, 1977.

Volume VIII, The Interim Government, 3 July–1 November 1946. London: Her Majesty's Stationery Office, 1979.

Volume IX, The Fixing of a Time Limit, 4 November 1946–22 March 1947. London: Her Majesty's Stationery Office, 1980.

Volume X, The Mountbatten Viceroyalty: Formulation of a Plan, 22 March–30 May 1947. London: Her Majesty's Stationery Office, 1981.

Volume XI, The Mountbatten Viceroyalty: Announcement and Reception of the 3 June Plan, 31 May–7 July 1947. London: Her Majesty's Stationery Office, 1982.

Volume XII, The Mountbatten Viceroyalty: Princes, Partition and Independence, 8 July–15 August 1947. London: Her Majesty's Stationery Office, 1983.

Unpublished primary sources that have been useful include the following:

Attlee Papers, Churchill College, Cambridge; and Lord Attlee Papers, Bodleian Library, Oxford; and his Cabinet Office Papers in the Public Record Office at Kew, Surrey.

Sir Richard Stafford Cripps Papers, Nuffield College Library, Oxford.

Lord Linlithgow Collection, India Office Library, London.

Lord Listowel Collection, India Office Library, London.

Lord Mountbatten Papers, University of Southampton Library, Southampton.

Lord Pethick-Lawrence Papers, Trinity College, Cambridge.

Lord (Richard Austen) Butler Papers, Trinity College, Cambridge.

Lionel George Curtis Papers, Bodleian Library, Oxford.

Geoffrey Dawson Papers, Bodleian Library, Oxford.

Ernest Bevin Papers, Churchill College, Cambridge.

Quaid-i-Azam M. A. Jinnah Papers, National Archives, Islamabad, Pakistan.

PUBLISHED PRIMARY SOURCE PAPERS

Churchill & Roosevelt: The Complete Correspondence, I, "Alliance Emerging, October 1933–November 1942," ed. Warren F. Kimball. Princeton: Princeton University Press, 1984; II, "Alliance Forged, November 1942–February 1944" (1984); III, "Alliance Declining, February 1944–April 1945" (1984).

Churchill, Randolph S. (pseud. Martin Gilbert). *Winston Spencer Churchill,* VII, "Road to Victory." London: Heinemann, 1986; VIII, "Never Despair, 1945–1965." London: Heinemann, 1988.

Winston S. Churchill, His Complete Speeches, 1897–1963, ed. Robert Rhodes James, VI, 1935–42. New York: Chelsea House, 1974.

The Collected Works of Mahatma Gandhi, vols. 65–90. Delhi: Publications Division of the Government of India's Ministry of Information and Broadcasting, 1976–1984; and M. K.Gandhi, *Delhi Diary.* Gandhi's Prayer Speeches from 10–9–47 to 30–1–48. Ahmedabad: Navajivan Publishing House, 1948; *Mahatma Gandhi: The Last Phase*, ed. Pyarelal, vols. I and II. Ahmedabad: Navajivan Publishing House, 1956; Tendulkkar, D. G., *Mahatma: Life of Mohandas Karamchand Gandhi*, 8 vols. Delhi: Publications Division, Ministry of Information and Broadcasting, 1954.

Bibliography

Selected Works of Jawaharlal Nehru, ed. S. Gopal, Second Series, 16 vols. New Delhi: Orient Longman, 1982–94; Nehru, Jawaharlal, *The Unity of India*. New York: John Day, 1942; *Toward Freedom*. New York: John Day, 1941; *Two Alone, Two Together: Letters between Indira Gandhi and Jawaharlal Nehru, 1940–1964*, ed. Sonia Gandhi. London: Hodder & Stoughton, 1992.

The Collected Works of Sardar Vallabhbhai Patel, ed. P. N. Chopra and Prabha Chopra, vols. VIII–XIV (1940–49). New Delhi: Konarak Publishers for the Sardar Patel Society, 1990–2000; Das, Durga, ed., *Sardar Patel's Correspondence, 1945–50*, 12 vols. Ahmedabad: Navajivan Publishing House, 1971–74.

Selected Works of Jayaprakash Narayan, ed. Bimal Prasad, 4 vols. New Delhi: Manohar, 2000–2003.

Quaid-i-Azam Mohammad Ali Jinnah Papers, ed. Z. H. Zaidi, 12 vols. Islamabad: Government of Pakistan, 1993–2005; *Quaid-e-Azam Jinnah's Correspondence*, ed. Syed S. Pirzada. Karachi: East and West Publishing, 1977; *Jinnah-Liaquat Correspondence*, ed. M. Reza. Karachi: Indus Publications, 2003.

End of the British-Indian Empire, "Politics of 'Divide and Quit,'" Select Documents, March–August 1947, ed. Manmath Nath Das. Cuttack: Vidyapuri, 1983.

AUTOBIOGRAPHIES AND MEMOIRS

Aga Khan. *The Memoirs of Aga Khan*. New York: Simon & Schuster, 1954.

Ambedkar, B. R. *What Congress and Gandhi Have Done to the Untouchables*. Bombay: Thacker, 1945.

Amery, Leo S. *My Political Life*. London: Hutchinson, 1953–55.

Attlee, C. R. *As It Happened*. London: Heinemann, 1954.

Attlee, Lord. *A Prime Minister Remembers*. London: Heinemann, 1961.

Azad, Maulana Abul Kalam. *India Wins Freedom: The Complete Version*. Hyderabad: Orient Longman, 1988.

Barnes, John, and David Nicholson, eds. *Leo Amery Diaries, 1929–45*. London: Hutchinson, 1988.

Birla, G. D. *In The Shadow of the Mahatma*. Bombay: Vakils, 1968.

Bose, Subhas Chandra. *The Indian Struggle, 1920–1942*. New York: Asia Publishing House, 1964.

Campbell-Johnson, Alan. *Mission with Mountbatten*. New York: E. P. Dutton, 1953.

Bibliography

Chagla, M. C. *Roses in December: An Autobiography.* Bombay: Bharaiya Vidya Bhavan, 1974.

Chopra, P. N. *The Receding Horizons: A Historian's Reminiscences.* New Delhi: Reliance Publishing House, 2001.

Gandhi, Indira. *My Truth*, presented by Emmanual Pouchpadass. New Delhi: Vision Books 1981.

Ghosh, Sudhir. *Gandhi's Emissary.* Bombay: Rupa, 1967.

Halifax, Earl of. *Fullness of Days.* London: Collins, 1957.

Hutheesing, Krishna Nehru. *We Nehrus.* New York: Holt, Rinehart, 1967.

Ismay, Hastings. *The Memoirs of Lord Ismay.* London: Heinemann, 1960.

Jinnah, M. A. *Speeches and Statements as Governor-General.* Karachi: Oxford University Press, 2000.

Khan, Liaquat Ali. *Pakistan: The Heart of Asia.* Cambridge, MA: Harvard University Press, 1950.

Khan, M. Ayub. *Friends Not Masters.* Karachi: Oxford University Press, 1967.

Mathai, M. O. *My Days with Nehru.* New Delhi: Vikas, 1979.

Mountbatten, Lord. *Time Only to Look Forward.* London: N. Kaye, 1949.

Nehru, Jawaharlal. *A Bunch of Old Letters.* Bombay: Asia Publishing House, 1958.

Nehru, Jawaharlal. *Toward Freedom.* New York: John Day, 1941.

Nehru, Krishna. *With No Regrets.* Bombay: Padma Publications, 1944.

Noon, Firoz Khan. *From Memory.* Lahore: Ferozsons, 1966.

Pandit, Vijaya Lakshmi. *The Scope of Happiness.* New York: Crown Books, 1979.

Prasad, Rajendra. *Autobiography.* Bombay: Asia Publishing House, 1957.

Singh, Khushwant. *Train to Pakistan.* New Delhi: Time Books, 1989 (originally *Mano Majra,* 1956).

Singh, Patwant. *Of Dreams and Demons.* London: Duckworth, 1994.

Wavell: The Viceroy's Journal, ed. Penderel Moon. London: Oxford University Press, 1973.

Wyatt, Woodrow. *Confessions of an Optimist.* London: Collins, 1985.

Zaidi, Z. H., ed. *Jinnah–Ispahani Correspondence, 1936–1948.* Karachi: Forward Publishing, 1976.

Bibliography

SECONDARY SOURCES

Ahluwalia, B. K., and Shashi Ahluwalia. *Netaji and Gandhi.* New Delhi: Indian Academic Publishers, 1982.

Ali, Chaudhri Muhammad. *The Emergence of Pakistan.* New York: Columbia University Press, 1967.

Ashraf, Muhammad, ed. *Cabinet Mission and After.* Lahore: M. Ashraf, 1946.

Bazaz, Prem Nath. *Kashmir in Crucible.* New Delhi: Pamposh Publishers, 1967.

Bhalla, Alok, ed. *Stories about the Partition of India,* 3 vols. New Delhi: Indus, 1994.

Bhaskaran, Krishnan. *Quit India Movement: A People's Revolt in Maharashtra.* Mumbai: Himalaya Publishing House, 1999.

Bose, N. K. *My Days with Gandhi.* Calcutta: Nishana, 1953.

Bradford, Sarah. *King George VI.* London: Weidenfeld & Nicolson, 1989.

Brecher, Michael. *Nehru: A Political Biography.* London: Oxford University Press, 1959.

Brecher, Michael. *The Struggle for Kashmir.* New York: Oxford University Press, 1953.

Brown, Judith. *Gandhi: Prisoner of Hope.* New Haven, CT: Yale University Press, 1989.

Brown, W. Norman. *The United States and India, Pakistan, Bangladesh.* 3d ed. Cambridge, MA: Harvard University Press, 1972.

Chatterji, Joya. *Bengal Divided: Hindu Communalism and Partition, 1932–1947.* Cambridge: Cambridge University Press, 1994.

Chopra, P. N. *The Sardar of India: Biography of Vallabhbhai Patel.* New Delhi: Allied Publishers, 1995.

Collins, Larry, and Dominique Lapierre. *Freedom at Midnight.* New York: Simon & Schuster, 1975.

Connell, John. *Auchinleck: A Critical Biography.* London: Cassell, 1959.

Cooke, Colin. *The Life of Richard Stafford Cripps.* London: Hodder & Stoughton, 1957.

Coupland, Sir Reginald. *The Cripps Mission.* London: Oxford University Press, 1942.

Dhar, Bimelandu. *The Sterling Balances of India.* Calcutta: Cooperative Book Depot, 1956.

Edwardes, Michael. *The Last Years of British India.* London: Cassell, 1963.

Estorick, Eric. *Stafford Cripps.* London: Heinemann, 1949.

Bibliography

French, Patrick. *Liberty or Death: India's Journey to Independence and Division*. London: HarperCollins, 1997.

Ganguly, S. *The Crisis in Kashmir: Portents of War, Hopes for Peace*. Cambridge: Cambridge University Press, 1997.

George, T. J. S. *Krishna Menon: A Biography*. New York: Taplinger, 1964.

Glendevon, John. *The Viceroy at Bay: Lord Linlithgow in India*. London: Collins, 1971.

Gilmartin, David. *Empire and Islam: Punjab and the Making of Pakistan*. London: Tauris, 1988.

Gopal, S., ed. *Jawaharlal Nehru: A Biography*, 3 vols. Cambridge, MA: Harvard University Press, 1976–84.

Gordon, Leonard. *Brothers against the Raj: A Biography of Sarat and Subhas Chandra Bose*. New Delhi: Oxford University Press, 1990.

Gupta, Sisir. *Kashmir*. New Delhi: Asia Publishing House, 1966.

Hamid, Shahid. *Disastrous Twilight: A Personal Record of the Partition of India*. London: Secker & Warburg, 1986.

Hardy, Peter. *The Muslims of British India*. Cambridge: Cambridge University Press, 1972.

Harriman, W. Averell, and Elie Abel. *Special Envoy to Churchill and Stalin, 1941–1946*. New York: Random House, 1975.

Hasan, Mushirul, ed. *India Partitioned: The Other Face of Freedom*, 2 vols. Delhi: Oxford University Press, 1995.

Hasan, Mushirul, ed. *India's Partition: Process, Strategy and Mobilization*. Delhi: Oxford University Press, 1993.

Hasan, Mushirul. *Inventing Boundaries: Gender, Politics and the Partition of India*. Delhi: Oxford University Press, 2000.

Hasan, Mushirul. *Legacy of a Divided Nation: India's Muslims since Independence*. New Delhi: Oxford University Press, 2001.

Hasan, Mushirul. "Partition Narratives," introduction to *The Partition Omnibus*. New Delhi: Oxford University Press, 2002.

Heward, Edmund. *The Great and the Good: A Life of Lord Radcliffe*. Chichester: Barry Rose, 1994.

Hodson, H. V. *The Great Divide: Britain–India–Pakistan*. Karachi: Oxford University Press, 1969, 1985, 1997.

Hough, Richard. *Mountbatten: A Biography*. New York: Random House, 1981.

Kamra, Sukeshi. *Bearing Witness: Partition, Independence, End of the Raj*. Calgary: University of Calgary Press, 2002.

Bibliography

Kaul, Suvir, ed. *The Partitions of Memory: The Afterlife of the Division of India*. Bloomington: Indiana University Press, 2001.

Khosla, G. D. *Stern Reckoning: A Survey of the Events Leading Up to and Following the Partition of India*. Delhi: Oxford University Press, 1989.

Korbel, Josef. *Danger in Kashmir*. Princeton: Princeton University Press, 1954.

Lamb, Alastair. *Kashmir: A Disputed Legacy, 1846–1990*. Hertingfordbury, Hertfordshire: Roxford Books, 1991.

Low, D. A., and Howard Brasted, eds. *Freedom, Trauma, Continuities: Northern India and Independence*. Walnut Creek, CA: Alta Mira Press, 1998.

Mahajan, Sucheta. *Independence and Partition: The Erosion of Colonial Power in India*. New Delhi: Sage, 2000.

Menon, Ritu, and Kamla Bhasin. *Borders and Boundaries: Women in India's Partition*. New Delhi: Kali for Women, 1998.

Menon, V. P. *The Story of the Integration of the Indian States*. New York: Longmans, Green, 1956.

Menon, V. P. *The Transfer of Power in India*. Princeton: Princeton University Press, 1957.

Mookerjee, Girija K. *Subhas Chandra Bose*. New Delhi: Government of India, 1975.

Moon, Penderel. *Divide and Quit: An Eyewitness Account of the Partition of India*. Berkeley: University of California Press, 1962.

Moore, R. J. *Churchill, Cripps and India, 1939–1945*. Oxford: Clarendon, 1979.

Moore, R. J. *The Crisis of Indian Unity, 1917–40*. Oxford: Clarendon, 1974.

Moore, R. J. *Endgames of Empire: Studies of Britain's Indian Problem*. New York: Oxford University Press, 1988.

Moore, R. J. *Escape from Empire: The Attlee Government and the Indian Problem*. Oxford: Clarendon, 1983.

Morgan, Janet. *Edwina Mountbatten*. London: HarperCollins, 1991.

Morris, James. *Farewell the Trumpets: An Imperial Retreat*. London: Faber & Faber, 1978.

Mosley, Leonard, *Last Days of the Raj*. London: Weidenfeld and Nicholson, 1961.

Nanda, B. R. *The Nehrus*. Delhi: Oxford University Press, 1962.

Neillands, Robin. *A Fighting Retreat: The British Empire, 1947–1997*. London: Hodder & Stoughton, 1996.

Bibliography

Norman, Dorothy, ed. *Nehru: The First Sixty Years*, 2 vols. London: Bodley Head, 1965.

Page, David. *Prelude to Partition: The Indian Muslims and the Imperial System of Control, 1920–1932*. Delhi: Oxford University Press, 1982.

Patel, I. J. *Sardar Vallabhbhai Patel*. Delhi: Government of India, 1985.

Philips, C. H., ed. *The Evolution of India and Pakistan, 1858 to 1947: Select Documents*. Oxford: Oxford University Press, 1962.

Philips, C. H., and M. D. Wainwright, eds. *The Partition of India: Policies and Perspectives*. London: George Allen & Unwin, 1970.

Prasad, Rajendra. *India Divided*. Bombay: Hind Kitabs, 1947.

Raza, S. Hasim. *Mountbatten and the Partition of India*. New Delhi: Atlantic Publishers, 1989.

Read, Anthony, and David Fisher. *The Proudest Day: India's Long Road to Independence*. New York: W. W. Norton, 1997.

Roberts, Andrew. *Eminent Churchillians*. London: Weidenfeld & Nicolson, 1994.

Roberts, Andrew. *The Holy Fox: A Biography of Lord Halifax*. London: Weidenfeld & Nicolson, 1991.

Royle, Trevor. *The Last Days of the Raj*. London: Michael Joseph, 1989.

Sadullah, Mian Muhammad et al., eds. *The Partition of the Punjab*, 4 vols. Lahore: National Documentation Centre, 1983.

Settar, S., and Indira B. Gupta, eds. *Pangs of Partition*. Vol. I, *The Parting of Ways*; Vol. 2, *The Human Dimension*. New Delhi: Manohar, 2002.

Singh, Amrik, ed. *The Partition in Retrospect*. New Delhi: Anamika Publishers, 2000.

Singh, Anita Inder. *The Origins of the Partition of India, 1936–1947*. New Delhi: Oxford University Press, 1987.

Singh, Keval. *Partition and Aftermath: Memoirs of an Ambassador*. New Delhi: Vikas, 1991.

Sisson, Richard, and Stanley Wolpert, eds. *Congress and Indian Nationalism: The Pre-Independence Phase*. Delhi: Oxford University Press, 1988.

Sherwani, Latif Ahmed. *The Partition of India and Mountbatten*. Karachi: Council for Pakistan Studies, 1986.

Tan, Tai Yong, and Gyanesh Kudaisya. *The Aftermath of Partition in South Asia*. London: Routledge, 2000.

Taylor, A. J. P. *Beaverbrook*. London: Hamish Hamilton, 1972.

Bibliography

Wainwright, A. Martin. *Inheritance of Empire: Britain, India, and the Balance of Power in Asia, 1938–55*. Westport, CT: Praeger, 1994.

Wolpert, Stanley. *Gandhi's Passion: The Life and Legacy of Mahatma Gandhi*. New York: Oxford University Press, 2001.

Wolpert, Stanley. *Jinnah of Pakistan*. New York: Oxford University Press, 1984.

Wolpert, Stanley. *Nehru: A Tryst with Destiny*. New York: Oxford University Press, 1996.

Wolpert, Stanley. *A New History of India*. 7th ed. New York: Oxford University Press, 2003.

Zakaria, Rafiq *Price of Partition: Recollections and Reflections*. Mumbai: Baratiya Vidya Bhavan, 1998.

Ziegler, Philip. *Mountbatten: The Official Biography*. London: Collins, 1985.

INDEX

Abell, George, 59, 96, 106–7, 112, 129, 133–34, 160
Abdullah, Sheikh Muhammad, 184, 186–87, 190
Aga Khan, 63
Ahimsa, 141, 159
Ahmed, Sir Sultan, 19
Ahmedabad, 45, 132
Alanbrooke, Field Marshal, 99
Alexander, A. V., 98, 100, 110, 112, 114, 161
Alexander, Field Marshal, 58, 70
Ali, Asaf, 20, 39, 99
Ali, Raja Ghazanfar, 133
Allahabad, 39–40, 45
Ambala, 133
Ambedkar, Dr. B. R., 44, 47, 75, 80, 101
Amery, Leopold (Leo), 16, 18, 30, 36, 40, 42, 48, 57, 59, 62, 68, 70, 72, 78–79, 85, 87
Amritsar, 4, 103, 131, 164–65, 170, 173, 177–78
Andaman Islands, 28
Anderson, Sir John, 131–32
Aney, Dr. M. S., 19, 55
Army, British Indian, 19, 23
    division of, at Partition, 156
Assam, 61, 65
Atal, General Hiralal, 185
Atlantic Charter, 67
Attlee, Clement, 1, 9–10, 15, 54, 70, 79, 89, 115, 117, 127, 129, 147, 161, 185, 188
Attock, 133
Auchinleck, General Claude, 60–61, 64, 90, 99, 119, 134, 156, 160, 170, 174, 186

Auden, W. H.   75
Azad ("Free") Kashmir, 184
Azad, Maulana Abul Kalam, 20, 23–4, 28, 32, 35, 38, 84–85, 91, 99, 105, 107, 110, 112, 139

Bajpai, Sir G. S., 28, 42
Baluchistan, 103, 169
Bangla Desh, 77, 141–42, 149, 178, 180
Bedlam plan, 106
Behn, Mira (Madeleine Slade), 44
Benares, 45
Bengal, 11, 39, 60–61, 65, 69, 76, 91, 119–20
Bengali, 180
Bharat, 141
Bhopal, Nawab of, 135, 150, 192
Bihar, 45, 120, 125–26, 141
Bikaner State, 167–68
Birla House, 191
Bombay, 41–42, 45, 63–4, 73
    Naval Mutiny in, 100
Bose, Netaji Subhas Chandra, 69, 93, 178
Bose, Sarat, 178
Boundary Commission, 167
British Commonwealth, 142, 146, 186
Brockman, Captain Ronald Vernon, 130, 155
Brooke, General, 60
Brown, W. Norman, ix
Burma, 39, 69, 75
Burrows, Sir Frederick, 119, 138, 142, 148

Index

Cabinet Mission, 98, 100ff., 109, 134, 137

Calcutta, 5, 11, 39, 42, 61, 77, 119–20, 149, 171, 180

Campbell-Johnson, Alan, 10, 129–30, 155, 167, 181

Candy, Surgeon-General, 64

Casey, Richard, 76–77

Central Provinces, 19

Chenab River, 164

Chiang Kai-shek, Madame, 55

Chittagong Hill Tracts , 179

Churchill, Winston, 2, 5, 9–10, 13ff., 16–17, 27–28, 32, 36, 46, 48–49, 54, 56–57, 59, 62, 64, 67–68, 74ff., 79, 89, 127, 131–32, 147

Clive, Bob, 131–32, 147

Clow, Sir Andrew, 123

Colombo, 28–29

Colville, Sir John, 63–64, 71, 91, 148

Congress Party, Indian National, 3–4, 7–8, 16, 20, 24, 35, 37, 63, 69, 72, 78, 80, 92, 94, 105, 109

Constituent Assembly, 105–6, 118, 125

Constitution, 105

Coward, Noel, 129–30

Cripps, Sir Stafford, 9, 13–15, 21ff., 25ff., 27–28, 33, 56, 91, 96, 98, 100, 102, 104, 113, 127, 129, 131, 141, 145

Dacca, 65, 180

Defence Department, 31

Desai, Mahadev, 44–45

"Direct Action" Day, 118–19

Dominion status, 96, 136, 146

Dow, Governor, 125

Dyer, Brigadier R. E., 4

East Bengal, 40, 123, 126, 178

East Pakistan, 79

East Punjab, 174–75

Eden, Anthony, 47

Eddy, Dr. Sherwood, 46

Executive Council, 120

Famine in Bengal, 60ff., 75

Ferozepur, 167

Fort William, 181

Galbraith, John Kenneth, ix

Gandhi, Kasturba ("Ba"), 44–45

Gandhi, Mahatma M. K., 2–3, 5–6, 7, 9, 16, 21, 27, 41, 43–44, 46, 50, 54–55, 58, 62ff., 65, 68–69, 71, 73–74, 81, 87, 93, 95, 101, 113, 119, 137–38, 139, 144, 152, 166, 171, 173, 185, 189–90

last fast, 191

assassination of, 191

Gandhi–Jinnah summit, 73–74

George VI (king of England), 10, 59, 86, 89, 115, 124, 129, 140, 170

Glancy, Sir Bertram, 20, 72, 84, 92

Godse, Nathuram, 191

Gokhale, Gopal Krishna, 3

Gracey, General Douglas, 186

Gujarat, 41

Gujral, Inder Kumar, ix

Gurdaspur District, 167–68

Gurgaon, 159

Gwyer, Chief Justice Sir Maurice, 117

Halifax, Lord (Irwin), 5, 42, 47, 49, 55

Hallett, Sir Maurice, 40, 56

Harriman, Averell, 17

Hasan, Mushirul, 176

Heath, Carl, 98

Herbert, Governor, 60

Hindu Raj, 91
Hindustan, 96, 106, 125
HMIS *Hindustan*, 100
Hoare, Sir Samuel, 7
Hope, Sir Arthur, 37, 60
Hopkins, Harry, 17, 32, 47, 58
Hull, Cordell, 55
Huque, Sir Azizul, 101
Husain, Dr. Zakir, 175, 177
Hydari, Sir Akbar, 101
Hyderabad, 23, 150, 163
    Nizam of, 136
Hysain, Fazl-i-, 77

India Conciliation Group, 98
India Office, 8, 10, 33, 39
Indian National Army (INA), 69,
    93
    Trials in Delhi of, 94
Irwin, Lord (Halifax), 5, 42
Islam, 134, 136, 187
Ismay, General H. L. ("Pug"), 129,
    134, 144, 146, 168

Jammu and Kashmir, 155–56, 163,
    183ff.
Jana Gana Mana, 181
Japan, 67
Jenkins, Evan, 59, 96, 122, 131–
    32, 133, 148, 160, 169
Jhelum Valley Road, 187
Jinnah, Quaid-i-Azam M.A., 2–3,
    5, 7, 9–10, 16, 20, 43, 47,
    57–58, 64, 68, 71–72, 73ff.,
    81, 83, 86, 90, 92, 95, 101–2,
    104–5, 110, 112, 115, 118,
    120, 123–24, 125, 135, 137,
    139, 151, 163
    Address to Pak Constituent
        Assembly, 168, 186–87
Johnson, Colonel Louis, 17, 30–31
Jullundur, 133, 178
Junagadh, 163

Karachi, 18, 65, 100, 146, 168
Kashmir, 103, 155, 157–58, 168,
    183ff., 189–90
Kaur, Rajkumari Amrit, 95, 111
Khan, Abdul Ghaffar, 104
Khan, Khizar Hyat, 131
Khan, Nawab Ismail, 104
Khan, Nawabzada Liaquat Ali, 81,
    84, 99, 104, 111, 123–24,
    135–36, 153, 161, 168, 180,
    185–86
Khan, Sahibzada Yaqub, ix
Khan, Sir Sikander Hyat, 57, 77
Khosla, Justice Gopal Das, 173–74,
    176
Kohala, 187
Krishna Menon (Menon, V.K.K.),
    94, 99, 129, 143–44, 154,
    156
Kurukshetra, 175

Lahore, 16, 133, 160
    Resolution, 18
    in flames, 148, 157, 159, 165,
        170, 173–74
Leathers, Baron F. J., 60
Linlithgow, Lord ("Hopie"), 6, 9,
    15–16, 18, 27, 30–32, 36, 40,
    42, 46, 48, 54, 56, 59, 77
Listowel, Fifth Earl of, 143, 158–
    59
London, 6, 22, 33, 39, 95, 128,
    148
Lumley, Governor, 43, 50

MacDonald, Ramsay, 5, 15
Madras, 37–38, 42, 60
Mahajan, Prime Minister, 187
Mahasabha, Hindu, 24, 141
Mano Majra ("Train to Pakistan"),
    ix
Marker, Ambassador Jamsheed, ix
Marwah, Dr. A. S., ix

Maxwell, Sir Reginald, 40
Mayne, General Mosley, 111
Menon, V.K.K. *See* Krishna Menon
Menon V. P., 150, 156, 162, 184
Messervy, General F. W., 134
Mieville, Sir Eric Charles, 130,
    134, 136, 148
Mody, Sir Homi, 55
Mookerji, Shyama Prasad, 141
Moon, Penderel, 176
Mountbatten, Lady Edwina, 129,
    134, 181
Mountbatten, Lord Louis
    ("Dickie"), 1–2, 10, 89,
    129ff., 134–35, 136–37, 140,
    145, 151–52, 156, 168, 170,
    176, 181, 186
Mountbatten, Pamela, 134
Multan, 133–34
Muslim League, 3–4, 7–8, 16, 24,
    35, 41, 57, 81, 84, 86, 94,
    105, 109, 114, 120, 151
Muzaffarabad, 184
Mysore, 150

Naidu, Sarojini, 44
Nanak, Guru,   22, 133, 164
Nankana Sahib, 164, 174
Navy, Royal Indian "Mutiny," 100
Nehru, Pandit Jawaharlal, 2, 7, 24,
    28, 30–31, 38, 84, 90, 94–95,
    99, 104, 110, 112, 115–16,
    117–18, 120, 128, 135, 140–
    42, 145, 153, 158, 162
  "Tryst with Destiny" address,
    169, 171, 173, 176–77, 179,
    183–85, 188, 190–91
Nehru, Pandit Motilal, 4, 83
New Delhi, 39, 60, 101, 125, 134,
    171
Nishtar, Sardar A. R., 104, 161
Noakhali District, 123
Noon, Sir Firoze Khan, 19, 44

North-West Frontier Province, 103,
    115, 161

Osman, John, 2

Pakistan, 16, 20, 57, 73, 76, 90–
    91, 93, 97–98, 101–2, 103,
    106, 118, 125, 134, 146
  Constituent Assembly of, 168,
    179, 187
Pandit, Madame, 158
Panikkar, K. M., 168
Panipat, 175
Pant, G. B., 24, 83
Partition, 153
  Administrative consequences of,
    156
Patel, Sardar Vallabhbhai, 2, 41,
    81, 93, 100, 104–5, 110, 115,
    136, 138, 145, 148, 153,
    156, 161, 174, 177, 179,
    190–91
Patna, 45, 141
Pethick-Lawrence, Lord Frederick,
    90–91, 93, 95, 97–98, 100,
    103, 105, 109, 111–12, 116,
    118, 124–25, 143
Phillips, Ambassador William, 55,
    67
Pilditch, Denys, 40–1
Pinnell, Leonard, 26
Plebiscite, 154, 186
Poonch, 183–84
Potsdam Summit, 89
Prakasha, Sri, 176, 189
Prasad, Rajendra, 40, 112, 161, 175
Princely States, 92
"Princestan," 79
Pune, 45
Punjab, 6, 11, 19–20, 65, 72, 77,
    91, 97, 103, 132–33, 148, 154
  Boundary Commission's Award,
    166ff.
Purna Swaraj, 137

"Quit India" Satyagraha, 44–45, 51, 69, 78

Radcliffe, Sir Cyril, 11, 157, 161, 165, 167–68, 175
Raisman, Sir Abraham Jeremy, 48
Raj, Siva, 83
Rajagopalachari, C. (C. R.), 29, 37–38, 42, 55, 65, 69, 73, 83, 86, 191–92
Ram, Jagjivan, 111
Rangoon, 39
Rashtrapati Bhavan, 134
Rawalpindi, 131, 133
Roosevelt, Eleanor, 55
Roosevelt, Franklin D. (FDR), 2, 13ff., 17, 28, 30, 32, 36, 40, 47, 55, 58, 67
Round Table Conference, 6
Roy, Dr. B. C., 180
Roy, K. S., 148–49, 178
Roy, M. N., 75
Royal Tolley Gunge, 181

Sapru, Sir Tej Bahadur, 55
Sarkar, N. R., 55
Savage, Gerald, 166
Savarkar, V. D., 24
Sheikhupura District, 174
Shone, Sir Terrence, 143
"Sikhistan," 22, 72, 103
Sikhs, 11, 20, 35, 72, 84, 91, 103, 133, 136, 154, 164, 169
Simla, 5, 75, 95
    Summit at, 80–81, 82ff., 85–86, 105–6
Sind, 18, 103
Singapore, 13ff., 19, 94
Singh, Baldev, 126, 128, 144
Singh, General Kalwant, 187
Singh, Hari, 183–84, 190
Singh, Khushwant, ix
Singh, Justice Nagendra, ix

Singh, Maharaja Sadul, 168
Singh, Master Tara, 22, 81, 103, 134, 166
Singh, Sardar Jogendra, 48, 101
Slade, Madeleine. *See* Behn, Mira
Smuts, Field Marshal, 56
Sri Lanka (Ceylon), 23
Srinagar, 185
States, Princely Indian, 26
Sterling debt to India,   50
Stilwell, General, 67
Suhrawardy, H. S., 119, 125, 141, 148, 174, 178
Sutlej River, 167

Talwar ("Sword"), Mutiny aboard, 100
Trivedi, C. M., 174
Truman, Harry , 89
Tuker, General Francis, 120, 177
Turnbull, Francis F., 97
Tuwana, Khizr Hayat Khan, 83
Twynam, Sir Henry, 19
Tyson, John, 142, 164

United Nations, 92
United Nations Commission on India and Pakistan (UNCIP), 186
United Provinces (Uttar Pradesh), 45, 125
United States, 67
Urdu, 180

Waddell, General Gilbert, 178
Wagah, 173
War Department, 31
War, first Indo-Pak, 183ff.
Wardha, 120
Washington, 67–8
Wavell, Sir Archibald, 13, 19, 28, 30, 32, 58–59, 61–62, 63–64, 68–69, 71, 75, 77, 79, 82,

Wavell (*continued*)
  84–85, 86–87, 90–91, 95–96,
    97, 100, 106–8, 113, 116–17,
    118, 123–24, 136
West Bengal, 179, 191

Wilkie, Wendell, 46
Wyatt, Woodrow, 130

Ziarat, 169
Zira *tehsil*, 167

The Blue Ice